SHAMANISM *for the* AGE ot SCIENCE

"This is a brilliant articulation of our limitless possibilities and how to realize them. *Shamanism for the Age of Science* is based on the history of inquiry into energetics, up to and including the findings of modern science. This book will vastly expand your comprehension of your own energy system and what it means to you and all your relationships. The fascinating journey of discovery described here is the most important story you can know about; it will impact every moment of your life. Prepare to discover the vast if not infinite resources that are available to all of us."

JAMES L. OSCHMAN, PH.D., AUTHOR OF
ENERGY MEDICINE: THE SCIENTIFIC BASIS

"Kenneth Smith illuminates the essential nature of being human, illustrates the basic mechanisms that we use to form separate realities, and offers us deeper understanding for establishing a healthier relationship in the world. This amazing book demonstrates the universality of the energy body by relating its dynamics to psychology, physics, sociology, and religion; and it helps to further establish the fields of bioenergetics, Energy Psychology, and Transpersonal Psychology. I can imagine the Toltec shaman don Juan announcing that *Shamanism for the Age of Science* offers us more than an ordinary path through the woods, since this is a path with true heart."

FRED GALLO, PH.D., AUTHOR OF *ENERGY PSYCHOLOGY*

"In the tradition of Carlos Castaneda, Kenneth Smith applies the energy body concept to a broad expanse of the academic landscape. Wisdom is a broadening and deepening of understanding, and the reader who participates in the spiritual exercise of this book will see the world differently."

JAMES F. DRANE, PH.D., RUSSELL B. ROTH PROFESSOR
OF BIOETHICS, EDINBORO UNIVERSITY OF PENNSYLVANIA,
AND AUTHOR OF *MORE HUMANE MEDICINE*

"Kenneth Smith eloquently reveals what we all need to know regarding the energy body—its nature, functions, and purpose. By embracing this perennial wisdom we are offered the rarest of opportunities: to once again experience the practical philosophy of the sage, the seer, and the shaman."

SIMON BUXTON, AUTHOR OF
THE SHAMANIC WAY OF THE BEE

"Kenneth Smith has methodically and thoughtfully written what we may be looking for to help lead us toward a revolution of thought and consciousness. Whether or not you are a scientist, practitioner, or lay person this book has something for you. I wish I had it years ago."

ERIK FISHER, PH.D., AUTHOR OF
THE ART OF EMPOWERED PARENTING

"If you want to change your life, simply change your mind. This simple truth is perhaps the greatest tool for personal change that remains unknown by most of the contemporary world. My hope is that *Shamanism for the Age of Science* might contribute to the understanding that we truly have a major role in co-creating our lives and our world, and it is a role that we can no longer neglect to take seriously."

KEVIN J. TODESCHI, AUTHOR OF
EDGAR CAYCE ON VIBRATIONS

"Dipping into this book, I'm fascinated, sometimes uncertain, and occasionally have my buttons pushed, thinking: that really couldn't be true, could it? But if it is . . . What a great mind-stretcher. Or, perhaps I should better say a great energy-stretcher."

CHARLES T. TART, PH.D., PROFESSOR EMERITUS
OF PSYCHOLOGY, UNIVERSITY OF CALIFORNIA, DAVIS,
AND AUTHOR OF STATES OF CONSCIOUSNESS

SHAMANISM
for the
AGE of SCIENCE

AWAKENING THE ENERGY BODY

Kenneth Smith

Bear & Company
Rochester, Vermont • Toronto, Canada

Bear & Company
One Park Street
Rochester, Vermont 05767
www.BearandCompanyBooks.com

Text stock is SFI certified

Bear & Company is a division of Inner Traditions International

Library of Congress Cataloging-in-Publication Data

Smith, Kenneth.
  Shamanism for the age of science : awakening the energy body / Kenneth Smith.— Expanded ed.
    p. cm.
  Revised ed of: Awakening the energy body. c2008.
  Includes bibliographical references and index.
  ISBN 978-1-59143-119-0 (pbk.) — ISBN 978-1-59143-977-6 (ebook)
 1. Awareness. 2. Consciousness. 3. Shamanism. 4. Bioenergetics. 5. Energy psychology. I. Smith, Kenneth. Awakening the energy body. II. Title.
  BF311.E235 2011
  131—dc22

                                                                                    2010041430

Printed and bound in the United States by Lake Book Manufacturing
The text stock is SFI certified. The Sustainable Forestry Initiative® program promotes sustainable forest management.

10 9 8 7 6 5 4 3 2 1

Text design and layout by Priscilla Baker
This book was typeset in Garamond Premier Pro with Versailles and Avenir used as display typefaces

Text illustrations of the energy body are by David Brown, with modifications by Jennifer Geib, and are used with permission of Biocognitive Technologies.

Unless noted, all other illustrations are used with permission of Biocognitive Technologies.

To send correspondence to the author of this book, mail a first-class letter to the author c/o Inner Traditions • Bear & Company, One Park Street, Rochester, VT 05767, and we will forward the communication or visit the author's website at **www .biocog.com**.

To Emma,
my beloved daughter,
and to her generation—
With thine maps
may thee securely saile.

Contents

Acknowledgments

For their kind influence on this endeavor, a tip of the hat to nurse and energy body researcher Caroline Coleman, bioethicist and educator Jim Drane, medical scientist and inventor John McMichael, biophysicist Jim Oschman, psychiatrist Maurie Pressman, and those shamans and scientists of near and far who revel in the dance of knowledge.

1

Shamanism for the Age of Science

Throughout the course of your everyday life, you live in the midst of infinity. In each moment, with each step, you have an infinite number of options at your beck and call. To illustrate, consider the circle, which is defined as an infinite number of points that are connected—a closed curve on a plane—with each point being the same distance from a fixed point, the center of the circle. Now, stand in the middle of a room. Keeping your feet in the same place (the center of the circle), rotate 360 degrees and end where you began. In so doing, you have formed a circle, and by definition you have the ability to access an infinite number of points or directions. You can therefore behave in an infinite number of ways. As though taking compass readings, from your starting point, any movement small or large, places you in a different space, a different orientation from where you started.

If you accept that you have an infinite number of options, questions then arise regarding how you can navigate this immensity, how you can relate to it, how you can move with it, how you can expand your reference to it, and how you can grow within it. The fact is that we limit our options, confining perception and behavior within a narrow slice of the possibilities. Breaking through these barriers is often a slow process.

We need to find out how to relate to the vastness of life so that we may continually awaken to new awareness, new knowledge, and new vistas—for the options are infinite.

REALITY

"Reality" is a human-made construct. It is a description of the world, born of imagination and defined by learning. Whether a view of reality is based on science, philosophy, religion, or anything else, it is a single canvas in a museum, or one book in a magnificent library. Each view of reality changes over time as individuals, groups, and the species evolve. What remains consistent is that the reality we experience forms from our perceptions of what we *think* reality entails. Since birth, we have each performed intricate maneuvers of learning, building, and consolidating a worldview. This is quite an accomplishment, even though we have created only a partial reflection of the vastness that lies before us.

The truth is that creation far exceeds our capacity to grasp it. Human-made reality is therefore a practical framework that enables us to survive and continue learning. Learning and survival go hand in hand. But to this end the current worldview is problematic. Humanity is at a crossroads, requiring a change in our view of the world in order to survive. One can argue, for example, that cyclical global warming has accelerated dramatically as a direct result of a human-made reality that renders humans separate from their planet and so the exploitation of natural resources for financial gain, rather than harmony with all aspects of the environment, now threatens social structures of all kinds, as well as the very existence of many forms of life. In a similar way, centuries ago a European "flat earth" view prevented exploration of oceans and continents, diminishing a new relationship with the world. Inhibited learning and lack of awareness caused the effects of both worldviews, modern and historical.

Answers to our contemporary challenges are emerging, however. People are growing more aware of cause and effect. Organizations are taking up arms on behalf of endangered species. And ethical debates abound. The intention behind this book is to contribute to the overall effort by providing information about a unique method of learning, which offers the possibility of heightened consciousness, expanded worldview, and new ways to participate with the world.

Shamanism

Based on my apprenticeship to Toltec seer don Juan Matus, and writing under the name Ken Eagle Feather, I have published five books about the Toltec worldview, a branch of shamanism in which the energy body is the principal component.[1] Based on this central theme, over some thirty-five years I have found that these ancient teachings reveal inherent processes of consciousness and perception, including how we form reality, and extend to us the possibility of purposefully cultivating ever-expanding worldviews. These teachings do not exist in a vacuum. They are rightfully an extension of established fields including philosophy and the sciences. They may also affect other disciplines and serve to significantly extend the boundaries of accepted knowledge.

Others have written about Toltec views and practices as well, elevating what was once-hidden to a recognizable position among an array of metaphysical literature. Since Carlos Castaneda's first book, *The Teachings of Don Juan,* published in the late 1960s, Toltec literature has gained ever-widening international recognition.[2] Toltec practitioners such as Victor Sanchez, Florinda Donner, Taisha Abelar, Miguel Ruiz, Susan Gregg, and others have since contributed to a growing body of work.

While Castaneda and his books gained a degree of notoriety, his work in providing an emic account (from the point of view of a participant rather than an outside, "objective" observer) of Toltec teachings earned him a doctorate in anthropology from UCLA. Contrary to a variety of assertions, Carlos Castaneda's doctorate has not been revoked.[3] The emic format is an essential consideration when evaluating Castaneda's work. He has been accused of intuiting or even inventing the content of his books. However, if we apply an emic standard, and so view his work as originating from inside the Toltec shamanic tradition rather than the more common observing and reporting by being seem-ingly removed from the experience under scrutiny, the expression of his training is entirely consistent with that body of teachings. His books may then be viewed as the culmination of a learning project where one is required to enact the teachings. And so rather than intuiting his books as ordinarily considered, he applied instructions for "dream-ing" given to him by his teacher, don Juan Matus. By doing so, he sig-nificantly extended communication and behavior into other realms of human potential. In this light, Castaneda's books represent a successful component of having learned and enacted the system, a true representa-tion of emic anthropology.

Shamanism for the Age of Science is not a "Toltec" book, though, as it does not provide practices related solely to that knowledge. Rather, it presents those aspects of the energy body that apply to everyone, not just to those with esoteric inclinations. It takes the essence of what Toltec shamans discovered regarding the basic structure of the human energy body—especially as it relates to individual and group learning—and then looks at it and its effects on consciousness through a lens of contemporary understanding. References to don Juan's teachings, the principal figure in Castaneda's books, are meant to provide continu-ity for this particular lineage. When Castaneda codified a once oral tradition, a new mold was cast, disrupting the sequence of how it has evolved; only time will tell the effects. Since the tradition is rooted in exploring the energy body rather than instilling a set philosophy, the Toltec strain of shamanism often takes different turns in the road. As don Juan said, "There is no official version of Toltec knowl-edge and the passage of time requires new ways of interpreting and elucidating it."[4]

One of the oldest practices of philosophy, healing, education, and other forms of expression relevant to the people it serves, shamanism has always been expressed in terms meaningful to the times. As we live in an era forged by science, the portrayal of shamanism in this book provides an opportunity for shamanism and science to have more than a casual encounter.

Science

Gerald Piel, founder of *Scientific American* and author of *The Age of Science,* eloquently depicts a world where dedicated men and women have mapped aspects of life once relegated to the mystic's and alchemist's dens.[5] Our knowledge of subjects such as light, space, time, genes, and geology, to name but a few, has undergone radical transformation due the explorations of resolute scientists.

As commonly considered, though, the worlds of science and shamanism remain separate beyond measure with those in each camp scratching their heads as they look at the other. It is difficult, if not impossible, to scientifically study philosophical propositions that exist only as mental constructs. The grist of what might be considered speculation is not empirical, not of the makings of experiment and observation, the bastion of science.

A New Collaboration

When specific conditions to be measured are provided, such as the energy body and its systems, then shamanism stands at the threshold of science as these items can be studied with the meticulousness that has gone into investigating other areas. A building block in the world of science is chemistry, for instance, whereas *intent*—focused energy— serves as a foundational component in shamanism. Scientists are now beginning to explore intention as found in remote healing or how an experimenter influences an experiment, and shamans may come to view chemical actions and reactions as refined manifestations of intent. In turn, the definitive energetic structures of human anatomy and cosmology observed by shamans offer scientists an opportunity to venture into uncharted scientific realms.

It seems things are heading in this direction. As exemplified by His Holiness the Dalai Lama's book *The Universe in a Single Atom,* we are at a point in our evolution where the worlds of scientific and ancient forms of consciousness research are merging.[6] Relating to this, there exists a straightforward compatibility between science and shamanism as both are methods to accelerate learning more about the way we tick and the world we live in. Science also complements shamanism by providing present-day, cross-cultural context and shamanism augments science by revealing new pathways of discovery.

Whether or not this collaboration occurs will not impede the progress of either. If it does not, it will just be a loss that each did not learn from the other. Science still has a land of infinite possibility to explore and shamanism will continue with or without the backing of scientific authority. It is in this vein that I blend shamanism with science as I've found that the combination provides a firm stepping-stone to increased awareness of human behavior and ability.

Consciousness

As part of this approach, you'll find reference to bioenergetics, a rapidly expanding scientific field that nicely meshes with advances in understanding cognition, or how we come to know and understand. This is laced with considerations of physics and neuroscience in order to better illustrate how the energy body regulates consciousness. But, as parapsychology professor and Zen student Susan Blackmore points out in her text *Consciousness: An Introduction,* actually defining consciousness remains one of the all-time riddles.[7] However, we don't need to define consciousness in order to use it to become more conscious. We do need the wherewithal provided by context and procedures that deliberately target the development and use of consciousness.

Blackmore also mentions that in the eighteenth century, psychology was regarded as a philosophy of mental life and in the nineteenth century took its first steps into developing as a science. Bringing to bear some of the many facets of psychology gives us another avenue to at least play with the riddle of consciousness and even derive further benefit by relating it to the energy body, especially given that shamanism has been referred to as "America's oldest psychology." This also applies to the various expressions of shamanism found around the globe as it remains one of the more widespread influences.[8] As a result, shamanism as well as science is rooted in cross-cultural meaning and carries relevance for today's world.

Philosophy

As different ages have come and gone, Toltec investigators of perception have continued their pursuits and delivered a sophisticated constellation of understanding about the energy body, providing concrete, consistent references that detail the energy body as an objective, measurable part of our anatomy. These perspectives also offer a unified perspective, enabling an accounting of the knowledge gained in the various metaphysical disciplines that also study the world as energy.

By its very nature, the energy body pertains to the entire sphere of human activity. Toltec considerations therefore allow us to examine anew the classic literature of other traditions, including the perennial philosophies of Buddhism, Hinduism, Islam, and Christianity. These branches of mysticism often have shamanic roots that span a spectrum from animism to pantheism to monotheism.[9] Shamanic findings also extend to examining time-honored matters of philosophical inquiry including topics such as ethics, free will, and the ontological state of *being*.

The Energy Body

The expanse of this perspective and the possibilities it highlights make this particular study of the human condition worth investigating. In a way, this is quite odd, as according to Toltec lore what became the highly refined worldview of today had begun to coalesce some 5,000 to 7,000 years ago deep in the heart of what is now a third-world country, Mexico. At the same time, what Toltec teachings represent doesn't reside in a vacuum. From modern science to homeopathy to ancient Taoism, other fields, cultures, and individuals have contributed to our knowledge of the energy body.

I have found that not being aware of our personal energy body is like trying to walk down the street without the use of our legs. There is that much more to being human that is awaiting realization. Developing awareness of our greater potential results in a profound shift in the way the world is viewed and subsequent changes in behavior. This enhanced relationship with our world permits additional learning, including new ways to learn. Learning hinges on how well you use the tools available to you as well as having the tools at your disposal to begin with. You may have loads of perspective and not have any experience that matches that context. Likewise, you might have plenty of experience that goes to waste because you don't have the means to apply and integrate the experience.

BOOKS

As part of our age, books are a dominant form of expression for information, education, and entertainment. They are projections of consciousness formed by energy bodies, with the type of book reflecting the nature of energy being presented. You can tell a book is a book just by looking at the shape, and you know the contents have been shaped in such a way as to convey some form of intelligence, just like energy bodies. Books communicate truths and distortions, all depending on the craftsmanship that goes into their formation, just like energy bodies. By focusing thought, feeling, and behavior books reflect as well as build realities large and small and for good or ill, just like energy bodies. And as comprehensive and accurate as any single book or even collection of books might be, they can't provide all that is known about any given subject; again, just like energy bodies. Yet books, just like energy bodies, can connect you with infinity.

This book stems from a synthesis of Toltec philosophy with a variety of scientific and academic fields, simultaneously revealing the structure and functions of the energy body and offering a context for a greater understanding of perception and personal growth. These new perspectives of imagination, intelligence, and memory don't obviate what is known. They augment awareness in the same manner that innovative technologies stimulate new concepts, behaviors, and products. The overarching theme of this effort is that what goes on within the energy body is the principal determinant in all that we see, feel, think, or otherwise perceive. While this discussion is informed by the strength, vitality, and value of the ancient Toltec tradition, the added references to various fields of inquiry support and guide the basic premise into modern context.

The requirements of this undertaking necessitate a technical rendering aptly reflecting the mechanics of the energy body and corresponding research. This method has purpose, as it is required to present the logic of how the energy body works, and how to usher it to its potential. If you don't grasp the intricate details, it won't hold you back from awakening your energy body. What comes first is having a sense of the matter and for this you just need to know your options.

In principle the options are no different from those arising from examining the various systems that comprise the physical body. For example, you'll find that dynamics of the nervous system and of the energy body reflect each other. Historical and modern research intersects, revealing more than what was thought to exist, while enriching the possibilities. That energy body processes can be related to a range of fields supports the premise that conditions within the energy body determine perception. The flipside is that these areas of study originate from the energy body as it focuses and generates perception. To examine this idea, each chapter forms a stepping-stone leading to an appreciation of our natural heritage, and how to develop proficiency in the care and management of your energy body.

From this approach, a few of the topics covered herein are the intricacies of projection, the interplay of learning and imagination, the basis of fundamentalism, the role of altered states of consciousness, and how to groom present-centeredness. Supportive procedures and exercises are sprinkled throughout the text and clustered in chapters ten and eleven. For additional perspectives and exercises, especially on the Toltec Way itself, you may find value in two of my other books, penned as Ken Eagle Feather, *On the Toltec Path* and *Toltec Dreaming*.

Lessons and Logic

This chapter is not simply an introduction to a book, perhaps something to be gently glossed over. Each chapter, including this one, is an integral component of the entire undertaking. As you will discover, when dealing with energy bodies, all influences, within and without, are essential. In this manner, each chapter and each section should be viewed as a part of understanding and using your energy body. At any one point in your life, you will reference a piece or a chunk of your knowledge as you develop consciousness. There is no linear time line for this; there is no standard for what must occur first or last. Each of the segments of this book is, however, connected by the intertwining thread of infinity.

Here we have set a tone, a guiding signal to carry us forward along a specific path to journey's end. Yet it is also a template reflecting and determining what is to come. For instance, in the next chapter, "A World of Energy," you survey an arena where science and metaphysics blend, where a shift in what we perceive as reality is occurring, and that provides context to further the legitimacy of the existence and influence of the energy body.

"Anatomy of the Energy Body" then outlines the components and perceptual abilities of our extended self. It also provides an overview of the mechanics of how thoughts create the bits and pieces of the reality of daily life and how feelings hold this tapestry together. Applied to an individual, group, or society, these reference points can help guide one and all to freedom or can unmercifully constrain us. To enable you to comprehend and command this process, "The Formation of Reality" offers insights into how models of reality are dynamically developed, encapsulating our view of the world and thereby giving us a world to view. In such a manner, this chapter reveals how reality forms out of infinity. "Expanding the Boundaries" details energy body processes in such a way as to bring to bear various ways to adventure into states of consciousness beyond group consensus, thereby extending the zone of accepted reality.

You may find that your beliefs are challenged every step of the way. Suspension of belief is at the heart of the scientific method, Eastern mysticism where the world is seen as illusion, and of Western Toltec thought where the world (any world) is considered to be just one of many real possibilities. This perceptual shift is the soul of objectivity. By learning to manage your beliefs, you can conceive of and even construct new orders of reality. In and of itself, this renews and invigorates your life, which is why "Stockroom of a Thousand Mirrors" delves more deeply into reality construction.

Some of the stultifying effects on learning produced by our ideas of reality are then examined in "Closing in on Fundamentalism." No one has immunity from fundamentalist behavior and this chapter should not be overlooked. In it, you will find that the formation of reality is always an active process, whether or not you subscribe to the existence of free will. "Building a Creative Life" then provides perspectives to help you enhance your energy and consciously form your reality, as well as gain understanding of the stages of growth you can anticipate and their intrinsic barriers to increasing awareness.

"Living the Unfolding Moment" looks at the overall result of developing the energy body. It deals with the immediacy of life, where personal consciousness intersects infinity. While this connection is ever-present, we are generally not conscious of it. Living this ongoing moment reflects quintessential human intelligence—*ontological intelligence*—and is usually described as the state of *being,* a state of fulfillment, awareness, and grace. The difference between the ability to talk about and intellectually understand a skill, for instance, and the ability to do, to experience, to perform that skill signifies the difference between academic and ontological knowledge. It is my sense that all of the classic mysticisms address *being* and, in so doing, focus on the natural human condition. What varies among them is their style of bringing this to light.

By now, the tone of this book will have become an understanding. "Energy Management Skills," then places more tools at your disposal that permit exploring your energy body. You may share features of the resulting experiences with others or they may be completely subjective. Either way, the material in the earlier chapters gives you the ability to make sense of them in a larger format of stimulating your attention, adventuring in imagination, and accelerating your learning. "The Heartbeat of Learning" closes off this exploration by examining central components of learning—memory, intelligence, objectivity, self-guidance—and finishes up with a learning posture to keep you attentive no matter the time, place, or circumstance. Learning, after all, is what awakening your energy body is really all about.

Purpose and Path

All said and done, the purpose of this book is to provide you the context and means to enhance your skills of awareness so that you may time and again revitalize your life, adding immeasurably to what that means for both individuals and groups. Imagination and learning provide the means for this, and context supplies the navigational reference. Fully realizing this quest rests on finding the energized moment of an energized reality; it means to fully awaken, to *be*. This is the point from which you access infinity.

2

A World of Energy

In the history of human development, there have been moments during which group awareness expanded and the world turned on its ear. These moments have often stretched over decades if not centuries, as new ways of looking at the world—viewing it as round instead of flat or revolving around the Sun rather than vice versa—have gradually found their way from idea to wide acceptance to established fact.

Reality is "simply" a matter of perception, of organizing an immense number of bits of data into a coherent form that both awakens and limits our sense of the world. Like taking a compass reading, our orientation to life provides the parameters of what is considered to be possible. For someone who sees the world as flat, a voyage across an ocean to distant lands is not possible, because it would mean falling to one's certain doom. The attempt is not even made. On the other hand, a worldview that incorporates the accurate movement of heavenly bodies allows for the possibility of safe navigation across seas and oceans and even traveling to the moon and back. In the light of new perceptions daring souls accept the challenge to go beyond what others say just can't be. And this sets the stage for others to join in.

We live in a defining moment of human history, a moment where the entire world, including us, is now seen as being made of energy. A quantum physicist will certainly tell you this, and be able to back up this claim with all the appropriate facts and figures. A laying-on-of-hands healer, an acupuncturist, or a homeopath will tell you the same thing, albeit in different ways based on their training. A traditionally trained biologist or medical doctor who is now on the cutting edge of his or her discipline may also portray the world in these terms.

The ramifications of this shift in worldview are beyond current imagination. It will usher in new paradigms of psychology, health, ecology, business, and technology. All areas of human endeavor will be transformed, as it will require a complete reassessment of actualities and possibilities. The implications of this revised worldview for health and healing alone are staggering. However, a survey of the various aspects of the changes that will result from the recognition that we—and the world—are comprised first and foremost of energy is outside the focus of this book. Instead, it tackles the anatomy and psychological mechanics of the energy body. This has application to any circumstance, any lifestyle, as it forms the backdrop for understanding changes in reality on any scale.

The energy body model presented here not only represents a unifying umbrella for all bioenergetic modalities and technologies but also offers a means to address personal and group circumstances, including those of creativity, health, and consciousness. As part of our natural being, the energy body not only connects us with our daily world but determines the complete range of our perceptions and behavior. Thus a substantial reorientation of conditions within the energy body results in a foundational shift in perceiving reality. The emphasis on healing in this chapter serves to show the practical bottom-line potential of this inquiry.

BIOENERGETICS

Bioenergy is at the foundation of a sweeping new field of inquiry, which suggests that the world is comprised of energy and that physical objects manifest a result of this energy. A branch of biophysics, the multidisciplinary field of *bioenergetics*[1] is "the study of the flow and transformation of energy in and between living organisms and between living organisms and their environment."[2] As the term indicates, it deals with biology (the study of all life) and energy (perhaps the underlying structure of all life) and where these two intersect. The meeting area between biology and energy is immense, extending beyond imagination. As virtually every area of human activity and every nook and cranny of our world is touched by bioenergy, it can form the basis of an entirely new cosmology.

Initially, the term bioenergetics was defined as "a form of psychology based on the use of kinesthetics and muscle testing to assess energy flow and levels," so the field first took hold based on physical anatomy. Physician Alexander Lowen popularized it with his book *Bioenergetics*. More recently, in his book *Energy Psychology,* psychologist Fred Gallo shows how the discipline has grown by revealing connections between cognition, energy, and behavior, and placing the movement and blockages of energy squarely in the center of why disorders manifest.[3]

The idea of energy playing a role within the body is well established. The principal communication mechanism of the central nervous system is electrical, brain waves are measured by frequency, and energy is at the root of metabolism. Elucidation of the role of energy within the body is becoming more enhanced. The specialty of biophysics evolved as a natural result of physicists furthering their research into all areas where energy plays a role. This discipline has grown to include topics including cellular communication, neurobiology, and the role of photons and electrons within the human body. At the same time, the world of technology is birthing devices that reveal and alter biologic energy fields, and even interact with the matrix of environmental energy.

From these types of investigation, we are rapidly increasing our appreciation of the fact that energy fields cause a wide variety of physical occurrences. In his landmark text, *Energy Medicine: The Scientific Basis,* biophysicist James Oschman points out that DNA's response to pulsing magnetic fields has been well documented. He also describes an *extracellular matrix* found throughout the body and its multifaceted relation to energy fields. This matrix "exerts specific and important influences upon cellular dynamics, just as much as hormones and neurotransmitters."[4]

While bioenergetics is a modern term, it has deep historical bindings. For example, as part of Traditional Chinese Medicine (TCM) acupuncture has been practiced for at least 2,000 years with some now dating its inception up to 5,000 years ago. At the heart of acupuncture are meridians, channels that form energetic circuits throughout the body. This flow is not unlike the movement of blood through the circulatory system, which requires proper regulation for health. Meridians are also the biological connection with *qi*, or life energy.[5] Needles are inserted into the skin along the channel routes in order to restore and regulate the natural flow of energy. Since acupuncture is performed with minimal invasiveness, adverse side effects are also minimal—a valuable consideration given the frequent toll taken by the side effects of pharmaceuticals.

Chakras comprise yet another energetic circuit within the body. In a basic view, chakras are energy centers occurring along the length of the spine, each accounting for a different mode of perception. The root chakra at the base of the spine, for instance, is often viewed as relating to physicality, whereas the crown chakra located at the top of the head corresponds to spiritual orientation. Many laying-on-of-hands practices, as with Reiki, use the chakra framework, which was developed in Eastern cultures thousands of years ago.[6]

A more recent model of energetic healing is found in homeopathy. In 1810, its inventor, physician Samuel Hahnemann, published the formative treatise, *Organon of the Medical Art,* in which he detailed the practice of using small amounts of a substance that corresponds to a disease in order to treat it, a "like cures like" principle. Through *succussing,* during which the solution is vigorously shaken, as well as repeatedly diluting the solution, the physical molecules are gradually removed until only an energetic trace remains, establishing another principle of "less is more." According to Hahnemann, this *potentizes* the formulation, which acts directly on the "vital force," the underlying energy of the patient. This causes the physical body to respond and heal.[7]

Homeopathy is credited with reducing the suffering experienced during the infectious disease plagues that swept Europe during the 1800s. Toward the end of that century, as scientific models of biology and chemistry gained popularity, homeopathy began to be viewed by many as quackery. Reflecting a revival of interest in the United States, however, the National Center for Complementary and Alternative Medicine (NCCAM), part of the National Institutes of Health, is now providing grants for the scientific evaluation of homeopathy. In Europe the practice of homeopathy is returning to its earlier popularity, typified by centers like the Paracelsus Clinic in Lustmuhle, Switzerland, which uses homeopathy as a main therapy in treating cancer and other illnesses from a biological medicine perspective.[8]

In the early 1900s, Royal Rife discovered a cancer virus, an accomplishment not verified by medical science until the late 1950s. He went on to find a specific electromagnetic frequency that, when targeted at cancer cells, caused their destruction, setting the stage for later considerations that every organism has its own electromagnetic signature or waveform associated with its genetic makeup. Rife's work was considered controversial, to say the least, with many agencies working to suppress it, but today it remains a focus of reference within the field of bioenergetics.[9]

A principal, and most compelling, feature separating many of these therapies from the allopathic biomedical model is that bioenergy-based modes of healing often require an examination of the total person and view illness as an expression of disharmony both internally and externally. Treatment in the Western allopathic model, on the other hand, is intended to antagonize the disease, which is seen as something separate from the patient. Often symptoms alone are attacked, causing harmful side effects, whereas in holistic models adverse side effects are purposefully minimized if not eliminated. I'm not arguing that one perspective is better than the other, as I think both models have value according to the situation.

As Clark Manning and Louis Vanrenan, authors of *Bioenergetic Medicines East and West,* point out, one of the difficulties for a new field like this is the lack of instrumentation to adequately measure effects and results.[10] Scientific tools to measure chakras, meridians, and associated energy systems have been slow to develop since these avenues of energy haven't found widespread acceptance in scientific thought. Chakras remain on the fringes of simple mention, let alone scientific study.

Although biologists are accumulating extensive data relating to different energetic processes such as cellular signaling, this pertains to accepted scientific inquiry. CAM methodologies such as homeopathy and acupuncture haven't been adequately measured, verified, and accepted by the broad medical science community. One reason technological invention lags, then, is because rigorous definitions of the energies to be measured are lacking.

NCCAM holds that energy-based therapies deal with two types of energy fields: *veritable* and *putative*. Veritable fields are those that can be measured and include visible light, magnetism, and portions of the electromagnetic spectrum. Putative fields are those that have yet to be measured and include energies such as the vital force and qi.[11] Lack of instrumentation pertaining to CAM-related biofields is being addressed on several fronts, though.

At the leading edge of this type of innovation is the SQUID (superconducting quantum interference device) magnetometer, a highly sensitive technology that can map biomagnetic fields produced by physiological processes within the body. Its development was spearheaded by J. E. Zimmerman, once a Ford Motor Company scientist. SQUID was the first practical electronic instrument to detect interference between the energy waves of matter and is currently considered one of the best detectors of magnetic flux. In conjunction with SQUID technology, special rooms to shield environmental energies have been built in order to examine extremely subtle magnetic fields of the brain and other areas of the body.[12]

Another invention comes from Konstantin Korotkov, a physics professor at Russia's St. Petersburg State Technical University. An expert in the field of bioelectrography, Korotkov developed a computerized device that permits what he refers to as Gas Discharge Visualization (GDV).

Based on Kirlian photography, GDV allows the observation of human energy fields, and can help in observing the changes in energy in a variety of situations, including when therapies are administered.[13]

Still another emerging technology with great promise for diagnosing physical and mental illness is Polycontrast Interference Photography (PIP). Invented by British researcher Harry Oldfield, it consists of a digital camera and proprietary software that tracks the energy emitted when two waveforms intersect. The resulting photonic discharge provides a picture that illuminates areas of disease and health. Chakras, meridians, and physiologic states are easily discernible, as are the effects of personal intention and a range of environmental influences. Oldfield has collaborated in the United States with physician Brian Dailey and in India with investigator Thornton Streeter, Director of The Centre for Biofield Sciences. In one study the crown chakra of a person diagnosed as psychotic was clearly split. In another profile, PIP mapped an experienced meditator's shifts as he went from normal waking consciousness into deep meditation and back to waking.[14] As with GDV studies, PIP measurements remain in the putative category as it isn't clear what energies are being monitored.

Bioenergetics is also now defined as the study of metabolic activity at the cellular level. Based on this, scientists at leading universities are demonstrating the role of energetic flow and transformation in disease and healing. The University of Colorado's Institute of Bioenergetics at Colorado Springs, for example, is building "a multidisciplinary approach to understanding cellular metabolism and cellular communication with the intention of treating or curing serious diseases."[15] The area of cellular signaling (how cells communicate) is also evolving from the study of physical processes—a hormone docking with a cellular receptor, for instance, which in turn sets a cascade of events into motion—to investigating energetic signaling where the first cause of the physical cascade is energetic in nature.

Another area of exploration is taking place in the laboratory of John McMichael, immunologist, virologist, and founder of Beech Tree Labs and The Institute for Therapeutic Discovery.[16] Decades of laboratory and preclinical studies have shown the value of a class of formulations that use low levels of naturally-occurring molecules—proteins and DNA, for instance—to potentially treat a wide range of disorders. The dosages are far above those used in homeopathy but far lower than those used in most current pharmaceuticals. Mounting scientific data regarding which receptors are influenced and which genes are up- or down-regulated (turned on or off) indicate this platform might result in a new understanding of how the body works.

After McMichael's novel invention for treating depression demonstrated efficacy in validated animal studies, scientists at the University of North Carolina at Chapel Hill also discovered that it didn't act through the biopathways associated with modern antidepressants. These findings drove speculation that the agent might work through a form of energetic communication that tells the body to restore balance. McMichael himself holds open the possibility that there may be an energetic circuit comprised of receptors in cells or in the extracellular matrix that plays a role in the restoration of *homeodynamics* (a more descriptive term for homeostasis), the body's natural harmony. As a result, his research now targets sub-molecular processes.

Also on the cutting edge of bioenergetics is *nonlocal* healing where the well-focused intent of an individual or a group may significantly affect the health of someone thousands of miles away. While this practice is often placed in a spiritual or religious category, the mechanism of nonlocal healing is usually viewed as energy-related, whether it is focused through dowsing, prayer, or other means. Among those who scientifically examine this mechanism of healing are physician Larry Dossey and research scientist Marilyn Mandala Schlitz of the Institute of Noetic Sciences, who have found promising albeit inconsistent results, a common circumstance when investigating putative energies.[17] Intentionality, the conscious application of intent, is often thought to be the common denominator of how the various approaches to nonlocal healing focus energy. Scientific mapping of intent remains on the horizon.

If healing practices and hardwired technologies—which cut to the essence of the human condition—are an effect of energy and require looking at the entire person as well as environmental influences, then the quantum physicist's "unified field" and the mystic's experience that "all is one" come together to suggest a common world. This brings us closer to the shared components of the human experience regardless of race, gender, or creed. While there has been an enormous amount of research on the energetics of living systems, for the most part this research has not been viewed in the context of Western European philosophical concepts and practices. This is changing. Science is catching up to what Toltecs have been saying about the world, and to the healing practices TCM has been offering the world, for centuries. It seems obvious, then, that the healing therapies of bioenergetics—often referred to as "energy medicine"—are quite diverse, have deep historical roots, and comprise an emerging multidisciplinary arena in the modern world of science.

If energy is in any way a determinant for biological actions and reactions, then new models, new variables for investigation, and new technologies for healing and wellness will continue to sprout. At the same time, these revelations are not casting an entirely new net of awareness over the scientific world. They are based on preceding knowledge. "The emerging concepts do not require us to abandon our sophisticated understandings of physiology, biochemistry, or molecular biology," maintains Oschman. "Instead they extend our picture of living processes, and of healing, to finer levels of structure and function."[18]

The human body constantly receives and emits magnetic electrical information and other types of energy-based signals. From taking in the Sun's energy and converting it to Vitamin D, to sound affecting regions of the brain, to receptors in the eye that detect photons, the body has an array of energy-detection apparatuses. Chemical reactions are set into motion by energy. Furthermore, there are over a hundred years of research behind the modern field of electromyography, the tracking of electrical currents behind muscle movement, which shows this type of activity occurs naturally within the body.[19]

Oschman, a recognized leader in the field of biophysics, says, "We are in a period of dramatic change in the healthcare system. Energy

Medicine has a huge role to play in this process. The reason is that conventional Western medicine is the only medical system in history that has virtually ignored energetics. Energetic concepts are part of nearly all of the complementary and alternative therapies that the public is enthusiastically moving toward." Quoting Albert Szent-Györgyi (who won a Nobel Prize in 1937 for his synthesis of vitamin C), Oschman continues, "'In every culture and in every medical tradition before ours, healing was accomplished by moving energy.'"[20]

As physicist Milo Wolff points out, "Nothing happens in nature without an energy exchange. Communication or acquisition of knowledge of any kind occurs only with an energetic transfer. There are no exceptions. This is a rule of nature."[21]

TRANSPERSONAL PSYCHOLOGY

The blossoming field of energy psychology is an aspect of bioenergetics as well as that of transpersonal psychology. The Institute of Transpersonal Psychology defines this discipline as "the extension of psychological studies into consciousness studies, spiritual inquiry, body-mind relationships, and transformation." It deals with the breadth and depth of perception and behavior. It is the fourth force of psychology, with behaviorism, psychoanalysis, and humanism being the others. The first three are often associated with B. F. Skinner, Sigmund Freud, and Abraham Maslow, respectively. Yet Maslow would later become dissatisfied with just a humanistic approach. As signaled by the first publication of *The Journal of Transpersonal Psychology* in 1969, a group of psychologists including Maslow, Anthony Sutich, and Charles T. Tart brought forth the fourth force.[22]

Traditional psychologies, such as Zen Buddhism, Taoism, certain denominations of Christianity, and the Toltec Way, are integral to transpersonal psychology. Each of these systems also offers practices of meditation, personal growth, and ways to consciously evolve beyond the mortal plane. When you add the various works of those like nineteenth-century theosophists C. W. Leadbeater and Madame Helena Blavatsky to the more modern writings of Barbara Brennan, Valerie V. Hunt, and

Fritjof Capra, the literature on aspects of the energy body, including psychological applications, continues to grow.

To date, religion and metaphysics have carried the banner of researching and explaining such things as the *mystical experience* where a person's consciousness expands well beyond normal limits and a profound oneness with all creation is directly experienced. The advent of a new division of psychology allows for the secularization of this study and is already providing common cross-cultural perspectives to further define it.

In addition, there is currently a strong movement to develop a science of consciousness. There are several quality books on this field, which is using rigorous scientific skills to examine what has been in the province of what some consider the soft sciences. Some of the most significant work has come from MIT Press, which has published a series appropriately titled *Toward a Science of Consciousness.* This series stems from discussions and debates sponsored by The University of Arizona that have brought together experts in fields such as cognitive science, physiology, psychology, and physics. Revealing the interest and depth of this research, Cambridge University Press followed with *The Cambridge Handbook of Consciousness.*[23]

From a wide-angle perspective, transpersonal psychology may be especially noteworthy, as it provides meaning for experiences beyond the currently accepted norms of daily human consciousness, including those of social consensus reality. In other words, it provides a telescope to examine the entire human experience and thereby enable us to look at how things are shaping up from an entirely different vantage point. It also reflects *positive psychology,* an area that Maslow has referred to as the psychology of the future, which deals with healthy, fully functioning people. In contrast to *abnormal psychology*—the study of dysfunctions—which has received the preponderance of attention, positive psychology examines the brighter side of human behavior including hope, happiness, and healing.[24]

While transpersonal psychology brings academic and scientific rigor to investigations of consciousness, the greater body of it currently presents intellectual perspectives, which help set the stage for new navigational charts. This may change. These charts, for instance, are yielding models of psychotherapy and an orientation to psychological health. The combination of bioenergetic perspectives with a branch of psychology that examines consciousness may enable us to develop a sophisticated model of states of pathology and their remedy. A practical effect of this work will be that the entire field of healing will change if not explode into new directions.

THE TOLTEC PARADIGM

This background demonstrates that an energy-based perspective of reality doesn't exist on the fringes of speculation; rather, aspects of the energy body already have a place within established fields. At the same time, it must be underscored that while these contemporary fields duly investigate aspects of energy, it is from centuries of efforts of metaphysical investigators from cultures around the world that provide the framework for a modern scientific examination of the energy body. By its very nature, the energy body offers a model that accounts for all states of consciousness, including those of healing, personal transformation, and cosmology. In this manner, the Toltec view consists of a coherent system of concepts and rules along with a set of propositions derived from observation that may be used to explain and predict.[25]

Components of the Toltec paradigm have been successfully implemented, verified, and refined for centuries by its practitioners. This perspective embraces philosophy as a means to acquire knowledge. It is also psychological, as it deals first and foremost with perception. It details a structure of the energy body with the elements that transform sensation into perception and then meaning. And it is now entering the domain of science vis-à-vis bioenergetics.

In great measure, Carlos Castaneda's work set the tone for subsequent Toltec literature as his books presented the essential framework of this metaphysical system.[26] In so doing, he also standardized much of the terminology in a manner similar to any other academic, scientific, or trade discipline. Mathematicians, biologists, or electricians, for instance, rely on common terms in order for practitioners within the respective fields to effectively communicate even though they are scattered throughout the world. And even though their lexicons may be arduous and tedious, their list of terms provides for more efficient communication and enhanced understanding.

The authors of contemporary Toltec books have similarly adopted much of the same terminology in their books, even though their individual relationships to the Toltec Way vary. I use some of this terminology in describing the energy body, while modifying some terms to provide a more descriptive or practical viewpoint. Most of the current Toltec literature retains the flavor and terminology of days long past. In many ways, this is well and good, but this practice of knowledge has much to offer—not just for its adherents—and deserves to be recast into more modern perspectives, a task very much in keeping with its teachings. Relating parts of the Toltec lexicon to those of contemporary fields shows the viability and value of this shamanic knowledge to one and all.

AN UPDATED HUMAN ANATOMY

The Toltec paradigm represents far more than wishful musings as the adherents established a view of extended, human anatomy applicable to everyone, as well as a schema that demonstrates how its components and systems influence perception. Energy body anatomy also provides the objective reference needed to enable hard science skills to be employed in investigations that are on empirical measurements. Bioenergetics is the bridge connecting science and shamanism as both these camps focus on exactly the same thing: energy and its relationship to life.

The energy body as a whole has four main components: *uniformity,* or its shape; *cohesion,* which reflects the overall coherence of energies within it; the *assemblage point,* which provides a reference to the type of cohesion; and *core,* the innermost area of the energy body, the cool spot of the flame, our direct connection with infinity itself.

Various dimensions of awareness reside within the energy body. The physical body is one segment of the energy body, for example. It is experienced when cohesion stabilizes in a certain way. If you move cohesion just a little you might experience a change of mood or have different thoughts. If you shift it more so, and reform cohesion to a greater extent, you might then experience other dimensions of reality or perceive the world from completely different perspectives, as during an out-of-body experience.

Cohesion results from a variety of influences. One of the primary determinants is uniformity, the container that holds together the internal energies. Each member of the human species has a similar uniformity, as do other species. This shape changes over time, which provides a useful perspective on evolution. Since a change of shape in uniformity changes cohesion, this causes new perceptions, new behaviors, and new physical attributes.

The assemblage point offers a reference for what type of cohesion has been formed. The assemblage point of a person having a strong intellectual bent will be positioned in a certain area, while this area of a nervous or unstable person will wiggle about, not being able to rest or stabilize in a specific location. A specific mental or physical disease is marked by the assemblage point being in a position corresponding to the particular disease, and health is likewise evidenced by a certain position. The assemblage point thereby indicates the pattern of cohesion.

Whether one uses a homeopathic remedy, acupuncture, Reiki, or a scientific medical technology, in terms of Toltec views, the mechanism by

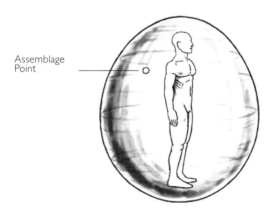

Figure 2.1. The Energy Body
The energy body has a definitive form but not a hardened boundary.

which the therapy works is the same: the energy of the healing modality affects the energy of the person, altering coherence. An effective treatment builds on this and changes the person's overall cohesion, which is reflected by a movement of the assemblage point. Traditionally, a shaman learns how to shift a person's assemblage point back to the "health" position by utilizing a range of procedures, which are based on a view of the world as being comprised of energy, sometimes using the word "spirit" in lieu of "energy."

Given that cohesion and the assemblage point are not part of traditional medical training, a physician approaches healing from quite a different vantage point. From an energy body perspective, however, both shaman and doctor have the same effect, that of shifting the assemblage point. No matter the technique, then, the concept that all perceptions and states of being derive from the mechanics of the energy body forms a basic premise of this book. This applies to each and every person walking the earth. This knowledge alone could foster new and varied industries of research, education, and technology.

TWO SIDES, THREE FIELDS

Knowing the two sides of the energy body is basic to understanding its structure and use. Simply, they are the right and left sides. In terms of bioenergetics, they are the *first* and *second energy fields*. In terms of psychology, they are the *conscious* and *unconscious*. In Toltec terms, they are the *known* and *unknown*. *Learning* and *imagination*—which respectively emphasize stability and rapid expansion of awareness— are the two fundamental, integral approaches to develop both sides of the energy body. In these terms, Castaneda referred to learning as "stalking" and imagination as "dreaming."

Developing the two sides may lead to awareness of a *third energy field,* a dimension that exists outside the energy body yet impacts it as it puts pressure on the energy body, giving it shape and substance. Emanations of energy arising from a single source, the source of all creation, form an underpinning of this field. These packages or streams of awareness have powerful influence on the shape of the energy body and what happens within it, thereby determining the assemblage point position. This falls neatly within the definition of bioenergetics, as the flow and transformation of energy between the energy body and the environment is taken into consideration.

The third energy field can also be understood as the *supraconscious,* a domain of awareness that contains the other two fields, yet extends into a far vaster environment. Purposefully tapping awareness of the third field created a line of demarcation between the ancient and modern Toltecs. Doing so eventually removes you from the craft of Toltec practices and places you in a more sublime arena, that of the *self-actualized* person, someone who has achieved a fundamental transformation in his or her energy body by activating the full range of innate abilities.

While Maslow put forth *self-actualization* as the capstone of psychological development, C. G. Jung regarded this as *individuation.*[27] In essence, both approaches look at becoming more human as determined by a natural order of how one is created rather than by the definitions and confinement of human-made order. Although I don't think either had the energy body in mind, in principle there is no disparity; all of these viewpoints deal with fulfilled, complete, psychologically healthy people. That there can be common denominators among established lines of thought only serves to demonstrate the viability of continued investigation concerning what it means and what it takes to achieve this level. The founders of transpersonal psychology have suggested that the study of actualization should be a new branch of psychology called *ontopsychology,* a hybrid term incorporating ontology and psychology.[28]

Ontology can be defined in many ways. Here it pertains to your relationship with life as a whole. It is part of metaphysical inquiry that deals with *being,* with essence. Metaphysics applies to those time-honored philosophical traditions that concern the nature of reality, including the underlying principles of reality formation. Focusing on deliberate awakening, these approaches to understanding the expanse of the human condition invoke *metacognition,* or thinking about thinking and being able to know that you know as well as how you know.[29] Transpersonal psychologies and some energy-based psychologies find a natural place within this field. The energy body perspective of consciousness serves to advance ontopsychology, and its subdivisions, in providing objective references and schematics regarding how to become self-actualized or individuated.

Regardless of its divisions, branches, or schools of thought, psychology is still psychology. If we use the root derivation of the term, it is "the study of mind." Perhaps the energy body as a whole is what philosophers call "mind" and at the core of it resides what theologians call "soul." And perhaps the two sides also correspond to the left and right hemispheres of the brain, while the three fields relate to the vertical partitioning of the brain into the reptilian, paleomammilian, and neomammilian sections.[30] In days to come, this extended bioenergetic anatomy could provide a more in-depth basis for many disciplines.

SELF-REFLECTION

Modern Toltecs focus on the unrelenting quest to awaken their entire energy bodies as a means to engage the third field, not to mention for the sheer adventure of doing so. But you don't have to be a Toltec to embark on this voyage. Anyone can set his or her mind to it. The principal way to facilitate this journey is to manage *self-reflection,* the almost constant mental and emotional referencing of ourselves to ourselves, others, and our world. When management of self-reflection combines with stopping our thoughts, the flow of our mental energy, it delivers a one-two punch that knocks out the images of our preconceived world. All other perspectives and procedures fall secondary to this challenge.[31]

No matter what the scheme of things—flat earth, shamanism, bioenergetics, or otherwise—the world we perceive bubbles forth from a network of interlocking thoughts that form a grand composite. What we think the world is becomes a self-fulfilling prophecy where we verify our own thoughts and feelings day in and day out. The trick, then, is to stop thinking . . . at least long enough, and regularly enough, to break apart the composite—the cohesion—in order to allow new perceptions to enter into our conscious world, to allow new thoughts to form, and then to repeat this time and again. It therefore supplies a means of discovering what exists, not what we think exists.

NEW FIELDS OF INQUIRY

Most current bioenergetic methods speak to physical health and healing. Only when we bring in other areas of science does this expand to an entire modern worldview. Even then, our knowledge is limited as to the range of known bioenergetic circuits in the body and environment. By updating human anatomy, we vastly expand the meaning of bioenergetics and the frontiers of science. We can apply the structure, function, and processes of the energy body to virtually any endeavor. Understanding how uniformity, cohesion, perception, and experience interact affects the practice of medicine, all forms and schools of psychology, ecology, and technology.

As presented here, all of the pieces for this already exist. It's a matter of consolidation. The foundation of this enterprise consists of:

- a cosmological environment that is comprised of energy, such as detailed by physics and Toltec shamanism;
- the anatomy of the individual energy body, including the functions of its parts and systems, as outlined by scientific and metaphysical disciplines;
- the processes to facilitate and guide these interactions, as provided by several psychological models, traditional and modern, with applications ranging from the abnormal to the positive; and
- the discipline of bioenergetics examining all aspects of the flow and exchange of energy from individual and environmental perspectives, which brings it full circle.

As an example of the many possibilities that collaboration between mysticism and science holds, relating energetic anatomy to consciousness studies might yield a multidisciplinary field such as *transpersonal bioenergetics* (or a similar term that encapsulates the study), in which the enduring, highly valuable work of indigenous traditions are made accessible to everyone by integrating their perspectives with the best knowledge from contemporary fields. Stretching this further, such a new endeavor would reexamine afresh the doctrines of the classic metaphysical traditions in light of what has been learned from transpersonal psychology, physics, religious studies, and related disciplines.

A NEW WORLD

Combining multiple fields to reveal more of what occurs is not unheard of and may be occurring more frequently, as in the case of University of Maine research that brings to bear evolution and ecology in order to reveal how other species are responding to human environmental interference.[32] From such like-minded efforts, we might then reveal a world where examining the interactions of energy among all aspects of life, and perhaps beyond, is commonplace. The results of applying these perspectives to your life could be quite astonishing.

The chapters to come offer you ways to look at and feel the world around you, take stock of yourself as you learn what you are made of, discover processes of exploring uncharted territories, and determine the directions of your life. This is the journey. If you stop learning, crashing is inevitable, rapid entropy assured. If you continue, be prepared for transformations of many kinds, as you leave your known world behind, bit by bit, then leap by leap.

All said and done, the beckoning of awareness is all you have. Eventually it will take you past all known channel markers, beyond all current models as you embark on an endeavor that will take you beyond your known world and deliver you to the infinity that is within and without, residing right here, right now, no matter what you are doing. There you have it: a new world, a world of energy, and one that has been within you all along. The means to access this world and better understand the creation of reality is to awaken your energy body to its fullest capacity in order to live a full and conscious life. For this, you need to know what it is, how it works, and a collection of basic management skills. What happens along the way is up to you.

3

Anatomy of the Energy Body

An energized world is a reality. We live in a world driven, consumed, and managed by energy. From the Sun's rays to wind to batteries to medical technologies, virtually nothing in our lives escapes the domain of energy.

It is also clear that this reality is being continually revealed and applied. In simple terms, engineers are learning how to better harness Sun and wind power, physicists now deal with scalar and vector energies and measurements (a vector is linear and finite, whereas scalar energies emanate instantaneously everywhere), and medical scientists have demonstrated that pulsed magnetic therapy has value for healing bone fractures.[1] All of these applications fit into a bioenergetic view of our world. It is less of a stretch, then, to view human anatomy as being comprised of energy.

We typically view the world as made up of material, solid objects. Perceiving the world as external objects hinges on the agreements we collectively make about the world, agreements that have been handed down unchallenged for centuries. We have a world based on a collection of assumptions *about* reality. We have inherited a description of reality so powerful that we have validated it time and time again without ever understanding what it truly is, let alone stepping beyond it.

Bioenergetics offers a fresh option: a universe comprised of energy.

As with any paradigm, it's possible to make an extensive categorization of various types of energy and their effects. If we hold that the world is energy, then each person, place, and thing in the world is energy. And each group of items, such as humans, trees, and clouds, has its own energetics. Then there is another set of processes for how they interact. The more you recognize these dynamics, the more you will become aware of yourself, your circumstances, and your growth.

To enhance this exploration, you need to know the mechanical structure and capabilities of your conveyance, just as it is important to know that if you want to travel three thousand miles in one day, an automobile isn't the best vehicle. In like manner, flying a small propeller-driven plane requires different skills than flying a jet airliner. And not knowing how to use the rigging of a sailboat during a storm leads to major trouble. In each case, knowing the nature of the craft—its capacities, its structure and layout, and how it functions in part and in whole—provides for a better journey.

Here, the craft is the energy body, which is sometimes referred to as the "light" or "luminous" body, reflecting metaphysical teachings that humans are comprised of a more rarified energy than just material form. This is in part referenced by science in that cells both emit and absorb photons. A photon is the basic unit of light and an elementary particle, and therefore governed by quantum mechanics. It can be gauged as a wave or a particle, and acts ". . . as a 'messenger' particle, conveying the electromagnetic information between particles of matter."[2] It thereby transmits information that may cause any number of things to occur. A *biophoton* is light emitted from a biological system. It is not bioluminescence, which occurs in species such as fireflies, glow-worms, and some marine life due to chemical reactions.

The physical body is considered by Toltecs to be an effect of the energy body and only one option of human awareness. Human anatomy is thus far more extensive than what is usually understood. The following exploration of various aspects of energetic anatomy, such as the nervous system and chakras, provide a better sense of this extended perspective. This prepares us to more fully enter into a Toltec-based worldview and examine the major anatomical components of uniformity, cohesion, assemblage point, and core.

The Toltec model didn't pop into consciousness out of the blue; from the contributions of other cultures you can see an energetic anatomy is not the idea of one group of people. It is valuable to understand that we are also reviewing the structure of the environment—the universe of energy—to help us connect with and perceive it, just as knowing the physical models of planets, solar systems, and galaxies enable us to better perceive the physical cosmos.

PHYSICAL-BODY ENERGY SYSTEMS

An overriding consideration is that there is already an established framework for understanding human perception and behavior as described and measured in terms of energy. There is acceptance of and scientific research on energetic aspects of human anatomy, consisting of the nervous system, brain waves, and acupuncture meridians, for example. The elements mentioned here by no means represent a complete list of what researchers around the world are tackling. But a brief review helps make the point about the viability of an energy-based model of humans. Awareness of the components of the energy body and of the energy body itself may then be regarded as an extension of what is already known.

The Nervous System

The human nervous system principally divides into central and peripheral parts. The *central nervous system* consists of the brain and spinal cord. It performs an array of functions, from processing information to generating reflexes to higher cognitive functioning. The *peripheral system* connects the central nervous system with both outer and inner environments; it is further divided into sensory and motor functions. Sensory functions, including taste, touch, sight, and so on, regulate the various forms of environmental energies that affect the body, while motor functions pertain to body movements such as intentionally turning the pages of a book.[3]

Another aspect is the *autonomic system,* which is the watchdog of

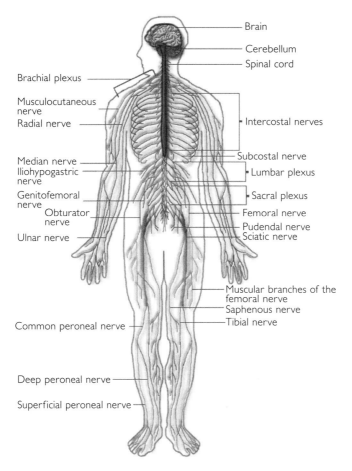

Brain

Cerebellum

Spinal cord

Brachial plexus

Musculocutaneous nerve

Radial nerve

Intercostal nerves

Median nerve

Iliohypogastric nerve

Genitofemoral nerve

Obturator nerve

Ulnar nerve

Subcostal nerve

Lumbar plexus

Sacral plexus

Femoral nerve

Pudendal nerve

Sciatic nerve

Muscular branches of the femoral nerve

Saphenous nerve

Tibial nerve

Common peroneal nerve

Deep peroneal nerve

Superficial peroneal nerve

Figure 3.1. Nervous System
(Illustration courtesy of Wikimedia Commons)

all internal neural functions. This divides further into the *sympathetic* and *parasympathetic systems.* These work together; for example, the sympathetic system tightens the gastrointestinal sphincters and the parasympathetic system loosens them.

Communication within the nervous system is performed by cells called *neurons.* This communication is studied in terms of electrical energy—"action potential" and "states of excitation," for instance—that describe the movement of electrical signals and information along the same neural pathways that also convey chemical substances.

Brain Waves

Measuring the electrical activity of the brain provides one way to discern behavior. The electroencephalograph (EEG) provides an indication of states of consciousness by registering activity associated with several bands of brain wave frequencies measured in hertz (Hz) or cycles per second. Different studies may list different frequencies; however, they usually vary only within a range of .5-1Hz. One schematic of brain wave frequencies consists of delta (.5–4Hz), theta (4–8Hz), alpha (8–13Hz), beta (13–30Hz), and gamma (30+Hz). Dominance of any band often indicates a certain state of awareness, such as relaxation, mental activity, agitation, reverie, various stages of sleep, and even peak athletic performance. An EEG pattern provides a map, or at least a sense of what a subject is experiencing.[4]

Other Physical Systems

Stemming from the work of physician Robert Becker, author of *The Body Electric,* Oschman has described a *perineural system* consisting of the connective tissue surrounding the nervous system.[5] Controlling the repair of injury, it acts in a more wide-reaching capacity with expansive nonlinear properties where communication and effects proceed rapidly throughout the whole of the body, while the nervous system is linear with information and activity directed along specific pathways.

In addition, biophysicists, engineers, medical doctors, educators, and other professionals with common interests formed an alliance to study *biologic closed electrical circuits.* Members focus on the use of a variety of energy-based therapies—electrical, magnetic, and thermal, for instance—to treat an array of diseases. Their work centers on circulating, self-regulating loops of energy within the body that use a number of physiologic pathways for healing.[6]

Meridians and Acupuncture

Referring to acupuncture as a medical science, the World Health Organization recognizes fourteen meridians with 361 classical acupuncture points.[7] Traditional Chinese Medicine (TCM), of which acupuncture is a part, deals with recognizing and treating disharmony among the various elements of the body that have been singled out over thousands of years of research.

Fundamental textures of qi, blood, essence, spirit, and fluids—along with their individual and collective effect on homeodynamics—are all taken into account. Each texture has several aspects. Qi has positive and negative functions relating to nutrition, protection, deficiencies, and stagnation. Blood is the yin-yang opposite of qi. Whereas qi energizes, blood relaxes. Essence deals with the intrinsic nature separating animate and inanimate worlds, and spirit is the defining quality of humanness. The fluids of the body moisten and nourish.[8]

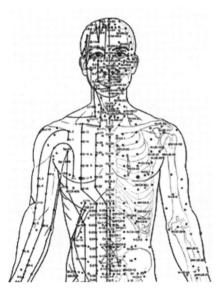 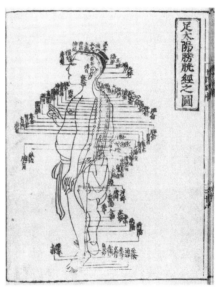

Figure 3.2a Meridians	*Figure 3.2b. Acupuncture chart from Hua Shou* *(fl. 1340s, Ming Dynasty)*
Acupuncture involves the manipulation of meridians—the channels of qi—to help restore harmony throughout the body. Charts like the one above serve to guide the placement of acupuncture needles. (This illustration is used with the kind permission of Devatara J. Holman, Marin Oriental Medicine, Sausalito, California, www.marinorientalmedicine.com.)	This image from *Shi si jing fa hui (Expression of the Fourteen Meridians)*. Tokyo, Suharaya Heisuke kanko, Kyoho gan, 1716. (Illustration courtesy of Wikimedia Commons)

A refinement of this practice occurs when viewing textures in relation to organs, another principal part of TCM. The liver, for instance, connects with blood as well as tempers qi. The kidneys provide the foundation upon which water or fluids may work with the rest of the body.[9] It is also interesting that scientific studies have revealed that the body's communication along the meridians occur at least 1,000 times faster than known signaling processes of the nervous system, perhaps conducting energy approaching the speed of light.[10] Simply on the face of it, this research supports metaphysical considerations of a "light" body.

Chakras

Chakras are energy generators, each associated with a specific function. Traditionally, seven centers comprise the chakra system. Located in proximity to the spinal column and ascending from the bottom of the spine to the crown of the head, some research presents the chakra system as a nonphysical loop of energy entering the bottoms of the feet, traversing upward, leaving the top of the head, and flowing outward and back down. Some investigations portray the chakras as having physical correlates with specific organs, often those of the endocrine glandular system, while other investigations relegate them to general locations not necessarily associated with physical organs. Invariably, though, chakras are seen as affecting the physical body as well as connecting the physical body to physical and non-physical environments inside and outside the energy body.

Each chakra has a vibration, perhaps a composite of several resonant frequencies. The higher along the spine a chakra is located, the higher its frequency range. Thus chakras extend from the base level of red

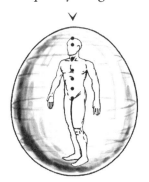

Figure 3.3. Chakras
This is one representation of chakra locations.
The "V" represents environmental influences.

through the physical light spectrum to violet. Accordingly, within your body you have a rainbow, the shade of which varies according to the person. These centers, combined with additional vertical channels of opposite polarity, are often referred to as the *kundalini system* or *tract*.[11] They may also be thought of as discrete dimensions, or planes of awareness. Working with these dimensions helps you achieve a more powerful relationship with your entire energy body and your life.

Some systems present as many as thirteen chakras, with additional chakras located at the knees, ankles, the top and bottom of the energy body, as well as between the top of the head and top of the energy body and between the bottoms of the feet and the bottom of the energy body. Combined, they are the bandwidth of human perception. Different systems also ascribe different meanings for each chakra. The following model is fairly generic. The idea behind it is not to provide a detailed map, but a simple schematic to offer a sense of the different aspects of our being.

Location	Color	Perception
Base of spine	Red	This energy pertains to the physical world.
Abdomen	Orange	Here we find emotional energy. Some systems place sexual energy here; other systems place sexual energy in the first center.
Solar plexus	Yellow	Mental or intellectual energy. The beginning of the power of discrimination, of making refined intellectual distinctions.
Heart	Green	This energy connects us with the world outside of our personal self. We begin to feel unity with the world.
Base of throat	Light blue	Communication energy. Also, this is often regarded as the entrance into more abstract regions of awareness, the initial realization of God.
Forehead	Dark blue	Psychic energy, often referred to as the *third eye*. Some metaphysical systems regard this as *will*.
Crown of the head	Violet	Spiritual dimensions. The link between the personal self and more-than-human regions.

To further elaborate:

Red, at the base of the spine. This is raw power, the baseline for physical-body and physical-world manifestations. Life as we know it extends from this primal world. Some energy exercises focus on this chakra to explosively release energy through the entire kundalini system, pushing awareness deep into unrealized territory.

The first chakra is often considered the densest of energies. It may be the densest within the ordinary human experience, but there are denser energies in the cosmos. Arcane and scientific literature detail regions of immense density, far outstripping the normal physical world we experience.

Orange, at the abdomen. This chakra ties in with emotions. As the energy of emotion, it directly relates to dreaming or imagination. Where red is the wellspring of the physical world, orange is the wellspring of the dreaming, creative world.

Yellow, at the solar plexus. This is the energy of classifying. As the chakras represent dimensions of awareness, the first, second, and third chakras build a three-dimensional world. Wanting to control your environment is the downside of the third chakra. You have such a sense of control, it's hard to let go in order to experience more . . . such as the fourth dimensional energies of the heart.

Green, at the heart. This energy enhances feeling. By developing it, you directly perceive subtleties, nuances, refinements. The trick is to get out of yourself long enough to sense them. The fourth chakra opens you to worlds beyond yourself. And yet these worlds are also you.

The first three chakras represent the personal self: the physical, emotional, and mental parts of individual awareness. These energies have to be groomed in order to find your conscious sense of self. From this point, you may enter worlds beyond your immediate personal dimensions. Therefore the fourth chakra takes you into, and connects you with, your environment. The more you activate the fourth chakra, the more you balance with and feel part of the world, not a three-dimensional object separate from it.

Light blue, at the base of the throat. This is a curious energy, which deals with verbal communication. Charismatic people tend to have good control of this energy, and their voices are often mesmerizing. Whereas the fourth chakra opens you to your environment, this energy begins to connect you with an out-of-this world environment. Elevating your perception of the environment, you begin to step outside of the physical world and into nonphysical dimensions. For this reason, it is sometimes considered the entrance into God realization.

Dark blue, at the forehead. Tapping this energy gives you entrance into psychic functioning as is why it is often referred to as the third eye. You may experience visions, telepathy, or precognition. Becoming psychic means you have greater ability to work with nonphysical energies. However, this often results in getting stuck. You have power, and don't want to let it go. To become actualized, you must manage the energies of the entire spectrum.

Violet, at the crown of the head. Whereas the first three chakras represent the personal self and the second set of three represent your environment, the seventh chakra is your entrance into worlds beyond the normal human domain. You may enter heavenly dimensions of bliss, or have mystical experiences. Since the energy is of a higher vibration, it translates to the physical body as ecstasy. It is for this reason that it is often considered the spiritual chakra.

Some schematics localize additional chakras at different areas of the physical body. For example, the palms of the hands as well as other areas of the body are often viewed as having chakras. As light is *seen* emanating from the hands, the interpretation is that there must be a chakra. Remember, however, your entire being is energy, which may be perceived as light. While the palms have openings to allow the movement of energy, they don't produce energy in the same manner as do chakras; rather, they are conduits of energy. Laying-on-of-hands healing utilizes this capacity to direct the flow energy, and perhaps the perception of this stream is interpreted as energy emanating directly from a chakra. Confusion regarding what is or is not a chakra might originate from defining points of the *nadi* schematic as being chakras.

Nadis

Nadis—energy pathways throughout the body—were detailed thousands of years ago as part of traditional Indian medicine. Nadis transport *prana,* the energy equivalent of qi. These channels emanate from the chakras and gradually become thinner the further they extend out-

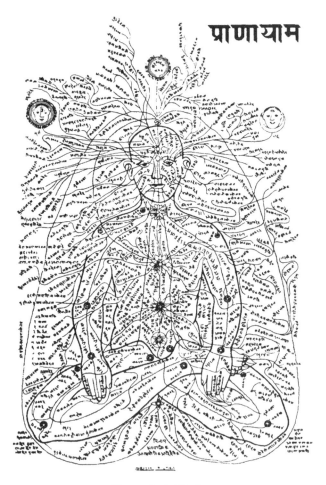

Figure 3.4. Nadis
An ancient depiction of the nadi energy pathways.
(Illustration courtesy of Wikimedia Commons)

ward.[12] This configuration is similar to the nervous system in that the chakras correlate to the central nervous system and the nadi pathways correspond to the peripheral nervous system. Although comparable to meridians, nadi pathways are more numerous than meridians and there are also thought to be over 72,000 points of stimulation along these routes compared with the 361 acupuncture points listed by WHO. On the other hand, there are three primary nadis whereas there are fourteen principal meridians.

THE ENERGY BODY

It is accepted by many quantum physicists that physical particles form as an effect of wave structures, and that the particles and objects of the physical universe spring from nonphysical energy. Atoms themselves are waveforms, not particles.[13] If the universe is inherently an energetic wave structure then the physical body could be the particle emanating from the human waveform.

If so, this gives credence to a view of the world in which: a) the physical body results from, or is an effect of, the energy body, b) states of health are the effect of conditions within the energy body that then find expression through the physical body, and c) the energy body is an objective, measurable form, not just the effect of physical-based emissions of energy.

As mentioned, Toltecs have provided a comprehensive view of the energy body, including uniformity, cohesion, assemblage point, and core. This schematic offers a discrete picture of the energy body as existing independently of the physical body, given that one influences the other. Let's then take a look at these elements and the environmental fields affecting them.

Emanations
Specific vibrations or energy lines known as emanations are generated by a cosmological source energy.[14] Each aspect of creation has its own emanation; there is an emanation for planets, for humans, for plants,

for trees, for bugs, and so forth. Emanations are energy streams emitted from a source, be it from an individual or of cosmic origin. They may be a single vibration, a bandwidth comprised of various frequencies such as the chakra energies coming together to form human life, or the emanations that bundle together to form planet Earth. Whether a single strand or a composite, an emanation carries within it the natural essence of a person, place, or thing. Emanations sustain your energy body as well as your environment, ranging from your living room to multiple dimensions to all creation.

From this perspective, *dark energy* represents the conditions of emanations. A recent discovery, dark energy is thought to comprise almost three-fourths of our universe and to have a direct influence on our world and us. This energy is called "dark" as it hasn't been directly mapped; it is thought to exist due to certain effects that may account for its existence. It could determine the shape of galaxies, for instance. That it appears to spread evenly throughout the universe makes it difficult to isolate, and considerations of both matter and dark energy may be necessary to explain the interconnectedness of all forms of matter. Another interpretation is that from the perspective of Earth an uneven expansion of the universe lends itself to perceiving a cosmic void. This void produces the effects that have been interpreted as resulting from dark energy.[15] With either interpretation, we have not only the impact of environmental conditions but the influences of perception as to how we view the environment.

Stretching through infinity, emanations contain the realization of potential. What they contain is what they contain; what we know they contain is a different matter as this is often open to various interpretations. As one becomes more conscious of an emanation, the potential within it translates to the actual, to the usable. While some emanations directly affect the energy body, others, which exist beyond the domain of human awareness, have indirect influence; still others may have no affect whatsoever as they don't connect, directly or indirectly, with the human band of energy.

Auric Field

Just as there are emanations that produce life, humans emit vibrations that generate what are often referred to as *auras*. This is the energy extending outward from the entire energy body. Oschman postulates that it is a field of ionic vapor surrounding the physical body.[16] An apt analogy is that of an incandescent lightbulb. The filament represents the physical body and the glass represents the outer edge of the non-physical energy field. As the energized physical body (filament) interacts with nonphysical energies (gas inside the bulb), the entire energy body (bulb) emits energy: the aura.

Some healers have schematics that associate states of health with the colors and clarity of the auric field whereas others may isolate only brightness and clarity to make their determinations.[17] The aura, how-ever, is not the energy body itself. It is the light emanating from the entire organism that reflects the energetic conditions of that being.

Coherence and Cohesion

Cohesion is the overall pattern of energy within the energy body. It reflects the vibrations from all of the things, the meanings, and the conditions that influence you, conscious or not. Coherence relates to the interworkings among all of these influences. Let's boil it down to the chakras, for an example. Each chakra represents something: physi-cal, emotional, mental, and so on, and carries its own dynamics, its own set of circumstances. All of these energies interact to produce coherence and form cohesion. It's easy to see that it is quite a balancing act to cho-reograph many separate forms of energy so that they act cooperatively. When we add the pushes and pulls found in daily life, the task becomes seemingly overwhelming. Coherence, then, reflects the orchestration of a number of influences and results in the cohesion that provides your perceptions and interpretations of reality.

Scientific studies indicate that if coherence among the body's sys-tems reflects well-integrated and stable energies, the person probably is in good health; if coherence is weak, discord and possible illness may be evident.[18] As cohesion results from all influences within and without, any energy assessment needs to take into consideration all factors, including the combined energies of the chakras, the meridians, the biological electric circuitry, and the environment. A greater understanding of all influences and how they influence each other and the whole might well be the focus of future scientific research.

In review, the keystone of understanding this energetic anatomy is recognizing that your cohesion determines exactly what you think, feel, or otherwise experience. It is the first cause of perception. At the same time, cohesion forms from our experiences. New experience permits new cohesions; new cohesions provide new experience. Meridians and chakras also play a role as they reflect and influence your state of health and so affect how cohesion forms and vice versa. While cohesion is the underlying factor of perception, it can be managed.

Cohesion dictates meaning. It drives behavior. Your job reflects a particular cohesion, as do your family, hobbies, religious life, and every other aspect of your life, whether dysfunctional or positive. When they are in harmony, so is coherence and vice versa. Learn to manage coherence and you learn to shift your cohesion; as a result, your experience changes. Shift cohesion enough and you may enter new worlds. The many forms cohesion takes are ultimately governed by uniformity.

Uniformity

Within infinity, our energy bodies exist within a certain bandwidth, as do the energy forms of other species.[19] The nature of an emanation is the environment that gives birth to and sustains the organisms of that energy field. Uniformity is the attribute that provides basic shape and definition to the organism, just as the regions or specific bandwidths of the AM and FM radio frequencies each have their own nature: FM consists of higher vibrations and clearer reception but generally does not travel the distance that AM frequencies do. The use of one or the other depends on what you want to listen to. Uniformity is an overarching condition that influences perception and behavior. It molds that which is within it and therefore determines the possibilities of cohesion, which determines the possibilities of perception.

One line of thought is that the energy body was once narrow and elliptical, is now more egg-shaped, and is evolving to a pure sphere. If so, this provides another example of how uniformity, the shape of the container, affects cohesion, the conditions inside the container. Perception and behavior were more narrowly constrained in the days of old, as exemplified by the ancient Toltecs' unrelenting emphasis on power for the sake of self-aggrandizement. In the modern era, considerations about humans residing in a multidimensional landscape are becoming more commonplace as uniformity expands toward a more spherical shape. Medicine is becoming more holistic, and more people are waking to new modes of perception and avenues of thinking. We're gaining breadth and depth of perception.

Assemblage Point

Cohesion can be identified by the location of the assemblage point. In the same manner that an EEG map of brain waves registers coherence among various frequencies and indicates a state of consciousness, for example, the assemblage point's position indicates the type of overall cohesion.[20]

The assemblage point is an area within the energy body where all the elements that go into perception come together, all the properties of coherence unify. It is a focal point, where perception is brought into focus as internal energies intersect external emanations. This intertwining and assembling of a number of influences focuses awareness and is the essential process of cohesion. The energetic pattern that forms, the cohesion, directs what you perceive.

It was once thought that the assemblage point determined perception rather than acting as a maplike representation of one's state of consciousness, but after generations of examination Toltecs realized a greater perspective. The term has taken root as reflected in the works of others, including groups of non-shamanic, alternative healers known as "assemblage point practitioners."

Personal awareness originates through the pressure of external emanations of energy impinging on the energy body, says don Juan. The pressure produces an alignment of energy lines inside the energy body with those outside it. This coherence energizes a specific area of the energy body, the point where cohesion becomes organized and perception results. There are myriad factors influencing this process such as extent of your learning, personal desires, environments near and far, and your goals, to name a few, all coming together for assembly by the force of cohesion.

While this is the centerpiece for the formation of your perceived reality, it is not the formation of perception itself. The title of a book is like the assemblage point. It indicates the focus of the book but is not the content, the cohesion, the internal organization that gives rise to the title. A book also has uniformity; you know a book when you see it.

Change cohesion of the energy body and you change the location of the assemblage point. Sleep results in a natural shift in cohesion from the right side to the left, from physical into nonphysical regions. When this occurs, you *see* a corresponding shift of the assemblage point. Common experiences with *seeing* include perceiving patterns of energy resembling heat rising from asphalt or more directly *seeing* the light of cohesion that, to me, appears like bundles of fiber optics.

Throughout the course of a day, the assemblage point tends to move around, albeit in small measure. For many, it may constantly quiver. This results from not having a stable relationship with the world. When the assemblage point moves, you may initially feel disoriented. This is due to having no conscious points of reference for

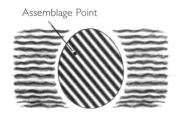
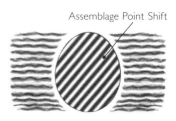

Figure 3.5. Assemblage Point Shift

your new cohesion. Anxiety, for example, can result from a shift of cohesion to an unconscious awareness; the physical body translates this shifting energy as the feeling of anxiety. The more experience you have with this new awareness, the more it becomes conscious and the less you experience anxiety.

As mentioned earlier, states of health or disease, which are inherently types of cohesion, are reflected by the position of the assemblage point. Medical scientist Jon Whale, author of *The Catalyst of Power,* actively investigates cohesion. He uses two forms of technology: one using crystals and intent, the other using a well-machined, modern medical device that filters light through gemstones. He bases his selection of a particular gemstone for a specific condition on ancient Ayurvedic healing practices. With these technologies, he has demonstrated rapid and remarkable healing. He accounts for the results of each therapy as a shift of the assemblage point to a state of health.[21]

Core Awareness

The essence of an individual core equates to a direct connection with infinity. Considerations of what is internal and external cease to have ordinary meaning as your inner-outer references melt away, leaving you with full experience of your life rather than thoughts about it. The further you stretch awareness, the more you are able to touch your core. From another perspective, core and a completely awakened energy body are synonymous.

First Energy Field

This is the known world, that which has been actualized. You may also think of it as that which is most familiar to you, the order of your life. In essence, the first field contains the order that has been formed out of potential energy. In most circumstances, our relationship with the first field forms through reason; it provides the capacity for self-reflective order and thinking is the enhancement of this reflection. But reason and thinking are but a portion of what's available to human awareness. The more you suspend reason, the more you become adept at expanding the first field as you have not relegated yourself solely to the prevailing known world, the reality formed by group consensus.

Usually we behave within a very narrow margin of the energy body, and so have relatively few options of behavior. It is therefore unreasonable to be able to *see* auras, to heal with a simple movement of energy, or to imagine entirely new worlds into existence. The more you expand through your energy body, the more order and knowledge you have at your disposal. What once was unimaginable becomes the order of the day. Stepping out of reason's self-made order you rest more easily within a universal natural order.

Second Energy Field

The second field pertains to the unknown, to the potential that has yet to be actualized. This usually comprises the more expansive area of the energy body. By expanding the first field, you reduce the second field. The unknown becomes known. One perspective maintains that the first field needs to be constantly extended into the second field through learning. Another view holds that the second field pulls at, and expands, the first field through imagination. In either case, you are realizing more of your innate potential.

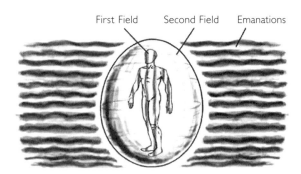

Figure 3.6. Energy Fields
First Field: Physical energies; order; the known world.
Second Field: Nonphysical energies; the unknown world.
Emanations: Some exist within and without the energy body; others reside completely utside ordinary human awareness and are therefore unknowable.

Both the first and second fields contain properties of awareness, attention, and intent. Awareness relates to consciousness, attention to focus, and intent to directing energy. All enable the general management of your resources.

Third Energy Field

In relation to normal awareness, this represents the unknowable, as it is beyond human anatomy. In the same way the second field is potential to the first field, the third field exists as potential to overall perception. Postulations of its existence stem from those who have developed their energy bodies in a manner as to temporarily step beyond ordinary human confines by pushing their assemblage points outside of their energy bodies. An alternate description is that they have temporarily pushed uniformity into another domain. Extending beyond normal human endeavors, the third field may provide a basis for theological and philosophical doctrines dealing with life after death.

TYPES OF COHESION

Cohesion can take the form of *conditional* or *natural energy fields:* the energy of form or unbounded potential. Conditional energy forms from the stipulations humans place on themselves and the world. These hard and fast rules intertwine to develop cohesion. Reality then unfolds from what we have conditioned ourselves to perceive, an *inventory* to which we consistently refer. Based on our education, perception is usually restricted to what we believe we are entitled to perceive.

Any given reality is a conditional field. Accordingly, for good or ill, reality by any measure is contrived. The underlying conditions of a reality establish the boundaries of possibility; they form a blueprint for a complete sequence of events. But unless we participate with the conditions forming a reality, it remains in the realm of potential. Only by behaving in accordance with it, says don Juan, does it become realized.[22] For Toltec shamans, the energy body is a fixture of their reality, while it doesn't even exist in other realities. Yet this shamanic knowledge has no effect at all unless behavior incorporates it.

How we relate to mind serves as an example. Don Juan defines mind as our inventory, the sum of what we hold to be true and how that is expressed. Moods, for instance, are frames of mind. Blackmore points out that the prevailing scientific consensus regards mind as the personalized form of brain functions. And philosophers may define mind as either the individual self, which feels, reasons, believes, imagines, and so forth, or a general nonmaterial, metaphysical substance, which pervades all individual minds.[23] No matter the scope of the definition, it still boils down to inventory: what we call to our attention and how we do it. If we include the energy body, we enlarge our inventory and expand our mind.

Most often, we have accepted the condition that the world is made of material, concrete objects. And from there we build aircraft and automobiles to enable our energy bodies to travel. In a different version of reality, we might learn to travel by actualizing potentials of imagination. Learning to transport their bodies through time and space solely by using innate resources, without a material vehicle, was one of the ancient Toltecs' great discoveries. They were able to do this because they not only accepted an expanded reality; they acted in line with that worldview.[24]

Another type of cohesion, available to us all, is the natural energy field. This is energy that has no form and yet contains form. Put another way, this energy can form in myriad ways. As we realize its potential we keep growing beyond the conditions that we encounter at each stage of growth. Evolving to a natural state means that we have grown beyond all form particular to any reality. We can *be* without the context and guidance of a worldview. Having a natural field means we are fully connected to, and are in harmony with, source energy: the quintessential natural field.

A natural field results from awakening the complete energy body. The further we extend the first field, the closer we are to achieving a natural field. From a different angle, the more we blend the first and

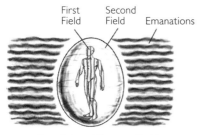

Conditional Energy Field   Natural Energy Field

Figure 3.7.

The diagram on the left symbolizes how a conditional energy field blocks
perception from the external world. A natural energy field supports
harmony between self and the world.

second fields, the more we cultivate a natural field. The activation of
core is equivalent with having developed a natural field. As mentioned
earlier, this is consistent with Maslow's concept of self-actualization and
Jung's thoughts on individuation.

A conditional field may or may not resonate with a natural field.
One conditional field may cause poor coherence within the energy
body while another strengthens coherence. One value of the classic metaphysical systems is that they provide conditional fields that
resonate with the natural field, allowing an awakening and integration of natural field cohesion. By pointing the way to individuation,
they employ a cosmology and means that provide a foundation to step
outside the cosmology and method employed. For this to fully occur,
at some point we must leave even the most helpful system behind.
Otherwise, the conditional field remains in place rather than acting
as a stepping-stone to a natural field.

CORNERSTONES OF
PERCEPTION

Another unique offering of the Toltec paradigm is that of presenting
a distinct organization of perceptual abilities, which I call *cornerstones*

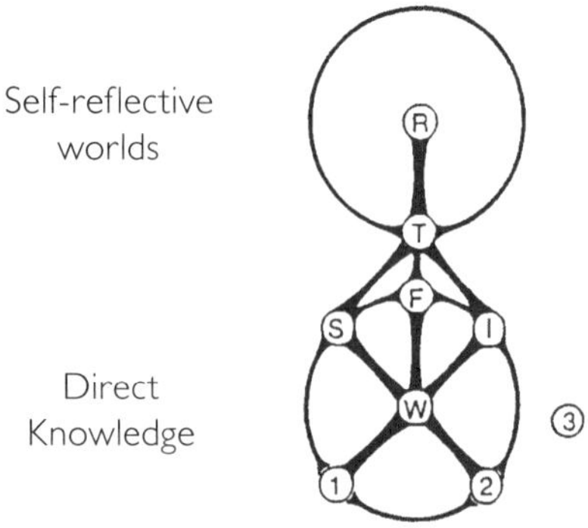

Mode	Energy
R	Reason
T	Talking
S	*Seeing*
F	Feeling
I	Imagination
W	*Will*
I	First Field—Conscious
2	Second Field—Unconscious
3	Third Field—Supraconscious

Self-reflective worlds

Direct Knowledge

Figure 3.8. The Cornerstones of Perception
This diagram indicates the spheres of influence regarding the abilities of
perception outlined by Toltecs. (This diagram is used with the kind permission
of publisher and author, Norbert Classen, *Das Wissen der Tolteken,*
Freiburg, Germany: Hans-Nietsch-Verlag, 2002.)

of perception and don Juan called the *eight points of the totality of being.*
They are reason, talking, feeling, imagination, *seeing, will,* and the
three energy fields. While don Juan taught of the third field, he did
not use it to describe the eight points. I include it in the cornerstones
to highlight its importance in examining our range of possibilities. The
cornerstones are scattered about the body, not in a straight line as are
the chakras.[25] Yet all perceptions of the chakras may be accounted for
by the cornerstones and vice versa. It is easy to work with both, as each
is energy-based. In this manner, they share a common origin. The value
of knowing both languages is flexibility.

Each cornerstone has a specific location in the physical body.
Reason and talking are in the brain, for instance, while imagination
is found in the adrenal glands and *seeing* is relegated to the pancreas.
There are instances where both Eastern and Western metaphysical
systems place a perception at the same physical area, such as ascribing imagination (dreaming) to the adrenal glands and feeling to
the heart.

Cornerstone	Location	Perception
Reason	Brain	Organizes information from the intellect and five physical senses. Produces human-made order.
Talking	Brain	Indirect representation of the world. Translates and expresses information from the other senses.
Feeling	Heart	The affective aspect of sensing of self and environment and corresponding aspect of emotions.
Imagination	Liver	Dreamlike perceptions, both spurious and concrete.
Seeing	Pancreas	Direct, immediate awareness of energy.
Will	Abdomen	An integrated and focused cohesion activates this direct connection with the environment. It manages the other cornerstones.
First Energy Field	Right side of the body	Realized, learned order of the known world.
Second Energy Field	Left side of the body	The potential of the unknown.
Third Energy Field	Outside human awareness	The unknowable. Energy that has no connection with ordinary human awareness.

To further elaborate:

Reason. Reason offers a way to make order out of the immensity of existence. It collapses infinity into a usable format. However, it is enmeshed in subject-object relationships and therefore provides indirect, or representational, awareness. Perceptions of something "out there" are measured in relation to oneself. The world then becomes objectified. While it is a marvelous tool, this cornerstone takes command of perception and inhibits awareness of direct and intimate connections with the world.

The brain, the location of this cornerstone, is but one part of the body. Our complete body connects us with infinity, while reason is responsible for only that portion of infinity that has thus far been rendered reasonable. It offers a delectable slice of the pie but it is only a slice. When we have a more full-bodied relationship to ourselves, we awaken our innate, and often latent, capacities of perception.

Talking. Talking, whether it is internal reflection or outward speech, maintains order. We tend to take the ordered sensibilities of reason and then constantly bounce that information around inside cohesion, like bouncing an image off a set of internal mirrors, and then in a more complex way we do the same with others. The reflection becomes what is viewed as being real, and it really doesn't have to be reasonable; it just needs to sustain focus to have an effect on behavior. Talking may then restrain awareness by keeping us in a self-reflective world. For all its majesty, talking, like reason, becomes a force to harden cohesion; it removes awareness from infinity rather than offering steps to encounter it.

There is an order beyond thought and reason. It is the order of the natural cosmos, the order resting within potential. Interestingly, talking about potential makes infinity seem reasonable, and reflecting on the world from a variety of angles helps make it possible for us to drop talking and reason in order to awaken other cornerstones. The more we discover the relativity of worldviews, the less sway they hold.

Feeling. This is the affective part of us, both the seemingly passive perception of listening to the world in a different way and the vibrant emotive ability. Each influences the other and "feeling" and "emotion" are often used interchangeably. Feeling is a principal navigational tool in a world of energy. It connects the physical and nonphysical worlds as well as those aspects within human anatomy. Oschman holds that there is a biomagnetic field associated with the heart that extends indefinitely into space.[26] This field connects us directly with the world and enables us to better sense, and make sense of, our environment. Recognizing the existence of this field of energy and then doing something about it adds weight to a view of consciousness that accounts for the value of harnessing this cornerstone.

The relationship between talking and feeling is intricate. The more perception is focused in reason, the less we are able to feel. Educating feeling provides wide-varying experiences that help expand worldviews.

A casual review of history demonstrates that human-inspired order changes, along with entire frameworks of reality. Feeling is a way to accelerate an ever-expanding sense of order. Through feeling we can tap the essence of a situation. We can also stretch ourselves beyond normal conditions and enter new worlds.

Rather than remain in the reflective world of thought, feeling lets us connect with the world. One of the recent advances in understanding the human condition emanates from the literature concerning the complexities of feeling, emotion, and thought. Led by Daniel Goleman's breakthrough book, *Emotional Intelligence,* there are now a number of books tackling various components of this complex realm, such as how emotions affect health, leadership, and the organization of reality.

Goleman points out interrelationships between thinking and feeling. He says that thinking plays a large role in determining our emotions and that our emotions are critical for effective thinking. He also offers evidence that people often make terrible decisions because their emotional education is inadequate. Furthermore, he connects both thinking and emotions to specific areas of the brain, and says that the brain holds two intelligences: rational and emotional. He presents emotional intelligence as a set of skills, including control of impulses, self-motivation, empathy, and self-awareness. When intellectual and emotional intelligence complement each other, both increase.[27] It might be that the brain that deals with emotions directly relates to the heart. If so, we have further correspondence of scientific and Toltec models. This offers another hint of the types of investigations that could catapult awareness into new realms.

In her provocative work, *Infinite Mind: Science of the Human Vibrations of Consciousness,* scientist Valerie Hunt makes the case that emotions organize the "mind field," the inherent capacity for deliberate consciousness. In *The Feeling of What Happens,* neuroscientist Antonio Damasio documents emotions as being a key aspect of reasoning. And in *Molecules of Emotion,* research professor Candace B. Pert offers a biological model of how emotions affect perception. She asserts that there is no objective reality. To handle the immensity of existence, we must have a filtering system to assess what is important; emotions "decide what is worth paying attention to." Emotional intelligence is therefore the meta-program of rational intelligence.[28]

Imagination. Imagination enables us to directly explore our energy body. As used here, it does not mean flights of fancy, but rather refers to a sophisticated, disciplined mode of viewing self and world. It may be a simple, fleeting image, a rigorous problem-solving technique, or even a full-bodied experience. In this manner, imagination is akin to entering *heightened awareness,* a state characterized by increased intensity of experience, keenness of perception, and an accentuated feeling of being alive. In Toltec literature, imagination is often referred to as *dreaming.*[29] Used in this way, dreaming is a sophisticated activity with many levels synonymous with the learned use of imagination.

For example, sufficient intensity makes it possible to have awareness of a body, some type of form, which travels within imagination itself. This faculty has been called *astral projection,* the *dreaming body,* and the *out-of-body experience* (OBE). In these experiences, perception doesn't leave the physical body; rather shifts of cohesion, and the degree of the shift, produce different states of imagination.

Seeing. This native ability perceives energy. It results from consciously realizing the connection between oneself and emanations, or between internal and external energies. It also corresponds to awareness of or about something and provides immediate knowledge and understanding of what is being observed. One might say it is accessing a different bandwidth of energy.

When *seeing,* it is normal that the daylight world becomes darker or a night environment lightens up. *Seeing* auras often precedes *seeing* the full energy world. While the aura is a bona fide energy, it represents a deeper level. When we fully *see* energy, the world may seem comprised of packages of energy. Humans may be represented as oblong, well-contained blobs of concentrated light. No physical objects are present. Everything appears as variations of light.

While Eastern metaphysical systems tend to place *seeing,* or third eye, capabilities in the pineal gland, the Western Toltec system associates it with the pancreas. The common denominator is that both pancreas and pineal gland are in the endocrine glandular system. It may be that using this mode of perception activates that entire network, a full-body effect, which then permits us to *see*. Another common denominator is that the perceiver must recognize a sense of oneness with the world for *seeing* to activate. Yet another is that we must step out of thinking and reason in order to engage the world directly.

Will. The cornerstones of feeling, *seeing*, and imagination are all direct modes of perception centered at *will*, while reason and talking are indirect aspects centered in the brain. This separation of abilities is not a Toltec artifice; it has been expounded upon in classic Eastern and Western philosophies. In his book, *The World as Will and Representation*, for example, nineteenth-century German philosopher Arthur Schopenhauer makes a case for direct and indirect faculties of perception.[30]

Will is also the raw energy existing throughout the universe. Maybe it is the *Star Wars* "Force." Through personal *will* this energy is at our disposal. The ability to change awareness and manage *will* results from the application of intent. Through intent we shift and then restabilize our cohesion. We can intend to walk, for example, or to imagine. The basics of it are that we can intend and that intending has effects.

Will is a dominant part of human energetic anatomy, the central energetic system. It commands the other cornerstones. In the Toltec model, the central nervous system (brain) is a minor epicenter and the *will* (gut) is a major epicenter of human perceptual anatomy. The "brain-gut axis," as it is called, is scientifically well-documented.[31] Of note is that there are chemical compounds, neurotransmitters, in the human intestines that help form a pathway of significant influence between the central nervous system and the *enteric* nervous system found in the gut. A reaction in the intestines (due to a milk allergy, for instance) could affect the brain and influence behavior. The Toltec model might be a more advanced rendering of how the gut affects overall perception.

Will is energy, not a concept. It is not dedication, commitment, or persistence. It's a force. It's the binding vortex of the cornerstones. As energy, it connects us with that fluid world. Managing our cohesion and our cornerstones—achieving various alignments of energy—is performed with *will* and intent.

Will is the substance of energy with emanations carrying the intents that affect us in many ways. In its various material forms, we can touch and smell it, taste and hear it. If it is dense enough, we can sit on it. Or we can mold it and fly through the air in it as we do with airplanes. In the more rarified forms of perceiving energy, we can feel it and *see* it. Emanations are the stuff of the cosmos, forming creatures upon creatures and worlds upon worlds. Personal *will,* then, places us at the doorstep of the universe. Opening the door is one thing, stepping through it is yet another.

The three energy fields. The three energy fields are the final cornerstones of perception. Their operation can be better understood by considering them in the light of the compelling psychological map detailed by psychiatrist Carl Jung.

THE PSYCHOLOGY OF AN ENERGETIC ANATOMY

Jung helped illuminate the nature of the psyche, which he thought of as our complete mind and all knowledge contained in it. However, he did not equate it with the conscious part of awareness, as he recognized that in large measure it functions unconsciously.[32]

He also thought that, while mind and body influence one another, they have separate dynamics. Jung also put forward a model of what mind is and how it works, a schematic comprised of the conscious, the unconscious, and the personal and collective attributes of each. Models, according to Jung, are a means of exploring fields of inquiry. They do not make something so; they allow the observation of useful constructs.[33]

As a result of Jung's work we have another perspective with which to assess the Toltec map. The separate dynamics of mind and body Jung cites correspond to the functions of the energy and physical bodies, for instance. The personal and collective aspects of the conscious and unconscious pertain to individual and group processes of the known and unknown. And the conscious and unconscious elements of the psyche correlate with the first and second energy fields.

The Conscious: First Energy Field

Jung articulated his view that humans have a type of consciousness where the unconscious predominates and another where self-consciousness prevails.[34] Superimposing the shamanic schema over this, the first energy field represents the conscious region of overall awareness. Its refinement enables an ever-expanding sense of the natural order and provides a stepping-stone away from reason into a fuller utilization of the psyche. The first field is also that aspect of consciousness ruled by self-consciousness or that which has become known. Usually only a slice of the first field has been awakened. This is mirrored physiologically, in that only a small portion of the brain is used.

The Unconscious: Second Energy Field

The unconscious compares with the unknown or second energy field. It has significant influence, but in ways a person cannot account for as we often reduce our awareness of the second energy field. Boiled down, Jung's concept of the unconscious is everything that is available to perception but not known. It is also that which is capable of being made conscious or known. In addition, he held that the unconscious contained potential; an order reflecting a real, metaphysical reality.[35] From this viewpoint, potential may also be considered to be an existing order, which has not yet been learned and therefore not yet made conscious. The parallels with a depiction of the energy body appear obvious.

Jung also held that the unconscious constitutes a "different medium" than the conscious. The unconscious contains both personal and collective aspects, with each pertaining to an individual's psychic connection with others.[36] Cohesion and uniformity, then, may relate to both the personal and collective unconscious domains. Uniformity establishes the boundaries of what the collective may form into realization. Cohesion may either influence, or be influenced by, the collective.

The Supraconscious: Third Energy Field

We begin to step away from Jung's work when introducing the third field, the supraconscious, which is a dimension beyond typical considerations of the human psyche. In like manner, it exists outside the structure of the energy body. At the same time, this enhanced view offers authenticity as it supports rather than obviates his efforts.

The third field contains the conscious and unconscious, the first and second fields, and yet is vast beyond human measure. It is the unknowable, that which is beyond the veil of ordinary human consciousness. However, there evidently are procedures for placing the assemblage point in the supraconscious. In the works of Castaneda, this ability is mentioned as a hallmark of a new cycle of Toltecs who rejoice in the pursuit of pure freedom. They aspire to awaken the entire energy body so that personal consciousness can be fully placed into the supraconscious. One transcendent application is being able to burn with "the fire from within." This involves completely entering the supraconscious and leaving this earthly existence behind and taking the physical body in tow.[37]

If true, this possibility adds further credence to considerations of the physical body being predominantly influenced by the energy body. A shift in awareness—such as the fire within that produces a resurrection, if you will—highlights marked control over the physical body, even the physical world, and carries with it knowledge of virtually any sphere of human activity.

As an educational tool, just the concept of the third field stimulates continued reexamination of the human condition. It also becomes the basis of a learning posture, an orientation to remain open and honest, as well as humble, because most of existence is beyond the human capacity of knowing.

4

The Formation of Reality

As we have seen, bioenergetics deals with the flow of energy within an organism and between the organism and its environment. This interplay of energies forms the basis for our examination of the perception of reality. For an individual, "within" pertains to all that is inside the energy body, including cohesion and the assemblage point, and "its environment" relates to everything else, including other people, groups, views of reality, all aspects of nature, and emanations. The meeting point is uniformity, the boundary of the energy body. This framework provides for a deeper understanding of how a tiny spark of energy—the human organism—deals with the surrounding immensity of the cosmos.

Two fundamental processes within the energy body—learning and imagination—correspond to the first two energy fields. Learning is that which has been actualized or realized, to what is known: the province of the first energy field, no matter how large or small the cohesion, no matter the subject. Imagination is of the second energy field. It permits rapid expansion of awareness, stepping beyond what is known into what can become known. It is a dance with potential.

Integrating the first and second fields via learning and imagination has the effect of bringing more of our energy body to life. The third field serves to highlight the vast expanse of what may be learned and imagined.

ENTRAINMENT

Learning and imagination are both impacted by *entrainment,* or *alignment* as it is sometimes called, which centers on the ability to shift cohesion. Put another way, entrainment describes the process of one type of energy influencing another by their coming into *resonance.* Just as the heat from burning wood in a fireplace influences the temperature of a room, all forms of energy influence the internal and external environments of the energy body. The entraining effect may be a condition or other energy. For instance, books—especially textbooks—are significant forces of entrainment. In sociology, it could be viewed as resulting from peer pressure or institutional learning. Your arithmetic teacher entrained your thinking along the lines of addition, subtraction, and so on. In physics, entrainment applies to two oscillating bodies entering into phase with each other. In meteorology, it pertains to one wind stream capturing another.[1]

Our social world develops through an enormous number of entraining influences that combine to form what we consider to be reality. Confining perception to a physical world of objects results from entraining to that model of reality. When natural abilities surface, such as *seeing* (perceiving energy), we have been taught to disregard those observations because they do not fit the world we have been entrained to perceive.

The culture of your upbringing holds dramatic sway over your perception. If you consort with criminals, you stand an increased chance of entraining to their energy. If you associate with people who are principled, you are influenced to be this way. If you overly entrain to a worldview, you become fundamentalist. If you entrain to source energy, you might step into a mystical experience.

Even though learning and imagination are both subject to the mechanics of entrainment, together they form a powerful way to manage it. Learning is the process of transforming potential into actualization, which, in a sleight-of-hand manner, also includes the use of imagination. In turn, imagination expands perception beyond the known limits of reality and helps to quicken learning. Imagination can therefore be applied to break the chains of conditional energy fields. Integrating the resulting experiences requires learning. Without this coordination, you can't form deep and lasting relationships among aspects of self, between conscious and unconscious, and between self and environment. Without learning, you may become lost in imagination. Without imagination, you may become lost in dogma. In leapfrog fashion, learning and imagination work together to stimulate, shift, and stabilize cohesion.

IMAGINATION

In this context, imagination is concrete. It is not flightiness or something to be easily dismissed as not pertaining to serious matters. Imagination is necessary to solve problems, to entertain new relationships of every kind, and to provide the necessary charge for personal growth. Its home base is the second energy field. Imagination permits you to access and manage potential. This is found in both the conscious and unconscious aspects of your life. Through the imagination used in your daily, waking world the second field feeds into your first-field physical reality. What has been potential becomes actualized and what has been unconscious becomes conscious.

While imagination relates to directly working with the second field, being *imaginative* pertains to procedures of imagination, and *imaginings* are creations or inventions originating from the use of imagination. Imaginings may be first or second field activities. Buildings, automobiles, and scientific laboratories are first-field imaginings. Artists often speak of waking from a dream and penning or painting a masterpiece. Scientists may speak of the role played by imagination in their discoveries, as did Albert Einstein. The concepts that precede these manifested technologies and skills were imaginings residing solely within the second field. They were ideas floating in imagination until someone plucked them out and placed them in this world by being imaginative, by being able to stabilize their assemblage point within the second field and then bring that awareness into harmony with the physical world. Imaginings exist as potential until actualized.

One of the most powerful tools of human consciousness, imagination connects us with the world about us, be it of the conscious or unconscious realms. It allows the perception of potential and as such produces the worlds to come. How much potential may become realized hinges on a number of factors. Here we will focus on the disciplined use of imagination, something that provides a fundamental reorientation to self, society, and life.

LEARNING

Characteristic of the order found in the first field, learning requires rules and methods to gather and make efficient sense of perceptions. This is where logic and reason enter; they have the ability to organize thought. Whether for computer programs, scientific inquiry, or journalistic reporting, logic requires the formation of a consistent set of beliefs or valid arguments. Without consistency, we can't build on what has already been learned.

Although the pursuit of logic may seem at times tedious, an understanding of logical fallacy—a mistake made in a line of reasoning that invalidates it—is invaluable. It is wise to be watchful of the logic that shapes an argument, for it ends up shaping your world. It is a fallacy of logic to say that you are correct based on the use of force, for instance, or that you are correct because you are an authority on a subject, or when you appeal to pity in order to sway another.[2] Jumping on the bandwagon of what has come before or what everyone else is up to commits yet another fallacy of logic; it uses an appeal to what is generally considered to be true as proof that something is true. Even the argument "the scientific community knows this to be true" is a fallacy of logic. In practice, this type of argument may prevent what has been held as true to become obsolete, or it may prevent discovery. This is why fallacies should be removed from learning.

These examples are often deemed *universal fallacies* because they apply to all forms of logic, even those used by various professions, which have their own systems to build on prior knowledge. Different disciplines vary widely in their overall approach to what is being studied, the technical terms that render meaning, the inherent structure or logic, and the applications of knowledge. Measuring psychoanalysis against mechanistic physics isn't appropriate while applying universal fallacies to test their integrity is not only appropriate but necessary.

Pertaining to the energy body, logic determines coherence, the harmony or imbalance of the various bits that go into cohesion. The strength and therefore the utility of cohesion hinge on well-crafted logic. Without this, cohesion is ill formed and dissipates. This is a key to understanding learning, the stabilization of a new cohesion. Awareness of the fallacies of logic guides us to avoid weak-kneed coherence by providing strength through objectivity. Through well-ordered logic we form the strongest, most resilient cohesion. Knowledge of the procedures and effects of building cohesion then forms the foundation for awakening the entire energy body. Without objectivity, we go hither and thither, spinning on a wheel that has no true reference to the natural human condition.

Objectivity is a tricky thing. Damasio makes the point that while the conscious mind is real, it must be investigated as a subjective experience. Don Juan says the individual assemblage point position determines a subjective experience and yet the world itself is objective; in other words, there is a uniform, constant domain of energy that is perceived differently by individuals. Two people may observe the exact same building, for example, but their experience varies. At the same time, different people may also share experience due to having similar assemblage-point locations. Common experience allows buildings to be constructed, scientists to achieve agreement, and cultures to form consensus. Don Juan goes on to emphasize the need for sobriety, for clear-headedness, of which objectivity is a part. Knowing the subjective side of interpretation provides a measure of objectivity.[3]

The scientific model offers an exquisite example of a procedure for learning, a method that instills objectivity. In its rarified form, nothing is arbitrarily dismissed or assumed to be true. This approach enables a highly detailed investigation and elucidation of the heretofore-unknown aspects of mind, body, and environment. The prevailing view of reality in our contemporary world has been markedly influenced by scientific inquiry.

Yet in practice science often becomes *scientism*. When practitioners become unduly glued to their thoughts, mental rigidity prevents discovery. Novel inquiry into new models of reality and new modes of perception stultifies. At this point, the revelations of science become something other than science. This takes a high toll on individuals and groups, such as when certain forms of medicine may be delayed in finding their way into the hands of those in need, or different views of the nature of time, space, and our relationship with a greater world are summarily dismissed.

By its very definition, the scientific method is based on rational logic. Reason, though, is like the channel markers leading to and from a port. It offers direction and context; it isn't the thing itself. But what if you were to use other forms of perception, such as those permitting direct access to that which is being studied? Might you then have more data to examine, to formulate, and to use? And what if these skills had been honed over centuries to a professional level producing a new method of rigorous inquiry?

This is exactly what occurred during the growth of Taoism and the Toltec Way. Because more avenues of perception were used, learning was accelerated. And thus they were able to imagine, feel, and *see* and accurately map the energy body. Considerations of meridians and cohesion began to influence healing practices. In wider context, they produced a worldview, which included principles of learning such as those outlined here. As with any approach to learning, the new principles were based on their new worldview. Yet they did this in a way that they remained opened to further exploration and willing to let their view of things become obsolete; a hallmark of objectivity. This reflects the very purpose of recognizing fallacies of logic—to have some measure in order to better learn.

Enhanced learning is an effect of the Toltec method, and logic is a part of the mix. Comparing the two approaches—scientific and shamanic—serves to illustrate the greater process of building reality. Both views, whether we are talking about the behavior of planets or of energetic waveforms, are based on empirical observation. Toltec shamans simply use different capacities for observation, which result in different data, different learning, and different knowledge.

Enhancing Awareness

As important as learning and imagination are, the more the energy body wakes, the less meaning they have. Each is real, as real can be, and yet "real" is arbitrary. What is considered to be real hinges on a number of factors, including personal and cultural meaning, survival imperatives, and the current map of reality, to name a few, all of which reflect environmental factors impacting cohesion. As the conscious area of the energy body expands, a new dynamic unfolds. Learning and imagination are then equal parts of an active awareness that brings us closer to *being*. In this light, imagination and learning are part of a practical *method* to enhance awareness.

Learning applies to integrating awareness within the first field, and imagination provides great stimulation by generating more options. Imagination, on the other hand, develops the second field. It also concerns expanding awareness and therefore supports learning. Stretching the first field solely by learning more of the same known world occurs slowly. Deliberate use of imagination adds a vibrant dimension to learning as it brings into awareness substantially more and varied references. When used with the other cornerstones, learning and imagination offer a chance to dramatically leap into previously inconceivable vistas.

Imagination lends itself to rapid assemblage point shifts characterized by new cohesions. In a nutshell, imagination supplies the conditions to move the assemblage point; learning holds the new cohesion in place. The inordinate time needed for reason-based learning can be offset by the cornerstones of *seeing,* feeling, and imagination. *Seeing* permits unparalleled perception of the mechanics of the second field. Feeling provides the sense of the experience, a relationship for personal balance and direction, and guidance for deriving meaning. Imagination offers conscious exploration of unconscious domains.

The crux of becoming more conscious is to learn through imagination that we live in the midst of infinity, a perception that awareness of the third energy field stimulates. Not recognizing this may lead to stagnant perception and could be the harbinger of our species' demise, as we might not be able to adapt to the significant challenges facing us as we remain stuck.

Imagine Learning

As commonly understood, learning often involves developing a wider and more detailed picture based on that which is already conscious, or at least readily available, like new information found in a library. Learning in this sense is more like hardening a veneer of awareness than actual learning.

To a significant extent, learning in any form requires imagination because learning necessitates opening further to something. Even if what you are learning is the ABCs, you must awaken to new possibilities that the alphabet exists and that it can be used for something. Moreover, nonrote problem solving is centered in imagination; novel solutions are inherently imaginative. Integrating the first and second fields simultaneously indicates the grounding of imagination and the opening of learning, and the correlate expansion of imagination and stabilization of learning. Imagination permits going beneath the surface of current assumptions into the unconscious to allow new propositions to be entertained, possibly to the point of their becoming concrete imaginings.

Once the value of imagination is acknowledged, then it can be refined. Learning solely through reason has become overaccentuated to the point that we have lost connection with imagination, even though it is one of the most reasonable aspects of the human condition.

Learning to Imagine

The utility of imagination hinges on how well you explore the potential of the second field and then integrate that experience into the first field; that is, how much potential becomes actualized, how much of the unconscious becomes conscious, and therefore how much is learned. In this pursuit, we can exhibit works characteristic of genius or we can become lost. While the focus of this book is positive development, awareness of the conscious-unconscious interactions also sheds light on many cognitive disorders. The writings of mystics and psychotics, for instance, are often similar. Yet mystics are able to integrate their otherworldly perceptions into their daily life while psychotics are ensnared by them, because they are unable to discriminate between potential and actual.

Imagination furnishes a way to shift your assemblage point. As it moves, you become aware of the nature and effects of the assemblage point, which reveals not only the mechanics of the energy body but the relativity of reality. Since interpretations of reality result from projections of the known world, imagination allows you to become more fluent with perception and less bound by psychological *projection,* a topic covered in chapter six. *Seeing* accelerates the shift and restabilization of the assemblage point, as you directly perceive the energetic causes and effects of your observations.

The intensity of the everyday world often hinders imagination. Ordinary tensions and worries, requirements of making money, upholding your place in a physical universe, and by the gravity, as it were, of trying to hold on to your worldview bind perception to a simple layer of life that only resembles being conscious. When this intensity diminishes, it's like a screen is removed, revealing a free-flowing, vibrant universe of energy. It is not that your worldview is an illusion; it is as real as anything else and yet is only one of many possible cohesions. The energy required to hold a singular assemblage point position in place may drain your resources to an extent that you can't reach other versions of reality.

Since our education normally does not include imagination as a principal feature in the formation of reality, it is all the more difficult to translate the unconscious into the conscious. Compounding the matter, we are often taught to dismiss imagination or at least relegate it to a minor role. Fortunately, thinkers such as Einstein provide us other options, if only in the often quoted, "Imagination is more important than knowledge."[4] Imagination, then, is not making things up; it is finding out what exists beyond the current boundaries of accepted reality. It delivers more consciousness.

The learning of imagination is like learning any other skill. You need a context to understand its nature, a desire to make it blossom, a sense of meaning that indicates why you should invest your time pursuing it, and a means to produce it. Then you practice and learn.

LEVELS OF IMAGINATION

In the course of learning, imagination achieves different levels, which indicates the ability to manage more of your energy body. These are adapted from Toltec *dreaming gates*. Don Juan taught that there are seven gates and in *Toltec Dreaming* I have outlined these and others. In this light, dreaming and imagination are one and the same, different terms that both mean the stimulation of the second energy field. To illuminate energy body function, I will outline the first four.[5]

These levels also reflect incremental expansion of the first field through the energy body. Learning is often defined as a lasting change in behavior,[6] and this is exactly what stretching out the first field produces as changes in behavior reflect having developed new cohesions. With each new level, more insights and abilities are gained. How these are expressed in your daily world depends on the individual. Because of the human species' uniformity, however, most everyone experiences common features.

Level One

In waking life, imagination makes itself known in an assortment of ways—intense imagery, flights of seeming fancy, and so on. Level one, though, is that of consciously entering the home ground of imagination, of intentionally accessing the second field.

In the beginning, imagination is akin to meditation. Meditative exercises often begin by sitting quietly and relaxing with eyes closed. To stimulate this level of imagination, pay attention to the emerging darkness as though you were falling asleep. Attend to the darkness until you find yourself immersed in a heavy, but not unpleasant, blackness. This is the precursor to properly tapping imagination. It also recharges your energy; being in this state for ten hours may seem like mere minutes. Being able to reside in the blackness marks a significant step, so don't think you aren't accomplishing anything just because "nothing is happening."

The next step is to entertain whatever images emerge from the blackness. At first, you may not notice images. Gently gazing in the direction of your forehead with your eyes closed may help. Let the images come and go as they may. Practicing with purpose and patience will help you to turn the corners of perception. Eventually you will learn to stabilize and direct these images, to control your dream.

Level Two

Attaining the second level allows you to behave from within imagination. It rests on having learned to maintain the stream of images. You may even find yourself entering the stream of images and flowing with them in a manner similar to waking life. This is characteristic of *lucid dreaming,* or becoming awake within a dream.[7]

In level two, you can also control your imagination by changing the terrain. Normally, dreams change: dream to dream, scene to scene. At this level you have choice; you have intentionality within the dream. To advance, don't get lost in the details or in obsessing about your magnificent achievement. Don Juan advises us to remain attentive to the experience without succumbing to it.[8]

When you center in imagination you gain a stillness that allows you to imagine from within imagination, to have another dream from within the dream. This is the way to prepare for level three: imagine a completely new environment from within imagination. From this vantage point, you are confronted with the multilevel nature of reality. It is also yours to enjoy. The steps to do this are simple: know you want this to occur, and then intend it.

Level Three

An interesting aspect of imagination, this level embodies astral projection, or what is commonly referred to as an OBE, and involves using an imagination body—an imagining—to travel, whether the destination is in imagination or the physical world. This helps you solidify your imaginative gains.

An OBE is just one form of other-than-physical-body experience. A key point is that these experiences are within the energy body. While you may have the perception of being out of your physical body, OBEs occur within the wider scope of human anatomy. There is no projecting into another external dimension. However, there is a shift of cohesion, which enables you to focus on different parts of the inter-dimensionality within you that correspond to the extra-dimensionality of emanations.

A classic OBE has three components. First, consciousness is exteriorized away from the physical body. You may view your physical body from your bedroom ceiling or from across a room. Second, the localization of this nonphysical perspective has form of some kind. It might resemble your physical body in that you experience having arms, legs, shoulders, and so on. This is most often the case, probably due to the ingrained habit of how we participate with the world. It might also take some other form like that of an animal, often an effect of someone who is firmly on a traditional shamanic path. The longer you stay in this state or the more frequently you engage it, the form tends to shift to a sphere. From this perspective, viewing a 360-degree panorama is common. If you choose, you can also replicate your physical senses. You can see, hear, smell, touch, and taste. Third, the form is animated and has emotions.

A spontaneous OBE may leave a person wondering what occurred. Without context, without an inventory that includes them, repeated OBEs may cause a person to think he's losing his mind. Such was the case with Robert Monroe as outlined in his notable book *Journeys Out of the Body*.[9] Investigating the phenomena, he expanded his inventory to include them and so expanded his mind. OBEs then became "normal."

Out-of-body experiences are not dry in the sense of just being aware, which may be the case in other types of psychic ability such as *remote viewing*.[10] As a distinct mode of perception, the OBE carries the capacity for different kinds of movement, feelings, and emotions. As a result, you can interact with your surroundings as you would from your physical body. The similarities to perceiving from within your physical body, plus the enhanced capabilities, make OBE a great way to learn.

Since learning is the perception of ever-increasing order, if you learn OBE you've expanded your perception of order and can thereby participate in more enhanced structures of consciousness. Through learning, you connect with potential, which consists of order existing outside the conscious part of mind but is still a natural part of our makeup, and in this manner the unknown becomes known. OBE, then, serves to illustrate a process that applies to all learning.

From a bioenergetic perspective, OBEs indicate a shift of coherence that then produces a cohesion enabling different perceptions. The first two levels of imagination rely on purposefully shifting cohesion by creating constructive coherence. Level three requires you to stabilize coherence, which intensifies the experience. Level four takes it all to a professional level.

Level Four

This is when you target your OBEs to precise locations in your physical world, such as deliberately traveling to another city. Level four indicates a marked ability to merge the first and second energy fields: an OBE is of the second field; when you can place your experience in your daily world, you hook together the two fields. You are managing your resources. At this point, a new process based on synthesizing these fields unfolds. It therefore reflects a major step in awakening your energy body and places you firmly on the path toward actualization and *being*.

Advanced Levels

The next levels of imagination continue a step-by-step method of bending the energy body's uniformity away from the conscious and unconscious and into the supraconscious. This highlights the work of the modern shamans: an examination of the human condition magnified by explorations of the third field. Each level represents a shift and restabilization of the assemblage point, another marker of learning. At a certain point *will* activates, thereby permitting further ability to manage the energy body.

In these arenas, imagination is vast and the experiences powerful and often tumultuous. The realm of imagination has always been so; but in these levels it is personally witnessed. Each new assemblage point position also changes your orientation to reality. It becomes possible to perceive regions of existence that were at one time literally beyond imagination.

Humans have a natural drive toward completion. The levels of imagination provide a means to take on the adventure of fully bringing your energy body to life. Your known-conscious world will collapse—or expand, depending on your view—time and again. Knowing the dynamics serves to buffer the turmoil and integrate the new. It is all a matter of learning.

HEIGHTENED CONSCIOUSNESS

There comes a time in learning when the energy body has been made sufficiently conscious that heightened awareness results. Colors are deeper, shapes clearer, and there is the recognizable emotional sense of connection with the world. In addition, this state also enables the use of imagination in the midst of any activity, lending a dreamlike quality to waking consciousness. As a result, some investigators refer to this state as *dreaming awake.*[11] This is appropriate, as in heightened consciousness the general landscape has a sense of viscosity that is characteristic of dreams.

This is not necessarily a *peak experience* where one may have a sense of a transcendent reality or at least that of an enhanced awareness of human potential.[12] Peak experiences embody more transient, almost euphoric events, while heightened consciousness is more calm and lasting. They are related, though, as aspects of peak experience bridge heightened awareness and also mystical experience, a transcendent state of consciousness, which is covered in the next chapter.

Stepping purposefully into imagination equates with entering heightened consciousness. Doing so enables you to use imagination more skillfully as well as explore other modes of perception. *Seeing,* for instance, is not as difficult in imagination because the bindings of perception are automatically loosened, not unlike the Hubble telescope being able to take clearer pictures of deep space because Earth's atmosphere doesn't cloud the view.

When the conscious domain extends significantly beyond the beginnings of heightened awareness, you enter another level of growth. Then

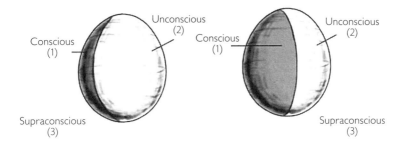

Figure 4.1. Heightened Consciousness
Stimulated by imagination and anchored by learning, the conscious domain
expands throughout the energy body. At a certain level, waking awareness becomes
heightened due to the conscious intermingling of the first and second fields.

the terms learning, imagination, first and second energy fields, and all the explanations and details bringing them into focus, become obsolete. In general terms, one of two things occurs. Either consciousness begins dealing with yet another model of reality, or you transcend reality as a model altogether. It is the latter that speaks more directly to *being*. You have reasoned your way out of reason and are in experience itself rather than experiencing a description of reality.

This illustrates the importance of not getting lost in the schematics and blueprints of terminology. The terms used here, for instance, such as "known and unknown," "learning and imagination," and "first and second energy fields" are different designations to help approach and understand central features of the energy body. Their purpose is to provide references to consciously explore imagination, to accelerate learning, and to properly engage discovery—not to bind perception along specific lines of thought. When you act in such a manner, individual effort is then on track to move this awareness into group consensus, accepted social reality.

GROUP CONSENSUS

Imagine all of the elements that go into designing and building a bridge, let alone all of the pieces that go into creating an entire culture. Take all the interlocking concepts of the energy body model and then expand that to include each and every aspect of your life. Then imagine what happens when a group of people validate and thus magnify the value of all these elements. The consensual worldview ends up becoming a version of reality that is almost impossible to break free of let alone see beyond.

Soap, hairspray, ships, automobiles, carpentry, education, medicine, the notion that the world is comprised of physical objects or of waveforms, God, and whatever else is part of individual or group consciousness are all parts of an inventory. The beauty of an inventory is that it provides meaning and relationship so you can engage the world. But inventories also constrict awareness by inhibiting the recognition that other inventories, other cohesions, and other worlds also exist. An inventory gives you things to look for, and if you see something that is not in your inventory you may not even recognize it.

Pieces of an inventory are established and connected through *selective cueing,* or deliberate focus on specific features of the world. Repetitive selective cueing builds and maintains inventories. Subject matter governs the inventory of an educational curriculum, for instance. An inventory can help you direct your attention by letting you know what options you have: yet at the same time it can limit your options. Imagination, though, allows new glimpses, pieces, and chunks of information to enter consciousness. How these are arranged and used is a matter of learning.

Group consensus is not necessarily born of objectivity. It is an aspect of collective consciousness; it is an effect of shared consciousness and subject to shared influence. There's great power when a group of people hold something to be true, but often the individual gives away autonomy to the group. At the same time, individuation not only requires finding and expressing a personal relationship with the world, it also hinges on finding meaning within the group and being able to constructively contribute to it. As social organisms, individuals are parts of the group. Not taking stock of this alienates you from yourself as well as limits the capabilities of the group.

According to Jung, a person who does not break out of group consensus will never realize individuation. This makes sense: how can you find yourself if you only relate to the group? At the same time, he argues that individuation "aims at a living cooperation of all factors." This falls in line with Maslow's concept of a hierarchy of needs, which indicates that basic personal and social needs must be met first in order for a person to progress to the higher needs of learning, knowledge, and self-actualization.[13] Please refer to the next chapter for a fuller explanation of Maslow's hierarchy.

On the other hand, the binding power of groups—from peer pressure to ethics to worldviews—entrains perception along preestablished lines and restricts inquiry from novel areas. This is the downside of social development. In terms of the energy body, the more you lock yourself into social considerations such as class standing, the less you actualize your own awareness. While there is great power in the collective, there is also immense power found in stretching into avenues not yet touched by it. You therefore need a balance of being simultaneously open and closed to all areas of life, while developing the art of knowing when to throw the switch in either direction.

This binary (open-close) requirement of learning reveals that new awareness requires openness, and consolidating the gains derived from awareness necessitates at least some degree of closing off. Both positions are necessary for growth, although the closed position tends to get more attention. While there is a natural drive toward forming the world into what is known, recognizable, and usable through enculturation, this tends to be overdone, causing us to step away from openness, to be less inclined to let go of one model in order to start fresh with another or to let more of the unconscious within self and society rise to a conscious level.

New social orders arise all the time. But if a new order is to be truly revolutionary, it must come from a deeper place within individuals who share a common bond. Otherwise, it is a rehash of what already exists. People need to be moved beyond the confines of collective reason and emotion by a greater force that offers enhancement of reason and emotion. Again, though, we have a blessing and curse, since a new movement can either liberate or ensnare.

The guideline for whether a revolution can become a blessing is that of maintaining positive individual governance—the opposite of any form of dominance—within a societal model that encourages flourishing. Collective consciousness—the heart of the group—would hold that authority is found at the core of each and every person. This value is synonymous with individuation and therefore serves to lead both the person and the group to higher states of actualization. Your life is not only a conceptual relationship between individual and society but extends beyond this, as it is also an energetic relationship between self and an all-encompassing environment.

Understanding these types of influences and relationships fosters better understanding of the mechanics of the energy body. Cohesion forms through the effects of the inventory, learning, imagination, and all other entraining influences within and without. As you develop the energy body, mental logic shifts to energetic considerations. In the interim, the world may turn topsy-turvy, meaning that constant vigilance is required to remain open or closed at any given turn in your path in order to maintain balance and harmony with yourself and the world.

MODELS OF REALITY

If you were to take only one lesson from this book, this section is the one to bank on. I say this because the first lesson in a shamanic apprenticeship often centers on learning that the world we hold to be real is only a description: a collection of ideas. Whatever that description is, it forms a model of reality. For shaman or scientist, knowing that this is factual produces a formative step in exploring consciousness.

Once you understand models, learning and imagination enter entirely new realms. This is because your current reality, as well as all other realities past, present, and future, are models, approximations of the overarching potential of what exists. Infinity has been reduced to "reality," to an extensive inventory that, even though forming an entire worldview, remains decidedly limited. Inventories are *about* something; they are not necessarily what *is*. A model is a bag of options that comes in all sizes. They are gestalts formed by culling interrelated elements of an inventory to form a representation of something larger.

Models are both solitary and influence other models. While interest in electricity and magnetism can be dated back to ancient Greece, the nineteenth century marked a historical turning point in the field of bioenergetics, for example. Many practical discoveries relating to different forms of energy and how they affect the human body were made during that period and the models associated with bioenergetics continue to be augmented. After Michael Faraday learned to harness magnetism to generate electrical current, Elias Smith patented an electromagnetic healing coil, Edwin Babbitt depicted energy fields surrounding the body and presented his work in the treatise *The Principles of Light and Color,* and Hahnemann developed homeopathy. Today we have magnetic resonance imaging and SQUID magnetometers. Over the years homeopathic *provings* (a method to determine the efficacy of a remedy) have increased. All of the information in this book is a model: that of an extended bioenergetic view of human anatomy. Within this, acupuncture offers a model, as do chakras, as do Western psychologies.

Within any discipline, models are often the benchmark to which new ideas, procedures, and products are measured, tested, and examined. By providing the means to intellectually grasp a system, models enable further study of the characteristics of that system, such as a mathematical model of atmospheric conditions, or a mechanistic view of the universe. A viable model explains, predicts, and adds to the knowledge from which it was born. The use of the Newtonian perspective of a mechanistic world reveals why an apple falls to the ground, enables the building of magnificent bridges, and helps to accurately forecast what will happen when something explodes or implodes.

Models both grow and fall to the side, though, because they are conditional fields and therefore invariably incomplete. The logic of a model consists of the arrangement of particular conditions. The practical effect is that a model always has limited applicability. For example, classical physics does little to make sense of teleportation. This form of travel—an area of investigation that is increasingly leaving the ranks of science fiction and entering science fact—finds home in the province of quantum physics. But to build this type of machine requires the knowledge of classical physics. Other models, like viewing our Sun as revolving around Earth, have become artifacts of an obsolete worldview.

At once resilient and fragile, models instill the means to have exquisite investigations or act as stumbling blocks to further research. These magnificently frail instruments capture the joy and the bane of trying to grasp what the world really is all about. All coherent intellectual perceptions rest within models, structures that reason uses to reflect, interpret, expand, and consider. Each model represents a singular cohesion and therefore an assemblage point position. On a grander scale, the interlocking of several compatible models forms a mega-cohesion, as it were, and is the driving force of group consensus reality.

Models come in all sizes. A laboratory bench model might be used to explain and measure the effects of adding one chemical to another. There are paradigms: expansive, wide-reaching models. Then there are worldviews, entire cosmologies that become so ingrained that they lead us to forget that the world that is being viewed is in fact a conglomeration of interpretations. The difference between a laboratory model that accounts for a chemical reaction and a model portraying a complete worldview is a matter of scale. Regardless of their expanse, as measured against infinity all models—be they of shamanism or science—are but single, isolated pictures of significantly greater circumstances.

It is worth repeating that each type of model, however large or small, is a reduced version of something larger. They exist as representations, symbols, or images, not reality itself. Any viable model functions as a principal determinant of what can be observed as well as focusing the results of that observation. Without this awareness of the role played by models, any approach to understanding can quickly degenerate into dogmatic fundamentalism. As physician Gabriel Cousens points out in the introduction to Richard Gerber's book, *Vibrational Medicine,* ". . . models are not necessarily real, but serve as conceptual tools to enhance a functional understanding."[14]

Models therefore need to be fluid. While they allow us to make practical gains in our understanding, they need to change to allow us to have new relationships to an ever-evolving universe, at least our ever-evolving perception of the universe. Without this malleability, submarines, airplanes, and healing technologies would have remained solely on the pages of science-fiction novels. When a more comprehensive model is developed, it is not that the new model is "right." It is that—in relation to the preceding model—it offers new perspective containing more potential.

For instance, the ability to specifically target cancer cells with minimal effect on healthy tissue, via new drugs and biotech advances, has produced a paradigm shift in oncology; physicians now approach the disease differently.[15] They have a new model, with matching technology, to specifically go after diseased cells rather than place the entire body under assault with broadly toxic cancer-fighting drugs. So-called "smart bombs," for example, distinguish between cancer cells and healthy cells, enter the diseased cell, and then explode.

Some models, however, are not all that useful in the first place. Engineering professor Henry Petroski says that including considerations of failure in a model is part of achieving success.[16] In the world of drug discovery, federal law usually requires animal testing for many new drugs in order to help ensure safety and efficacy. Because of the difficulties of correspondence between species, the type of data derived from these animal studies may be of only marginal value or even inaccurate, thereby throwing studies completely off the mark. By contrast, certain other animal models have proven to have better predictive value about what will happen when a drug is given to humans; these are known as "validated animal models." The validated models often provide a better basis for evaluation; however, the frequent lack of correlation between animal models demonstrates why possibilities of failure need to be part of investigations. You therefore have models within models within models. . . . This aptly reflects the complexity of constructing reality.

FROM MODEL TO REALITY

Reality formation and re-formation constitutes a process whereby one model gives way to another, one set of boundaries expands to establish a new region for exploration, and more of the world reveals itself. On a group level, inventories govern selective cueing as they determine the options of what can be called to our attention. The primary utility of models applies precisely to group consensus, which constructs and expresses reality. This may be on a small or large scale, and may be violent or peaceful. It gives us something to work with, to experience, and to guide our lives.

The history of the dampening and resurgence of homeopathy illustrates the role of models in learning. A key to the efficacy of homeopathic remedies is the transfer of the essence of physical molecules into water; the energy pattern of the molecule is imprinted in the homeopathic solution through succussing. When taken, a remedy acts on the vital force, the life energy, of a patient, which then leads to healing. The remedy resonates with energy fields in the body, which then entrain the organism to a healing response.

Homeopathy was once accepted in the United States, but during the early 1900s, pressure from a group of physicians who did not accept this model helped marginalize its use. Modern quantum theory, which can account for the imprinting of molecular energy patterns in solutions, is now beginning to explain homeopathy and other energy-based therapies of old.[17] With the reemergence of energy-based models within complementary and alternative medicine (CAM), homeopathy is regaining credence, as are acupuncture, laying-on-of-hands, and prayer.

Originating from the explosion of books and periodicals offering CAM information, consumers have been putting pressure on physicians to provide more options for treatment. Because of this grassroots movement, models based in various aspects of energy are blossoming. The energies of minerals, flowers, and aromas are applied to achieve particular effects. At the same time, some investigators in the scientific disciplines of medicine, physiology, and physics are tackling the role of energy in physiology and the field of bioenergetics is growing. By its very nature bioenergetics touches virtually every aspect of human endeavor; its healing dimension serves as a good example of this wide-reaching field. In part, these advances illustrate an individuated type of influence expressing itself constructively within a group.

This line of thinking also presents itself in the biophysical model, which holds that energetics provides a deeper level of understanding and description of the material world. If energy is in any way a determinant for physical actions and reactions, then new models, new variables for study, and new approaches to life will continue to sprout, eventually forming new ways of looking at the world in contrast to material, mechanistic perspectives. This is exactly what is taking form as evidenced by bioenergetic studies. As Oschman explains, "The medical and chemical-pharmacological models that have served us well in the past are not being replaced, but are being viewed within a more complete multidimensional perspective."[18]

MIT Professor Emeritus Thomas Kuhn writes in his book, *The Structure of Scientific Revolutions,* that only a crisis produces the need for practitioners to get out of their own way and allow new perspectives of inquiry to emerge.[19] The plagues of the nineteenth century provided such a catalyst. Kuhn also argues that a modern crisis has emerged from within humans due to the lack of answers that solve modern problems. The cost of health care and the debilitating side effects of many drugs may be providing an opening for new endeavors.

From the energy body perspective, models help form cohesions, which determine the ability to work with any given model. If you haven't integrated a sufficient number of elements that form a given cohesion's inventory, you can't relate. There is no resonance, no connection, no awareness, and no understanding. The reason that practices such as homeopathy, nonlocal healing, and other healing modalities have not been scientifically mapped yet is that there has not yet been a scientific model with which to develop hypotheses, theories, and then scientifically test these constructs—all of these being components of the model that makes science, science.

Once a model that accounts for the mechanisms and effects of prayer on healing develops, it may then be explained scientifically. Since healers often refer to the role played by energy, a bioenergetics model steps toward a scientific recognition as well as toward an entire worldview, for which quantum physics provides the groundwork. Discoveries in the field now paint entirely new pictures of how the body works and how it heals. Many investigators regard their work as revealing the very foundation of life where energetic occurrences, not material events, form the basis of life. But alas, it is still a model. It has been built from thoughts that eventually form cohesion. As a result, you *experience* the model. This self-validation lends itself to an interpretation that true reality is at hand.

Investigating the universe of energy will surely take us to new worlds, and will certainly provide a high adventure of discovery. An understanding of models boosts this process. While a world of energy may account for far more than that which has preceded it, and may therefore take us to a brighter day, waiting to be born are yet more discoveries, models, and ways of participating with the world about us.

5

Expanding the Boundaries

History reveals that consensus reality changes as circumstance gives way to new perceptions. From a flat earth to a geocentric universe to a quantum cosmos, our relationship with the world routinely undergoes upheaval. And yet the changes tend not to be immediately cataclysmic or transformative. It took some time before the ideas of Copernicus took hold, even after Galileo's validating efforts. Einstein thought aspects of a quantum universe just couldn't be right. Yet his legacy lives and breathes. And now adherents of the proposition that the world is fundamentally comprised of energy are helping turn the world upside down, or is it right side up?

STATES OF CONSCIOUSNESS

We can make this expansion of worldview function even better by understanding the process behind it. The work of psychologist Charles Tart helps to explain perceptual evolution. In *States of Consciousness,* a book ahead of its time, Tart puts forth the concepts of a *baseline state of consciousness* (b-SoC), *altered state of consciousness* (ASC), and *discrete altered state of consciousness* (d-ASC).[1]

In a nutshell, a b-SoC is your normal, waking consciousness, your normal cohesion. An ASC is a state of consciousness that in some way differs from a b-SoC and differs sufficiently to result in awareness outside of the norm; thus, an altered state. A d-ASC is a stable altered state. When you've learned how to use an altered state it becomes a discrete state. It is something clearly and consciously separate from your baseline consciousness yet may be returned to time and time again. With an ASC, such as your first OBE, you have minimal connection and coherence to a new area of perception. With a d-ASC, repeated OBEs have established a broader network of what they mean, and the increased coherence produces a cohesion allowing you to gain at least a modicum of control to induce and guide it.

This can be related to the Toltec paradigm, which elucidates the evolution of your energy body through different cohesions. Start with your stable cohesion that you use to get you through the workday, pay the mortgage, and raise a family: the cohesion and model—the baseline— of ordinary life. To change the entire baseline state, you need to experience a number of different cohesions. This is accomplished by plowing as many influences as you can into your energy field: art, literature, music, religion, science, and economics . . . whatever. How you address these, and the skills you develop, are between you and the world. That is the subjective element, the individual component of cohesion. The overriding practice involves exercising consciousness in many different ways. Doing so forms different cohesions, and when these are oriented toward a common goal they result in a profound shift in your baseline.

At the beginning stage of learning, a topic may be outside your daily reference. It may even be completely unrecognizable. An OBE, for instance, is something that is not usually included in daily inventories. If you have an OBE, you may even work hard to forget it because you have no context for it. At this point, the OBE is an altered state. However, if you have repeated, spontaneous OBEs, at some point you will no longer be able to turn your back on them. You might even start researching what they mean. You then continue your study and effort. Over time, you may learn to bring about an OBE whenever you wish. Then it becomes a discrete altered state; your efforts have helped shift, or entrain, your cohesion to express that ability. It is the same for learning any skill, esoteric or mundane.

Susan Blackmore presents another way of looking at this dynamic of innate potential becoming realized. In reviewing studies on the synchronous nature of perception, how bits and pieces of awareness bind into a single recognition, she indicates that "when unconscious information becomes unified it magically 'enters consciousness.'"[2] Put yet another way, when you have a sufficient amount of experience with related altered states, they organize to form a coherent discrete altered state.

Perhaps you have concurrently been learning how to solve problems using imagination, as well as how to fly an airplane, speak a foreign language, and conjure up various science-fiction-style cities for a novel. If you develop these to a knowledgeable level, each realm of exploration represents a distinct cohesion. In the beginning, each was an ASC, which developed into a d-ASC. Your b-SoC changes when they all have been integrated into a greater whole. You then participate in life from a new vantage point.

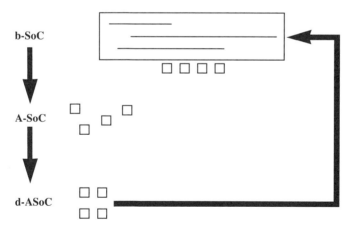

Figure 5.1. States of Consciousness

Altered states directly influence your daily baseline state of consciousness. They are part of developing awareness. The above box represents a complete worldview, with the small boxes representing aspects of that view. When the elements of a baseline are rearranged, you experience an altered state. When this arrangement has meaning, it becomes a discrete altered state. When you command a sufficient number of like-minded discrete states, your baseline changes; you've completed the loop.

STAGES OF AWAKENING

The change from a baseline state of consciousness through an altered state to a new baseline applies to the *stages of awakening* or what may also be regarded as levels of ontological development. As reflected by the different relationships of consciousness (i.e., ASC or d-ASC), each level represents new concepts and behaviors. Each new stage, for example, is an ASC until you can employ the skills associated within it with some degree of proficiency, whereupon it has become a d-ASC. When you have stabilized several related skills, such as various aspects of imagination, you experience a b-SoC shift, and have a new assemblage-point position. The main difference between specific skills and the broader cohesion of stages is the degree of expansion; put another way, differences among levels represent how much of your energy body has been actualized, how much of your unconscious has become conscious.

An ASC occurs principally due to the random influence of the second energy field. Some portion of imagination pops into consciousness, and then usually exits. A d-ASC and then a new b-SoC form when you have integrated this new knowledge into the first field, which means you have learned something about another part of your second field; you have learned to manage imagination a bit better. Again, the process is the same for handling a particular skill or enlarging your worldview,

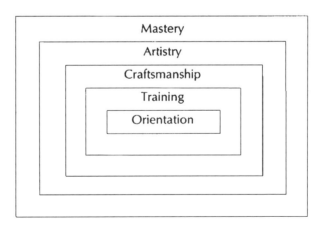

Figure 5.2. Stages of Awakening
Each stage contains the others.

just on different scales. Ontological development, then, brings entire segments of your energy body into awareness and you experience quantitative leaps of consciousness.

An ontological stage represents a major cohesion; it governs each and every feature of the reality you experience. Cohesion organizes your perceptions of the world and, in so doing, calls forth interpretations, values, ethics, habits, hopes, dreams, and states of health. With each shift in cohesion, these change. Intensity of daily experience magnifies at each new level.

Each stage is also a domain of self-actualization, of *being*. A self-actualization journey requires being oriented to core for each step. Only the degree of proficiency of stabilizing core awareness varies among levels. As you progress from orientation to training, and on to craftsmanship, artistry, and mastery, you can express more of your completeness. These levels are natural to humans in the same manner that moths have natural stages, growing from egg to larva to pupa to adult.

Cohesional or *energy body intelligence*—the ability to understand and manage your energy body—is a subset of ontological intelligence. Technically speaking, cohesion relates to the conditions within the energy body and ontological relates to the wider landscape of the human condition that also extends beyond the energy body. Both types of intelligence apply to skills of the energy body. Shifting awareness among cornerstones represents such skill as does the self-regulation of health. Applying this knowledge derives from ontological intelligence. For another nuanced understanding of energy body dynamics, cohesion and ontological may at times be considered synonymous as they both influence each other, depending on circumstance. Cosmology (the origins of the universe) is ontological, for instance, yet the considerations that are formed from such study stem from cohesion.

One way to begin expanding the boundaries of cohesion is to experience more. Engaging in things you are not fond of as well as those you enjoy builds connections within the energy body. Experience leads to learning and learning leads to knowledge, a condition where cohesion has been so well integrated that your relationship to the world—your ontological state of *being*—changes. The developmental stages represent leaps in expanding the conscious domain of the energy body. Each level also provides greater degrees of heightened consciousness as measured by the first and second fields blending. The more you have formed cohesional baselines for a range of distinct experiences and skills, the greater your overall cohesion. Practically, this means you are better able to *see* what you are up to and what effects your actions have. Put another way, *seeing* facilitates the experience of energy. Ontological levels instill meaning for this experience and this translates to more awareness. Each stage means you're that much more conscious of being conscious.

Each stage represents an immense amount of reorganization of perception, characterized by new insights and abilities, and also reflects the type and quality of coherence between internal and external energies. Working with imagination directly stimulates and develops the energy body; learning integrates the experiences. The results are yours to discover. Otherwise, there wouldn't be any individuation to discuss. At the same time, humans share uniformity and therefore to some degree share cohesion, so each stage has common properties.

Orientation

If you are in the orientation stage, you have a highly conditional field. Cohesion is unyielding and there is minimal fluency of perception. You wouldn't recognize an ASC if it bonked you on the head. Your reality is pretty much fixed in place like a window-store mannequin. Orientation, though, means that you have stepped onto a path such as one of the transpersonal psychologies. You might begin to meditate, practice yoga postures, or work to enter imagination. It means taking the first step toward learning about the world beyond ordinary constructs of reality. You now have some type of recognition that life is lacking and you are getting oriented to what other possibilities exist. Doing so carries the commitment to experience yourself as more conscious, more actualized. The dominant aspect of this stage is an orientation to learning a philosophy and set of skills; your formal training is about to begin.

Training

This stage reflects the beginning of movement, the remedy to stagnation. You begin to sense the intricacies of learning and growth. Whether you call it an apprenticeship or discipleship, this stage determines your relationship with your craft, be it Buddhist, Taoist, Sufi, Toltec, Christian, or whatever else that fits the bill. These all concern the development of awareness beyond the ordinary. While they may have different contexts, they often use similar methods such as meditation. It is a conscious decision to embark on this type of path, and whether or not you have a teacher you need to find entry by virtue of your own wits.

As an apprentice, you are fully yet clumsily engaged with your efforts to become more aware. Cohesion begins to be more malleable. During this adjustment you may feel like you lose touch with reality from time to time, which might be the case. Another way of saying this is that you are learning about the relativity of reality, and until you can find continuity in your means of constructing reality you may feel lost.

At first, seemingly mysterious events may randomly happen. You may have a spontaneous OBE or epiphany concerning a scientific discovery. As you grow, not only do you better understand how reality is an effect of cohesion, but you also begin to manage and use your experience at a more skillful level. You can begin to deliberately seek these types of experiences and begin learning in earnest how to transform altered states into new baseline states.

The training provided by your chosen system—including theory, context, and how-to exercises—is designed to further orient and stabilize perception. Your training offers the basics that not only lift you out of the orientation level but also provides the framework to advance to the other stages. In this manner, you will always be able to orient yourself, no matter the circumstance.

Craftsmanship

At a certain point, you gain a professional relationship with your endeavors. You now step away from training and learn through application as a practitioner of your craft. You have learned various elements of the craft to the point of being able to deliberately enact them. This process is characterized has having incorporated what once was unknown into something having meaning, or put another way as having traversed altered states to a new baseline state. You might therefore practice shamanism, science, or plumbing, for example.

From an ontological view, this means you're now more adept at using the resources of your energy body. No matter the extent of your craft, the management of personal resources is a main feature of this stage. You can shift cohesion when desired and remain alert and balanced while doing so. You have firm understanding of conditional fields and what it takes to develop a natural field. You have also integrated the worldview and techniques of the craft with the pieces of your life. Formerly latent cornerstones of perception are activating.

The elements of one stage don't become completely clear until you stabilize the next. And as you traverse the stages, you'll see that what once was effective no longer works. You always have to bring new skills to bear and behave in different ways to accomplish your objectives, a requirement for a craftsperson of any profession. Discipline is the key to moving through the stages toward self-actualization, and part of discipline is not getting lost in the system. The labels and rituals associated with a given discipline are not the work; they represent ways to approach the true issue at hand. The real work resides in the *being* of it. A traditional shamanic exercise of orienting oneself to the four cardinal directions and the meaning each has for you, for instance, may help you feel more emotionally centered. The ritual helped bring about the actual sense of it. The higher skill, though, is being centered no matter where and when without any extraneous support. This is the knowledge—the *being*—learned from performing the exercises. Remaining oriented to core energy governs further growth.

Artistry

Superior craftsmanship leads to artistry, rousing the energy body to the level of a natural energy field. A hallmark of this field is that learning and imagination are on equal footing. The first and second energy fields have merged to a degree that differentiating them is meaningless, not because you're disoriented but because you have lifted yourself outside their reference. This also means you have become individuated, to use Jung's term albeit with shamanic meaning. At this point, you are no longer bound to your craft. You can stretch your perception in any direction without the need for channel markers and supportive exercises.

While a metaphysical system offers a practical approach to engaging this range of humanness, embedded within the training is the path to grow beyond the path. Training engenders a specialized conditional field, while craftsmanship represents a level of skill commensurate with achieving membership. Entering the artisan stage means you've left the system behind. You no longer need that structure to grow. In artistry you are participating in an entirely new manner with the world. You have become a conscious part of it, an integral part, rather than removed from it, truly living the time-honored adage, "in the world but not of it." You are completely yourself and completely of the environment at the same time.

This is the domain of core, which contains all aspects of human intelligence. Conditional fields block access to this intelligence and interfere with the flow of information from it to conscious awareness. As a result, it remains in the realm of potential. Artisans rest easy at the core of their energy bodies, and life emanates from this vantage point.

As the energy body comes to life, the more you perceive the world from *will* rather than from reason. If you reach artistry via Toltec training, all of your cornerstones of perception will be awake. You will have moved away from the mental and into feeling as a principal means to navigate life. You will be using your complete anatomy. You adeptly manage your energetic resources. For modern Toltecs, this stage is the guiding light of what "shaman" means.

In general, whatever your craft, the potential you've labored to awaken is ready and available to be expressed. Logic constructed from personal and group considerations gives way to a natural order. This is another way of saying that you are more integrated with infinity. What happens next results as a statement of your artistry as you have learned to live in the thickness of imagination. You won't know how this will be expressed until you're in the midst of doing so.

Mastery

Whereas the artisan has arrived at his or her core, the master behaves from this center. Don Juan has indicated that this stage of development is that of the *seer,* involving the mastery of one's totality, which includes the whole of the energy body. The prelude for this stage, he says, is that of the person of knowledge, or what I have referred to as the artisan.[3] From this perspective, the principles put forth during orientation and training are the basics for learning mastery.

While *seeing* as a mode of perception is developed at each stage, a true seer completely engages a universe of energy as an integral, fully aware part of that universe. No matter how proficiently one *sees,* until a person enters mastery *seeing* may be relegated to part of the training needed to participate in a grander scheme of life. And therefore from a perspective of infinity, the master and apprentice are equal; however, from the perspective of these individuals, there are worlds upon worlds of difference in their awareness.

ABRAHAM MASLOW'S HIERARCHY OF NEEDS

As another model of psychological development, Abraham Maslow's Hierarchy of Needs provides useful references. His schematic is usually presented in pyramid form to represent steps of personal growth. The more we are able to fulfill what Maslow labels our "deficit" needs (shown in the bottom four steps of the diagram), the more likely we are to be able to fulfill our "growth" needs (shown in the top step). A self-actualized person can suspend the innate drive to satiate the deficit needs, for example. This person does not need social acceptance in order to complete a task. Conversely, a person may shun social acceptance due to psychopathology rather than for creative purposes.

The stages in this hierarchy are not mutually exclusive. A person can be reveling in creativity, yet when access to his or her studio is threatened, may drop levels and respond in terms of a basic need for security. As with other learning, the measure for whether a person has stabilized self-actualization is found in behavior. When someone lashes out at another, for instance, it is because of feeling threatened. A self-actualized person will recognize the threat but responds more in line with it as a solvable problem, perhaps to enter into negotiation rather than use violence.

According to Maslow, other key aspects of a self-actualized person are having stronger character, being more open to experience, having a sense of autonomy, demonstrating increased objectivity, being able to love, and *recovering* creativity (which indicates it was at some point lost during maturation). He also says that these healthy persons have a superior perception of reality, an appreciation of emotional reaction, and an increased acceptance of self and others.[4]

Developmental models such as Maslow's or the stages of awakening help us to orient, assess, and direct behavior of all kinds. These levels of ontological development also have the inherent value of providing stepping-stones toward self-actualization. Each stage brings to bear how much potential you can access, which is in direct proportion to your degree of individuation. These stages therefore contain both an intellectual and energetic logic. Talking about them facilitates entrainment

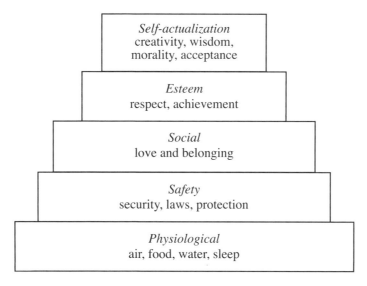

Figure 5.3. Maslow's Hierarchy of Needs

as you are reinforcing these channel markers of growth in your mental, emotional, and physical behaviors. You are also deriving guidance from them, which is an effect of entrainment. This builds cohesion, which entrains perception to new emanations and vice versa. This is the foundation of human perception, as participating with new emanations results in making the energy body more conscious.[5]

INDICATIONS OF GROWTH

Regardless of your stage of awareness, there are common traits that characterize growth. Only the degree of skill with these attributes separates one stage from another. Some of these qualities are:

1. Emotional equanimity, reflecting increased emotional intelligence. You have more peace and balance, both within and without your sense of self.
2. Fluency with logic, able to shift perception to at least entertain other viewpoints.
3. Holistic observation and participation with life, knowing yourself to be a part of life.
4. Enhanced sense of security.
5. Non-dogmatic approach to life; able to live and let live.
6. Well-defined principles to guide your personal life.
7. Goal oriented.
8. Engaged in learning.
9. A sense of *becoming* with an appreciation of *being*.
10. Behaving more spontaneous and less worried.

The stages reflect ever-increasing complexity of behavior, requiring the orchestration of different behaviors such as strategies, tactics, and general orientation. They also represent chunks of learning in both the first and second fields, and indicate the awakening of entire sections of the energy body. They pertain to how many emanations you align with and how well your internal energies resonate with them. The more cosmological emanations you touch, the more alive your energy body is;

the more refined and harmonious the connection, the greater the aware-ness. Figure 4.1 illustrates this process.

Your sense of reasonableness may also quicken. This, though, hinges on your ability to integrate new relationships. You need to understand group consensus while not succumbing to it, for instance. This in turn corresponds to stretching the first-field order of what is known further into your energy body. Learning and imagination must support, bal-ance, and stimulate each other. Reflecting this process, your baseline state of consciousness undergoes radical reformation at each level and often within a level.

EXPANDING THE BASELINE STATE OF CONSCIOUSNESS

While imagination plays a role in forming and sustaining consensus real-ity, the bulk of it exists beyond the zone of accepted reality. Entering this energy field revitalizes views and experiences of life. The following sec-tions put forth experiences that move perception out of its cozy nest by stimulating imagination and learning, and enhancing ontological growth as they provide experience with life beyond widespread accepted norms. Depending on the nature of the experience and level of skill, they repre-sent altered or discrete altered states. They also provide examples of vari-ous aspects of consciousness that, when integrated, help establish a new baseline state.

Psychic Experience

Psychic experience, or *psi* as academic and scientific literature refers to it, is most often segmented into two major categories: extra-sensory per-ception (ESP) and psychokinesis (PK). ESP consists of those perceptions outside the physical senses. The basic elements of ESP are clairvoyance (*seeing* beyond the range of ordinary vision), telepathy (direct communi-cation between minds), and precognition (the ability to know the future). We can add remote viewing (ESP using a specific method) as a distinct class. PK deals with the direct influence of mind on matter. Examples of

PK include OBE, firewalking, imprinting images on photographic film, and spoon bending.[6] Each facet of *psi* is a specific cohesion that deepens with the expansion of skill.

Scientific inquiry into *psi* began in the 1870s, and the field received a boost from the spiritualist movement (mediumship) when psychical research organizations were founded in Britain and the United States during the 1880s.[7] Today, while books on OBE, courses on firewalking, and psychic development classes can easily be found, scientific investigation has languished, with few institutions of higher learning providing courses.

Empirical research, however, points to a conclusion that some, if not all, *psi* is innate to humans and that it may not really be "extra" at all. For example, psychiatrists Gabbard and Twemlow have shown that prior to onset, 79 percent of those they studied or surveyed who had an OBE were emotionally calm and physically relaxed, that 89 percent wanted to have another, and that 86 percent said the experience provided a greater awareness of reality. Most OBEs weren't forced in any way; they were natural and spontaneous events.[8]

Moreover, it is now clear that U.S. governmental agencies have not only sponsored *psi* research but have trained people in its use. For example, a former military intelligence officer, Joseph McMoneagle, has revealed the inner workings of the once top-secret spy program, Stargate Project. Once a field operative, McMoneagle was later trained in a rigorous protocol of remote viewing. After demonstrating great talent, McMoneagle was designated Government Remote Viewer and Psychic 001. Decorated by the U.S. Army for his prowess as a psychic spy, McMoneagle now consults for corporations on projects such as finding the best geographic locations to drill for oil, as well as working with scientists in collaborations that have included contributing to the discovery of a new subatomic particle.[9]

The acceptance of *psi* hinges on the model of reality used: does *psi* exist or is it scoffed at? But this pertains to acceptance, not legitimacy. A model that accounts for it can be found in both the Toltec paradigm that references emanations, connectedness with the environment, assemblage point positions, and entrainment as well as in quantum physics theory, which puts forth energetic resonance, entanglement, and nonlocality.[10] Both theories hold that domains of energy connect with and influence other domains, that information from one energy field may be communicated or transferred to another, and that there is a dimension of reality that is not bound by ordinary time and space. *Psi* could therefore reflect having a more fluent connection with an extended environment. From this viewpoint, learning the various elements of *psi* becomes just that, learning. The groundwork for a worldview incorporating *psi* exists.

Mystical Experience

A mystical experience is one in which awareness expands to the extent that humans are perceived to be part of a greater, possibly divine, reality. Representing a cosmological rather than skill-based cohesion, it dismantles boundaries in favor of extensive and continual growth. It requires us to break barriers because it can't be contained. Personal accounts of mystical experience are often couched in religious terms, so this transcendent awakening usually finds a place in theological as well as psychological studies.[11]

A mystical experience awakens potential. It connects you with infinity. It stretches you further through your energy body and jettisons you out of your current condition field. It facilitates growth to a new level. The term *mystical* should not be equated with the term *occult*. Occult concerns the experience, use, and application of psychic forces. An occult view may enclose supernatural events to make sense of them yet do so without requiring you to expand your vision.

Although mystical experiences usually occur spontaneously, they can be facilitated by following a step-by-step path that leads to ever-widening awareness. All of the classic transpersonal psychologies contain their own staircase of logic. The information in this book serves as an example. At some point during a mystical experience, though, logic is suddenly and overwhelmingly supplanted by a gestalt of awareness. As pointed out by physicist Fritjof Capra in *The Tao of Physics,* however you arrive at a mystical experience, and regardless of whether you are a practitioner of mysticism or science, a common experience is that of having your reality shaken to its roots.[12] Over time, what is at first an altered state forms into a discrete altered state. Rounding out the procedure, the integration of the experience leads to a fundamental change in your view of reality, a new baseline state.

Researcher Valerie Hunt maintains, "Psychotherapists must envision this realm of consciousness as essential to an expanded, orderly relationship with self and the cosmic world." Noting that mystical experiences are often dismissed as emotional aberrations, she adds that they add to emotional intelligence and "are absolutely essential for comprehending life's profound meanings."[13]

Just as a certain pattern of stars indicates a particular constellation, a pattern of discrete perceptions indicates a mystical experience. If you were to have a mystical experience right now, you would notice several of at least ten distinct perceptions that combine to form this constellation, producing what might be an overwhelming gestalt of awareness.

1. A mystical experience is ineffable; words are not adequate to describe the experience. Although it is possible to recount the event to some degree, you clearly feel words portray only the surface.

2. There is a sense of surrender. You feel at ease recognizing creative forces molding your life. In addition, although you may have sought the experience, it came and went of its own accord.

3. As you touch the mystical, it enshrouds you in sacred wonderment. Knowledge beyond reason is yours, and the value of the experience is self-validating. You need no group consensus support to recognize its reality.

4. The experience is short-lived.

5. You are taken beyond ordinary time and space. While the experience is short, you may feel as though you have touched eternity. Gone, too, is the sense that you live exclusively in three dimensions. You now recognize a direct, inner connection with creation that does not rely on ordinary measurements.

6. You experience paradox, seeming opposites. You may feel as though you are in the midst of a fertile wasteland. The experience is rich beyond compare, yet there is nothing to hold. You tap direct knowledge that does not require thinking. You experience what you learn rather than apprehend it once removed.

7. You do not study knowledge; you are knowledge.

8. You understand the experience as positive and affirming.

9. You can integrate the experience. A persisting change in your personality prevents you from turning away from your new awareness. A mystical experience alters your life.

10. You feel fused with all life. You are no longer separate from your existence; the realization of oneness grants your life new meaning.

Some of these qualities are mentioned in the work of William James, often credited with being the father of American psychology. Abraham Maslow also mentions some in terms of peak experience. He states that a peak experience carries its own intrinsic meaning, includes disorientation (an altered state) of time and space, and is always a positive experience.[14]

While this list gives a general outline of elements of a mystical experience, the event is always unique, as though it were tailored to the individual. All of these qualities don't need to be a part of each mystical experience. Just as a cloud might prevent your seeing an entire stellar constellation, you might miss a few of the components. In any case, the authority of personal experience supersedes any guidelines. At the same time, knowing these elements is helpful, since you will become aware of each at some time in your growth through the stages of awakening. The mystical experience represents a symphony in which all elements harmonize.

A mystical experience not only opens and refines your perception but also clarifies your life. If you were to feel the sacred unity of all creation, you would naturally behave more ethically. Rather than use OBEs for self-aggrandizement, they can be used to explore the farthest reaches of the universe or the innermost depths of yourself. If you can integrate the experience in positive ways, you seek to express your knowledge in positive ways, too. Through your experience, and the manner in which you express it, you begin to travel within infinity. As you do, your horizons grow, you touch expanded impressions of reality, and you realize deeper regions of your being.

Mysticism

It is possible to live in a way that contributes to having mystical experiences. Traditionally, this has been the province of mysticism: philosophies, religions, and lifestyles that engender a mystical relation with the universe. These are high-end metaphysical systems that provide a way to reveal the wholeness of life, including its divinity. A mystical experience often results as a by-product of having this orientation.

Mysticism has heretofore placed the emphasis of religious experience on the immediate awareness of God. In Christian mysticism, for instance, Jesus serves as a model for direct participation with God-conscious. The mystical movement within Judaism produced the Kabbalah, a tradition of perceiving divine reality. And Islamic mysticism, often referred to as Sufism, holds as a principle the immediate intuitive knowledge of God. Similar constructs of divine communion are the defining element of mysticisms in other religions as well as in various philosophies.[15] However, the field of transpersonal psychology, which incorporates studies of mysticisms, demonstrates that a mystical experience need not be couched in religious terms or understanding; that is, the basis of mysticism may be considered in a secular light. Still, through history religion has kept alive this form of relationship with a higher order, no matter what it is called.

While the cognitive technologies found in transpersonal psychologies provide the means to open us to possibilities and hopefully lift us out of conditional fields, interpretations of the ensuing experiences result from the very nature of the technologies, be they material, psychological, or religious. Perhaps the experience is often rendered in religious context because religions have been the purveyor of information about mystical adventure. It then becomes a self-validating experience, as interpretation constrains the expanded awareness. A priest may touch the face of God, for instance, while a psychologist may glimpse the fullness of individuation and a scientist delve into a unified field of consciousness. On the other hand, perhaps religious doctrine emerges from prophets encountering the mystical and bringing form to it. Either way, the result is that the conditional field of the system (religion or psychology) is being used to pressure awareness into a natural field, into a direct alignment with a cosmic awareness. This is an example of craftsmanship that leads to artistry.

This is also a requisite point in understanding human consciousness. Even when consciousness attends to higher orders of human awareness, as can be found in areas of religion, philosophy, and psychology; it is still tuned to conditional fields. If they can push you to a natural field, then they are the ones to follow. If they can't, and you still abide by them, you will remain relegated to the conditions of an arbitrary human arrangement that does not represent a natural order—whether the order is of biology, physics, or all creation.

The natural energy field, a complete conscious state of human awareness, exists beyond the confines of those systems that are designed to help you get there. Once there, you are always on your own—just as you have been all along. The difference is that you now have balance and wherewithal. Mysticism therefore supports the quest of expanding consciousness and a mystical experience transcends the model that helped engender it.

Greek-Armenian mystic G. I. Gurdjieff described four main avenues of mysticism: conquering pain or commanding physical resources, faith and devotion, direct knowledge of consciousness, and a path that combines the others.[16] Yet in each branch, elements of the others are present. A person of devotion will realize more consciousness, for example, and vice versa. The various forms provide access to a greater reality for different personalities. Each avenue may express itself in elaborate practices or through very streamlined styles.

There are also cultural considerations. While the world's three major monotheistic religions—Judaism, Christianity, and Islam—share common ancestry, each has developed a unique form of mysticism. Even though they all engender a mystical relationship with the cosmos, they may not all consider paranormal experience or abilities to be viable for ontological development. Various denominations may also accept or reject *psi*.

The same applies to transpersonal psychologies. A Zen Buddhist may shun the high adventures of OBEs, a Taoist may allow them, and a Toltec may intend them. It is also interesting to note that meditative experiences vary among practitioners. Electroencephalograph (EEG) research has shown that a Zen master might stay alert to the simple rhythm of a metronome while remaining deep in meditation, for instance, while a skilled Yoga meditator's EEG doesn't register the physical-environment stimulation. Even with common overarching goals, different systems yield different results.[17]

Buddhist monk and psychologist Jack Kornfield presents two principal schools of mystical thought as *transcendent* and *immanent*.[18] A transcendent path strives for the higher order of altered states, including mystical revelations, while an immanent path doesn't place importance on altered states and teaches that everything needed is right here, right now, in ordinary time and space. Modern Toltecs are in the middle as they strive for a range of altered states to accelerate learning while recognizing that they haven't learned much if they can't apply their experiences in the here and now. As we have seen, the experience of altered states is needed for learning as without altering what you know, you don't learn. You need to expand the bubble of perception, by entering an altered relation with the world, and then integrating it to form a new baseline to where what once was altered is now normal. Immanent paths, however, de-emphasize the types of altered states that include *psi* and mystical experience.

Within the various forms of mysticism, some researchers hold that there are two major divisions, reflecting outward or inward orientation to mystical phenomena. This division is also referred to as plenum and void, or *catophatic* and *apophatic*.[19] Plenum may be described as pure potential, all that is, or the complete fullness of energy and being. The catophatic approach uses images to provide a human relationship to this expanse, which allows the mystical to make sense through material or emotional representation such as stained-glass renderings found in church windows.

The apophatic style, on the other hand, provides an imageless, abstract portrayal of something beyond the ordinary human condition.[20] The void is often described in negative terms: "that which is not" as opposed to "that which is" (plenum). Void is also considered to hold potential; beingness springs forth out of something else, which is beyond description. Meditating on a blank wall serves as an example technique.

Both methods reveal vital models. The scientific debate surrounding dark energy offers a good example for application to other fields. That is, the interpretation that dark energy spreads throughout the universe reflects a plenum orientation, whereas if dark energy is viewed as a perception of void then we're talking about an apophatic approach. The debate also serves our better understanding mysticism as when we're dealing with the essence of perception and interpretation: reality always perches beyond comprehension. Void may represent peaking into the unknowable where there are absolutely no references, known or unknown. It could therefore be an aspect of the plenum that exists beyond human capacity to touch it and is perceived as void. Or void could be the womb of potential and plenum; it could be emptiness that gives rise to form. Don't let interpretations get in the way of experience.

While worthy to distinguish the different aspects of mysticism, a significant point is that they are not exclusive. Despite their intrinsic differences, teachings of one method overlap with those of others. Understanding the whys and wherefores can help you latch on to the integrity of a school of thought in order to gain momentum. Doing so also helps you to avoid the trap of fundamentalism. All said and done, mystical systems share common denominators including:

1. Recognizing a greater reality that is far more substantial than a material world.

2. Defining a mystical reality. Within this schematic, we find the clear division between occult and mystical experience.

3. Portraying a psychology or philosophy that determines an individual's soul (which may be the energetic, anatomical core) to be similar to—if not identical with—the greater reality.

4. Offering a doctrine, system, or way to bring about the perception of the greater reality.

5. Providing means to align with, and experience, that reality.

From an energy body perspective, a mystical experience offers temporary freedom from conditional-field cohesion. It can be understood in terms of the assemblage point shifting more to the core of the energy body, corresponding with an alignment to emanations that uplift awareness. The grace of this interpretation is that since there are objective references of human anatomy, the causes and effects can be measured and then intentionally reproduced. In principle, this is similar to mapping out the cause of disease and then developing a technology to restore health.

Near-Death Experience

Yet another phenomenon that expands awareness is the near-death experience (NDE), which provides firsthand experience with reality outside of normal daily living. I had my first NDE when I was eight years old and a few more in a dream research laboratory.

The NDE that occurred when I was eight resulted from falling into a lake while fishing and nearly drowning. I experienced the lab adventures at The Monroe Institute, which is located in the foothills of the Blue Ridge Mountains of Virginia. They use a technology known as *Hemi-Sync,* short for "hemispheric synchronization." It was initially developed by Robert Monroe, a sound engineer and producer of several hundred radio network programs, as well as a person who gained notoriety by reporting his OBEs.

This bioenergetic technology uses sound to help balance the electrical activity of the right and left hemispheres of the brain. This automatically focuses attention, enabling the listener to more fully investigate aspects of consciousness. We could say that *Hemi-Sync* shifts a person's assemblage point, thereby shifting perception. Conversely, changing cohesion alters brain waves.

In recent years, scientific research has led to the popularization of a psychological model of brain functions, which allows us to clarify different modes of perception. In short, the right hemisphere of the brain perceives in a holistic, spatial, intuitive, and symbolically oriented manner. In contrast, the left hemisphere processes information in a linear, sequential, and analytical manner. The brain hemispheres, which correlate and control the opposite sides of the physical body, may also be related to the first and second energy fields, to the right and left sides of the energy body, with the left hemisphere corresponding to the linear, right side of the energy body and the right hemisphere to the potential and imaginative capacities of the left-side, second field.[21]

Hemi-Sync builds on the principle that the brain can follow, or entrain to, brain-wave frequencies—delta (0.5–4Hz), theta (4–8Hz), alpha (8–13Hz), beta (13–30Hz), and gamma (30+Hz)—as outlined in chapter three. To establish this *frequency following response,* slightly different audio frequencies are sent to each hemisphere of the brain, preferably using stereo headphones for increased efficiency. If a 100Hz tone is sent to one ear and an 110Hz tone to the other, the brain mixes these signals and automatically produces the difference between the two signals. In this instance, the brain generates a 10Hz *binaural beat.* The brain then resonates at 10Hz, thus producing more alpha waves. The person then becomes more relaxed and experiences more mental imagery—a state known to correlate with dominant alpha activity.[22]

To expand this, imagine simultaneously establishing binaural beats of 4Hz and 16Hz. At 4Hz the brain is resonating near delta, so the listener would gradually experience more perceptions characteristic of deep sleep. But a 16Hz beta wave is also being generated, leading the person to remain awake and alert, and able to consciously perceive what happens during the corresponding sleep state.

By entraining to specific audio signals, I had clinically induced mystical and near-death experiences as well as OBEs. In each instance, the laboratory experience corresponded to similar events outside of the laboratory while not using *Hemi-Sync*. The NDEs resulted while entraining to a 1.5Hz binaural beat, a frequency close to what is considered brain wave, clinical death. As I listened to the tones, I spontaneously found myself traveling in a tunnel with a vortex at the end and vanishing in the distance. At the end of the tunnel was a gentle but brilliant white light. I sensed that the light consisted of a uniform field of energy of indescribable proportions. When I exited the tunnel, I *saw* a huge ball of white light. Although I sensed it in impersonal terms, I could understand why many people who have had an NDE thought of it as a tremendous light being or entity, often deemed to be God.

Approaching the light, I *saw* it as pure energy, or as a void, depending upon my orientation, which I could easily shift. When I entered the light, I felt it could be used for any purpose, that it is passive and value-neutral. I had the realization that perception there is not intellectual although it might be possible to take the intellect along for the ride. I felt the light was the permeating energy of all creation, including the intellect. I then went completely through the light and found that on the other side of it everything was reversed. I found a mirror image of the physical universe I knew in my ordinary life. My mind recoiled at the intensity of this altered state and the experience ended.

I think it is interesting that my experience corresponds with the findings of Raymond Moody, later verified by other scientists. Moody found a constellation of experience that marked a classic NDE, including traveling through a tunnel, seeing a field of light or an entity of light, and OBE. As with mystical experience, not all of the elements of a NDE need to be present in a given experience to accept the legitimacy of the phenomenon.[23]

In the lab a couple of months after my first experiences, we again used the 1.5Hz binaural beat. Soon I kinesthetically felt a tunnel in my abdomen. I then *saw* the field of white light. This time, I felt that it was only one bandwidth in the breadth of existence, albeit the dominant band of the human condition. I understood that it was not God; it was the pinnacle of *human* awareness, the capstone of the chakra rainbow and God encompassed as well as transcended this domain. I also intuited that the physical senses downplay, or even blind one to, other perceptions. I had a knowing that the tunnel was a representation of a force leading to the white light and perhaps beyond.

Reflecting a discrete altered state, this time I dove directly into the light without hesitation. I discovered that we take ourselves far too seriously. I also touched what seemed like the deepest recesses of my being. Bridging a mystical experience, the realization that throughout creation all realities occur simultaneously and in the current moment then quietly exploded within me. This provided a principal reference for an eventual shift in my baseline state of consciousness.

Science

The process of acquiring knowledge and having it widely accepted is the same whether you're dealing with the outer edges of metaphysics or with culturally mainstream investigations. Even in science, it's often a matter of time before what once was hidden becomes widely known. Mario Molina, for instance, is one of the scientists who discovered the deleterious effect of chlorofluorocarbons (CFCs) on the upper atmosphere. He says that his early studies on ozone depletion were regarded by the media as "such an esoteric problem that who cares about it?" Even within the general scientific community, his ideas had no resonance; they were too abstract for others to get a handle on, as the ozone layer had not yet been explored. His work also bridged environmental politics, which crossed the line of true science in the thinking of some.

Molina's motivation to enter research rather than chemical engineering was based on his personal fascination of the problem rather than on the pursuit of money. Because CFCs are stable and don't readily dissipate in the lower atmosphere, his curiosity propelled him to examine what happened in the upper atmosphere as humans wantonly discarded these molecules, a situation he considered to be a case of "bad manners." Rather than close off investigation based on then current perspectives, he sought *more* science: this being a difference between scientism and science.

He discovered that even one CFC molecule destroyed hundreds of thousands of ozone molecules in a catalytic chain. It then took years before governments around the world had incorporated a sufficient amount of information to change their ways and enter into agreement to eliminate CFCs. Based on his forward-thinking work and its inherent value to the group, Molina, born in Mexico City, shared the 1996 Nobel Prize in Chemistry with colleague Paul Crutzen.[24]

Molina's initial evidence can be seen as an altered state as it was a significant departure from the known, at least at that time. Those who verified Molina's research represent discrete altered states as they could duplicate Molina's finding. As the scientific community gradually adopted these findings, the scientific baseline state of consciousness relating to atmospheric science changed. As is often the case with departures from the status quo, it required years before governments changed their political baselines and entered into a treaty.

MULTIDIMENSIONAL REALITY

Scientific evidence, mystical and near-death experiences, along with the many varieties of *psi* reveal that the daily world isn't always what it seems to be. These perceptions are rooted in experience, not solely on theoretical propositions concerning what the world is thought to be. To account for these experiences we must view reality as multidimensional, with more facets being revealed all the time. Their utility is governed by how they are spun into one model or another. From one angle, a report of *psi* is viewed as psychopathology, from another as advanced human potential. The bottom line of these experiences is that humans are capable of being aware of more than what is typically taught.

These perceptions can readily be accounted for as shifts in cohesion. The physical world reflects a particular cohesion, for example, with cultural orientations representing minor variations. These experiences can also pertain to other models such as chakras. A psychic experience may activate the sixth chakra, while a mystical experience brings more to life the seventh chakra. At the same time, the orchestration of all chakra energies forms cohesion. Awareness of other dimensions, then, hinges on the fluency of the energy body and the alignment of internal and external energies.

Integrating these experiences into a baseline state, and into a map of reality, is not different from any other form of learning. The entraining influence sparking the experience could be the desire to induce what is read about in a book, a spontaneous resonance with an emanation, or technologically induced. The accuracy and objectivity of communicating the experience hinge on how well cohesion entrains to the energy field being experienced (the clarity of the event), how well the observer has been educated in the nature of perception, the manner in which the experience is communicated to others, and how well biases are managed by listeners.

My lab experiences at The Monroe Institute revealed to me that we live in a universe where there may well be an infinite number of Earths, each representing minor to major variations in frequency from the others. My epiphany has some grounding in science. According to science writer Marcus Chown, a "many worlds" theory is growing in popularity with physicists "increasingly accepting the idea that there are infinite realities stacked together like the pages of a never-ending book." Any reality, he maintains, "could be very similar to another or vary in extreme difference."[25]

Another theory holds that only one material universe emerges from potential and all other universes remain only as probabilities. Yet another theory maintains that all possibilities are only that, and that it is only by the act of observing, of placing consciousness into motion, that a reality becomes evident.[26] Like any well-developed theory, each model provides at least a degree of utility to apply the science behind it, to make some headway in implementing practical outcomes. However, to gain the widest possible angle of vision of reality, the multiple universe theory appears more expansive, more accepting, and provides more accountability.

From an energetic perspective, a reality is a composite of frequencies, with each frequency producing an aspect of cohesion. An ASC is not only a departure from the baseline cohesion but is also the accessing of other frequencies that are part of another baseline. Because of its coherence, the many worlds theory signifies a d-ASC. If new technologies are formed on that basis, it will mean a new baseline is emerging or has emerged, depending on the pervasiveness of the technologies it spawns. The end result would be that what was once alive only in the realm of the unconscious is now conscious.

The progression of what is considered reality reveals this movement of consciousness. Sailors once recoiled from traversing the oceans for fear of falling off a flat earth; Galileo put forth mathematical proof that Earth revolved around the Sun; a three-dimensional world gave way to a view incorporating time as a fourth or perhaps a fifth dimension. Now, in order to unify all known phenomena, a fifth-dimension of hyperspace is giving way to "string theory" involving at least ten dimensions and as many as twenty-six.[27]

In his popular book, *Hyperspace,* physics professor Michio Kaku places ghosts and other paranormal experiences in the fourth dimension.[28] I would argue that OBEs are also fourth dimensional, as they command greater abilities in relation to our three-dimensional world. Kaku also reveals more about dimensionality by shedding light on why extra-dimensional activity is mind-boggling to those living in the lower dimensions. A three-dimensional creature can't directly see the fourth dimension, due to its inherent limitations. It will perceive the fourth dimension only in terms it can comprehend.

A quick review of your life will demonstrate that you live each day in many dimensions, in that you have many roles such as being professional, father or mother, son or daughter, friend, musician, artist, and so on. Plus, within your anatomy is the multidimensionality of the chakras. Then add the vertical and horizontal partitions of the brain, other physical systems, meridians, nadis, energy body, and so forth. If you also expand the three-dimensional model of reality to include ten or more dimensions, add a possible afterlife, other intelligent beings, other worlds, and so forth, it is not very difficult to imagine that we live in a multidimensional reality. And there may well be an infinite number of them.

6

Stockroom of a Thousand Mirrors

Understanding the energy body rests in recognizing the mechanics of interpretation. In essence, interpretation results from inner reflections of thoughts and feelings and their outward projection. As interpretation guides your steps through life, it is a principal interface between you and the world. It is therefore basic that you understand and manage reflection and projection in order to move your personal awareness toward the core of your energy body.

PROJECTION

Projection is the attribution of your traits and perceptions to another. From a psychoanalytic angle, projection is often accompanied by a denial, even to the point of dysfunction, if not pathology.[1] Associated with this, the amount of emotional reactivity often marks the degree that a person is projecting. From an energy body perspective, projection extends beyond simple attribution. It can be seen as the effect of cohesion spinning and shaping all perceptions as cohesion determines what is perceived, including interpretation. Projection, then, pertains to the mere act of interpreting anything, since doing so results solely from the type of cohesion in place at the moment.

Charles Tart holds that interpretation results from a process—in which the intellect and emotions both play a role—of filtering raw awareness into defined perceptions. He maintains that as we pick and choose perceptions the following interpretations are based on preexisting beliefs and feelings. Projected states, then, are a measure of reality. As German philosopher Martin Heidegger points out, projection determines what is possible in the first place.[2]

In this light, there are three basic types of projection: personal, group or collective, and species. Personal projection naturally results from individual cohesion. For example, a person might say, "He is angry with me," when the opposite it true; it is that person who is angry. A shared sense and interpretation of reality, or even a piece of reality, is group consensus. For example, a particular group might hold that Jesus is the sole Son of God, while another group regards him as being one in a long line of prophets. This single interpretation has wide-ranging implications including being a dividing point among major religions. Species-related projection pertains to the effect of uniformity on determining what can be perceived since the container plays an active role in forming inner cohesion. Perceiving the physical movements of heavenly bodies is one example of species-related projection. Based on physical observation, humans see a sun and moon. Ascribing meaning to this is an example of group projection—interpreting the movement from an astronomical or astrological framework, for instance. Taking species projection to another level, experiencing the characteristics of arms, legs, head, and so forth, is projection as physical form governs capacities of perception and uniformity governs physical form. Change uniformity sufficiently and you have a new physical form that gives rise to new perceptions and new interpretations of those perceptions. All three types of projection influence the others. Depending on time, place, and circumstance, each delivers an entrainment effect. Each contains the conscious and unconscious elements that shape perception. Each is therefore a reflection of cohesion.

Much of the work of the classic mystical traditions is geared toward interfering with this projective process, to removing the stranglehold that beliefs and feelings have on interpretation, in order for new perceptions to be brought forth, making it possible to eventually arrive at new formulations of reality. The skill of suspending beliefs is known in modern psychology as *deautomatization,* meaning that you interfere with the automatic responses and their associated interpretations, be they individual, social, or of the species.[3]

The dynamics of projection-interpretation are forceful; from them, entire worlds are built. The dark side is that you lose the mystery of the world as you criticize others and even deny that those same features are alive and well within you. These influences are also at the heart of creativity. But to tap their potential, you need to learn how to manage the inflexibility produced by conditional energy fields; otherwise your perceptions are predetermined by the prevailing view of reality. At best, learning occurs slowly.

Since being more deeply enmeshed in projection presents a higher capacity for denial, we could say that humans as a species are still trying to figure out our orientation. More so, as we destroy not only ourselves but our very home, the amount of denial could be considered pathological. There seems to be no prevailing awareness that a reality based on exploitation of material resources isn't working out. There is no compelling, wide-ranging consciousness that we need a new orientation to the world to survive, the most basic of needs. The value of the guidance provided by the stages is therefore readily apparent. We need to know how, why, and where we can learn and grow. In bioenergetic fashion, the more aware an individual or group becomes the more they develop awareness of the environment and the human relationship to it.

THE CONTINUITY OF REALITY

The source as well as the result of projection is self-reflection. It is the glue that binds cohesion. The intellect interprets, defines, and arranges the world into a neat mental pattern, preserved by the stream of thought. The emotional aspect forms, reacts, and arranges the world in its own way. This type of self-reflection forms from considerations of feeling better than or worse than someone or something. Both mental and emotional states reflect conditions within cohesion.

The relationship between uniformity and cohesion also influences self-reflection. It is as though the inside of the energy body were lined with a thousand small mirrors, each representing one inventory item on the shelves in your stockroom of reality. The mirrors reflect raw data into what we perceive physically, emotionally, and mentally. In short, how we interpret the world results from our anatomy, and then our thoughts and feelings bounce back off the mirrors and influence consciousness. From a wider angle, reality is a collective reflection of this stockroom of mirrors. Using a computer metaphor, our perception of reality emanates from how our hardware (physical and energetic anatomy) and software (thoughts and feelings) work together.

In psycho-sociological terms, thinking influences awareness and reinforces social reality. From a shamanic reference, this means that thoughts fixate the assemblage point.[4] If your assemblage point is at the position of "behavioral psychology," when you see people acting like they own the world, you might say to yourself that those people have been conditioned by their upbringing and by society to behave like that. If your assemblage point is at "Toltec paradigm," you might say that those people have too rigid a conditional energy field. If your assemblage point is at "mechanistic world," then the world is comprised of material objects. If it is at "quantum physics," the world is viewed as being comprised of energy.

Every time you label something—an event, a person's behavior, a theory, anything—you are interpreting the world though reflection and projection. You are supplying energy to hold your cohesion in exactly the same pattern that gave rise to the interpretations in the first place. Collapsing infinity into a usable arrangement for *mental continuity* is the hallmark of reason. Although what is considered to be reasonable reflects but a piece of the vastness that surrounds you, it provides a measure of stability; at least you have a stockroom for reference. The magic of maintaining cohesion is that entire realities are built from sharing a similar assemblage point position with others.

Our internal dialogue aims and maintains perception and provides continuity. Hence, stopping your thoughts allows you to manage projection. A lull in your stream of thoughts permits a natural shift in cohesion as it entrains to new emanations, making it possible to have different perceptions and interpretations. Shift it a great deal and you will end up in a different reality. The same effect takes place for an individual, the collective, or the species. By understanding the neatly woven wall of mirrors, you begin to better understand cohesion, which helps you understand the force behind it all. Then you can begin deliberately transcending that force. Please refer to chapter ten for an exercise to stop your internal dialogue.

One remedy for projection put forth by Zen teacher Shunryu Suzuki is to not believe in anything. This doesn't mean to believe in emptiness, but to suspend belief in arbitrary rules embodied in transient formations of reality. Ninety-nine percent of thinking, he says, is self-centered. To step beyond this, he suggests believing in that which has no form or color, but that which is waiting to take form.[5] He is advocating a stronger relationship with potential, with a creative force, instead of being limited solely to human contrivance.

However, mental agility and stability by themselves don't solve the problem because our feelings also act as a binding glue of reality. Reality has an *emotional continuity;* it is held together by emotional links, emotional commitments. Valerie Hunt refers to emotions as the "mind field organizer." Stemming from integrating a multitude of experiences over time, a person ends up with a well-defined energetic signature.[6] This cohesion spins perception along the lines of the influences that determined the signature, and so how you think of the world is bound by how you feel about the world. This is why all heck breaks lose when you challenge the underpinnings of another's reality.

In addition, consider *physical continuity,* or projection arising from the very physical world we inhabit. Our familiarity with trees, rocks, clouds, and all other physical-world elements exerts pressure to keep the assemblage point stable. Shifting cohesion to altered states of nonphysical dimensions—OBE, NDE, or mystical experience, for example—shatters this continuity.

The degree to which any worldview evolves hinges on projection.

A more expansive model requires more elements of projection, which are then applied on a more expansive social scale. But you may end up just creating a more complex world without really getting anywhere. Growth through the ontological stages is geared toward realizing your core; personal projection evaporates because you are paying more attention to potential, to ever-increasing abstract relationships. Individual growth thereby influences group reality.

LEARNING AND IMAGINATION

The stages of awakening—orientation, training, craftsmanship, artistry, and mastery—represent increasingly larger stockrooms, each containing more perspectives about life as well as greater capacities to *be*. Your inventory grows incrementally as you build a level, and then quickly expands as you stabilize the next. Each stage builds from projection, producing a conditional energy field consisting of those conditions (the inventory) that create the room. Each stage also acts as an echo chamber, providing both accurate and false readings about the nature of the room. The more self-reflection becomes self-centered, the more dysfunction you exhibit and experience. The echoes are phantoms rather than harmonics of reality; they don't have a solid point of origin. With shelves loaded with inventory, mirrors reflecting this and that, and echoes bouncing off the walls, it is easy to get lost. But that is what maps—such as the outline of these stages and of human anatomy—are meant to help us avoid.

When you first enter a new stockroom, you may feel at a loss. The vastness of the new territory is too large to grasp and too big to feel. The first glimpses of the new room are altered states and may have no meaning to you whatsoever, other than signaling that you have experienced an altered state. As you become more comfortable inside the room, your expanded consciousness changes your relation to the mirrors and more meaning is developed. You have therefore elevated your awareness to having a discrete altered state. You learn in bits, then chunks. When you know your way about the room, you have developed a new baseline state of consciousness. You are literally living in a new world, a process reflecting the accurate, harmonic echoes of projection. It is then time to knock on the door of the next stockroom.

You don't need to throw rocks at the mirrors and shatter them to become free or to learn. You can just stop what you are doing, release the effects of the mirrors, and let new information and experience enter. This is the essence of deautomatization, seen in the capacity of rivers to clean themselves after they cease being polluted. You need to let go and allow your intrinsic, core awareness to come forth. You then can arrange the new perceptions to reflect and project the new conditions, all the while knowing that at some point you will also need to let these go in order to reach yet another level of awakening. This dance of death and renewal, or release and regeneration, is at the heart of learning and imagination. It is the essence of the type of conditional field necessary to power you through the stages to a natural field.

Each level contains an energetic logic, with its own steps and measures, just as with intellectual logic. You can't truly understand until you either have the experience or a sufficient amount of like-minded experience to make the connections. And just like intellectual intelligence, energetic logic is subject to use and misuse. You may distort what is said based on your conditional field and likewise distort your relation to the world due to the same thing: an improperly aligned cohesion. Put another way, each stage contains its own nuances, traps, and blessings. Consistency comes when you are focused on your core, as that energy resides beyond conditional fields.

Core and Projection

Core can be defined as the absence of personal projection as well as the quintessential, natural human condition. Traversing all the stages of awakening is possible as a result of aligning with your core energy. The activation of *will* is a by-product of this orientation, which brings the energy body fully to life. Correctly maneuvered, each stage brings you to a better sense of trusting your resources, decisions, and place in this world.

Self-reflection produces many conditions of imagination, some purposeful and some not so good. If you are lost in despair or dwelling in psychological disorder, then your imagination will reflect this type of energy, adding to your despair. On the other hand, if your mirrors are well integrated and polished for growth, then your imagination forms productive experiences. In each instance, projection influences the quality and content of perception. The degree of pathology associated with projection indicates the degree of denial that projection is taking place.

Arrogance and fundamentalism come from perceiving oneself as being right in absolute terms. A person with expertise in one field may also project that knowledge and speak with absolute authority on subjects outside his or her expertise. Being well versed in the logic of one subject can blind one to the logic of another discipline. Core energy, by contrast, is more amenable to different views of the world; it connects with infinity and infinity holds all possibilities.

Maintaining core alignment is what enables you to sift through all the potential that doesn't apply to personal and social development, as well as to maintain a balance between relative and absolute. If you entertain the relativity of the universe too much, you won't be able to sustain your own nature. If you focus on the absolute nature of the cosmos, fundamentalism takes over.

Only when you reach the artisan stage have you navigated your way out of this type of pathology. Until then, you're in the throes of personal and group-associated projection and denial. A quest to reach core is a way to stay balanced and focused. From this posture comes the behavior that allows you to express and fulfill your innermost condition. Attaining this natural field reflects psychological health.

In the path of learning, closure and core need to be reconciled. Closure results from and produces projection. As a natural part of learning, it supports our capacity to focus. However, closure also closes off perception and limits imagination. Core awareness, on the other hand, opens the gates of imagination and accelerates learning. As a fully awakened energy body and core awareness are synonymous, a completely conscious connection with the world results. Anything off center and away from core is projection, and projection results from having a conditional field of one kind or another. At the same time, core is closed in the sense that it is the way you, and you alone, were created.

The more you align with your core, the more objectivity you have of yourself and the environment. This correlates with a movement of the assemblage point; the deeper you take your assemblage point into your energy body, the more you become aware of your environment. This is the same thing as simultaneously being at core and extended throughout your energy body. The effect is that you are aware that you are intimately connected with the environment and therefore are naturally more aware of the environment. Objectivity unfolds from this enhanced awareness. This is *being*-centered, not self-centered. The difference between the two makes all the difference in how you navigate life.

Another way of looking at this is to say that if you completely individuate, if you reach core, if you have developed a natural energy field, then you eliminate the effects of projection. Individuation first occurs at the artisan stage and is refined at the mastery level. At these levels, behavior emanates from core; it is not tied to a group consensus of reality or to what is known by structured teachings, metaphysical or otherwise. The person is knowledge and awareness, not the representation of them. The person is *being*.

When you reach the artisan stage, you possess an inner calm and quiet, almost a sense that nothing at all is going on while your world unfolds about you. Projection has ended and your connection with external emanations places you at infinity's doorstep. At the mastery stage, you have taken this awareness to a highly skillful level of managing your innermost abilities, to the extent that you can step into those emanations, some of which may be literally out of this world.

Timing

Time lies at the heart of our earthly experience. Even in simple terms, it is the measure of life as provided by our Sun rising and setting. In turn, *timing* grants awareness of time; it provides the opportunity and ability to saturate consciousness in this requisite dimension. It should not be surprising, then, that a principle feature of the stages is timing, the speed of your relationship with self, others, and the world. Timing is rhythm, harmony. It is characterized by your movements through time, space, and other dimensions. Good timing is difficult to pull off. Just think of having to orchestrate the pushes and pulls of several chakra energies to arrange them so that you may act in a consistent manner. And in our modern culture, how often do you find yourself moving too fast in response to the demands of daily life?

Timing reflects your relationship with core; it can indicate a natural *flow,* as in the case of a strong and direct resonance, or it can indicate discord. It is also an indicator of the type of energetic field you have, the location of the assemblage point, and which stage of development you're in. Within the energy body, timing reflects the degree of harmony between the first and second fields. It involves the opening and closing of awareness and the ebb and flow between learning and imagination. Projection, as it is not of core, reflects both poor timing as well as something that throws your timing off. On the flip side, reflecting on timing gives you something concrete to work toward.

Awareness of personal timing normally doesn't find its way into standard educational curricula, let alone instruction on the means to engage it. To understand the importance of timing is itself remarkable. To be able to exhibit good timing at an ontological level is exceptional as it means you're experiencing artistry, not just talking about it. Distinction between talk and doing makes all the difference in the world. For instance, one person might approach health from having extensive textbook training and a medical degree, while another person comes at it from the experience of it, the ontology or *beingness* of health. A physician may be quite adept in diagnosis and treatment of disease but have poor health-promoting habits, while another person is a shining statement of health but has no depth of medical science knowledge. Robust health signals at least some knowledge of timing as it demonstrates the harmony—the timing—of all systems within an individual.

Good timing requires the use of four-dimensional space, perceiving the whole of the environment, not just pieces of it. With self awareness, you can better adjust to the demands of the clock; you can navigate your job, relationships, hobbies, and other facets of your life that are governed by having to be somewhere at some time. Good timing by itself may not elevate your status in the world. It does, however, bring you more to life. A gesture given, a word spoken, or a laugh can all make or break any kind of interaction with others.

Timing is not something needing to be fixed or static. You don't have to act the same way all the time. Timing is a measure of the alignment of internal and external emanations, and alignments produce perception. In the same manner, timing both reflects and governs heightened consciousness. Thoughts determine habits and both influence cohesion. The assemblage point holds in a certain position when a sufficient number of logically interrelated pieces come together. The ability to move the assemblage point to a new location requires forming a new set of habits.[7] Timing is part of the puzzle of when to learn new habits, and how to enact them.

Habituation means you repeatedly experience something to the degree you become less sensitive to it.[8] The maintenance of habit keeps you from feeling the original sensations. Your actions become automatic, rote. Timing falls by the wayside. You then become dull and lifeless, not even noticing what once held keen interest. Deautomatization helps prevent this calcification of perception; it helps you step outside of preconceived notions, rules, and behaviors. Using feeling, as a means to guide your steps, is an example of deautomatization, as is taking a different route to work everyday . . . as long as you don't make doing so into another routine.

Deautomatization also offsets the effects of closure by refreshing, clearing, and opening perception. Each person—if not each and every organism—is in some way unique; each has a core signature, reflecting innate timing. This provides a distinctive relation to yourself and to myriad forms of the environment. Your core timing, then, yields an avenue of growth that can be used as a thread to navigate through levels of development.

You can use the stages of awakening to understand the relationship of timing to core.[9] In the orientation stage, life is somewhat random. Often a person has no purpose, no sense with which to measure anything. During training, you gain a direction in life. The capacity to tap into an initially elusive concept of core starts as you begin to place your life in order.

By the time you develop craftsmanship, you have a fairly well-tempered energy body. You can let go of preconceptions and entertain new possibilities; purposeful direction is well in hand. As you have removed tired and worn-out behavior, life takes on a more novel flavor. Your life has been tuned in a way that you connect with life hour by hour. At the artistry stage, a natural field has taken over all aspects of your life. The journey has delivered you to the moment at hand, and traveling in the moment is the only way to sustain this level. Timing provides the means for maintaining your gains.

BARRIERS WITHIN THE STAGES OF AWAKENING

Corresponding with advances in learning and imagination, barriers to unfolding perception are also found in each stage. Deemed "natural enemies," by don Juan, they are immobility, insightfulness, control, and aging.[10] These barriers may be found in anyone's behavior at any time; they are not necessarily isolated to specific stages. For example, a person still needs to deal with the constrictive effects of an inflexible cohesion after attaining craftsmanship. The artisan, then, must remain vigilant to the ins and outs of insight as being projection in order to maintain a natural field. And the debilitating physical and mental effects associated with aging can strike at any age or any stage. However, these barriers do characterize the ingredients of ontological development; assigning them to specific categories aids our understanding of their operation.

Orientation

If you are in orientation, you are trying to do just that: get oriented. This means that you have no foundational direction in life, certainly none in relation to your core. Your conditional field is therefore static and characterized by a lack of movement and suppleness, an excessive degree of closure, and the inability to form new avenues of perception.

The high-reflectively nature of perception often blocks awareness that it forms from projection. This augments the effects of closure. This general condition expresses itself as the feeling of fear; that is, when faced with a new prospect the inability of cohesion to shift translates through the physical body as fear.

One remedy for an immobile conditional field is to gain a wide range of experience. Each type of experience represents its own cohesion, so the more you are able to form a range of cohesions, the more fluid your energy body becomes. A guideline for this is to do exactly what you fear doing: in this way you face the rigidity head on. This doesn't mean being stupid, as in breaking laws. It does mean directly facing your life with courage. Over time, you will have a sufficient amount of experience to be well oriented in life.

Training

At this point, you have a sense of the major ingredients of your life. You have a path. Now begins the training. This could take shape in the form of a college education, an apprenticeship, or other formal training. From an ontological perspective, it means you know what type of transpersonal psychology or metaphysical philosophy is most natural to you. No matter your path, you are developing a new set of habits, and new meaning.

You achieved this level by expanding your cohesion, yet it is like an in-between world. In practice, your hard-won knowledge grants better insight, more clarity about yourself and the world, and you can now suspend projection to some degree. You are clear about the world; you finally have it sorted out. You more easily sense the potential of events and your imagination bustles with excitement. It turns out that that is the problem. Your clarity and decisions stemming from it may not reflect a firm relationship with your life. It is too soon to apply your insight, as there is much more to be experienced and learned before you are ready, and so you act too quickly or don't act when you should. You need more depth to your cohesion; otherwise you are reflecting and projecting from a training cohesion, not a professional one. It's like living in an altered state where your steps may not match the needs of your life. By the time you're ready to work with the next stage, you've learned not to let imagination get the better of you.

Insightfulness reflects the first significant step to heightened consciousness. But the fascination of experiencing heightened perception may throw you off the mark. Maintaining keen awareness requires an even better control and orientation to core to prevent you from thinking you know the definitive answer even when you are only flirting with a new cohesion. A way to groom balance is to remain a bit cautious, actively wondering about the depth of your insights, while still battling rigidity. After all, this stage is just another conditional field.

Attaining this stage also means you begin directly working with timing. To manage your insightfulness, you need to learn when to act and when not. Without timidity, carefully feel things out. Align your decisions with your core values. Allow yourself to learn. The rhythm for all this is found in discovering when to proceed or remain still, to be open or closed. Within the infinity of potential, you are now learning a high-wire balancing act of how, what, when, and where to engage your next steps. It is the beginning of managing your energy body.

To become individuated, everyone needs to find his or her own way. The skill is taking these concepts and applying them, then discovering what transpires, and then applying what you've learned. A path like this truly requires an independent drive to learn.

Craftsmanship

Craftsmanship indicates a high degree of learning and a sophisticated degree of managing the energy body. You can control that which is around you. By regulating cohesion, you determine the emanations you want to align with and thus determine circumstances. Now your energy acts as an external force to others.[11] Your now-stabilized heightened consciousness and insightfulness enable you to better perceive and assess what lies before you, enhancing your ability to shape your world or, more to the point, bend it out of shape.

According to don Juan, the ability to overly influence events to your desire makes this the most difficult of all stages.[12] It offers strong temptations that can lead you away from core. This is self-importance, not self-actualization. While you may have acquired knowledge well beyond the usual spheres of human activity, the cost is that of estranging you from the very quest that has thus far motivated you. For instance, as a person builds a career in business or politics, cohesion develops as the person learns and experiences more. A promotion or winning an election places the person in a position of power whereby it is part of the job to influence events. Ontological power is the same, yet more expansive as the person can manipulate the energy that determines the outward result. Each profession has its code of conduct, and abuse of any form of power estranges the person from core.

This ability of control opens the gate to the refined use of imagination, but remember that control also relates to closure. Resulting from having consolidated a large cohesion without orienting it to core, closure can easily turn into the abuse of power. This applies to all circumstances, large and small, where you hold sway over others. That kind of power is manipulation, not freedom. It suggests marginalizing life, not participating with infinity. The guideline to transcend it is simple: never use it. True power is derived from taking part in creation, not trying to determine it. A key to success is to focus on developing cohesion in order to enter the next stage rather than to stop and admire your abilities. While craftsmanship is the professional practice of what was learned during training, it is also training for the next stage. Awakening to infinity is a never-ending quest.

Until you've reached artistry, every perception—*everything*—is an effect of projection. As you progress, you clean the mirrors on your stockroom walls. The trick is to keep polishing until they become translucent, until your light passes through them to connect with the emanations. You then *become* light, not a reflection of it. Although you already *are* light, getting to the point of it being a conscious experience is full of deception. You automatically, and with an ironclad guarantee, limit your connections with potential by your thoughts and feelings of how you fit into the world. This remains firmly in place until you become the artisan and have removed yourself from the confines of conditional fields. At such time, you claim what has always been yours, but by now have removed the distortions of light's shadows.

Artistry and Mastery

Artistry forms a direct relationship with knowledge and awareness, not with collective consciousness; the artisan is a force of nature rather than of the group. At this stage you have gained the freedom and ability to imagine your own inventories, to stock your own room. You have come to understand the wall of mirrors as reflection and have transcended their influence.

A natural field results from your alignment with your core: how you have been created, not how your personality has developed amidst social pressures. Individuation, according to Jung, is arriving at your "innermost and incomparable uniqueness." This necessitates granting precedence to self-realization rather than to the considerations and obligations of the collective. At the same time, Jung was quick to point out that doing so is not selfish but the fulfillment of one's nature. This requires "a living co-operation with all factors."[13]

The mastery level becomes center stage when you've mastered your energy body to the degree that you step completely outside the stockroom. Everything that once was is now obsolete. Your experiences are yours alone. You may also step into the third energy field and attain a new sense of and enhanced objectivity about the human condition.[14] Whatever your circumstances in life, you can orient yourself to mastery anytime, anywhere. The stepping-stones then reveal themselves while realization waits.

Understanding at least the concept of the energy body begins during the orientation stage. From there, you traverse the stages step by step, with the full use of your resources being the hallmark of the mastery level. Your insightfulness is refined and your drive for power is in check. You are able to maintain *being* and have a keen sense of *flow* in all areas of your life. Your energy body is sufficiently fluent that you can gently enter and leave any circumstance by shifting cohesion to match those events.

To do this takes many years, so many that most of those who reach mastery are old and their resources are waning. Even though they have mastered their energy body, the barrier of age is insurmountable; they will die due to old age, if by nothing else.

Don Juan holds that if one who has traveled a path of awareness gives in to the desire to rest, this new orientation causes an energetic warp, which leads to feebleness. However, he adds that if the person can shrug off this tension, the door is opened to having the most refined cosmological experiences imaginable, thereby making the pursuit worth the heavy toll.[15] It is conceivable that such events supersede the current definition of mystical experience and may require a new category based on emerging psychological models.

It is the awareness gained by those who have developed their energy bodies to the artistry and mastery levels that has given rise to modern Toltec philosophy. This system has been forged over millennia from highly sophisticated individual and group reflection and projection, and aimed toward the goal of liberating perception beyond those very embankments.

7

Closing in on Fundamentalism

Fundamentalism is a type of behavior with common characteristics regardless of the context or setting. It results from a type of cohesion: specifically, a conditional energy field characterized by inflexibility.

When a number of facts are logically woven together, a picture of the world emerges, which might be a concept, theory, or entire worldview. In order for the picture to be useful, it needs to have a boundary, whether the size of its frame is small or vast. Therefore, closure—the aspect of perception that closes off a viewpoint—performs a vital role. However, when the picture is not only closed off but also placed inside an unventilated box, difficulties with learning and imagination arise. If we dismiss awareness of another model, perhaps one even more expansive, by confining it to the conditions of a smaller picture, then we suppress the new point of view. We then force all information to abide by the logic of the status quo.

An interesting example can be found regarding the Eastern concept of qi, for which mainstream Western culture does not yet have an equivalent term.[1] Not having this concept in our inventory prevents our forming an appropriate image and allows us to easily dismiss the existence of an energetic life force. To avoid this difficulty, we need a picture that includes *flow*, movement, openness, and discernment along with closing off. Otherwise we only reflect upon what is already known and do not grow.

On a more expansive scale, each stage of awakening reflects a new baseline, a larger picture of the world. At the beginning of a stage, the next stage is foreign. Time and training elevate the baseline through altered and discrete altered states until you experience major shifts of cohesion, such as realizing the world is not flat after all, or that the world is first and foremost comprised of energy.

CONDITIONAL ENERGY FIELDS

When you are locked in a specific cohesion, you can't see anything beyond the conditions that formed it. You reside in a world of mirrors as the self-validating effects of models aptly demonstrate. A model restricts what is under examination and the parameters of perception. It also defines the interpretations and results. This applies to whether you're focusing on an experiment, a religious theme, or an entire worldview. The stockroom of mirrors that both created the model and was created by it can tie perception into a little ball or point the way to unveiling more of the universe. If the mirrors don't let in light from other cohesions, other models, other worlds—all of which begin to form from altered states—then you are at the basis of fundamentalism. In short, a person with a fundamentalist cohesion—formed by religion, politics, business, healthcare, or anything else—is lost in a model that governs behavior rather than serves as a tool to enhance behavior.

As a result, your conditional field causes you to bend that which is being experienced into preexisting form. The field then prevents you from listening, recognizing, and adapting to new data and relationships. And it engenders castigation of those who may challenge the model as any challenge to the prevailing dogma is seen as heresy. The life of Galileo serves as an example; he spent the latter part of his life under house arrest for calling attention to facts that lay outside the accepted version of reality. For a variety of reasons, then, it is critical to learn how to use models, not be used by them. Reality is best used as a tool to help navigate life, not as something to lock you within a concrete prison.

Like the ancient mariners of Homer's day who either succumbed to or sailed free from the seductive and treacherous sirens, everyone who makes the voyage of infinity will find themselves having to navigate the world of mirrors, an enlargement of your personal stockroom. There simply is no other choice. The stages of ontological development offer channel markers to guide awareness, to groom and focus consciousness rather than to close it off arbitrarily.

CLOSURE

Closure, an effect of conditional fields, is a significant force. The biologic closed electrical circuits of the body reflect this innate aspect of humans. *The Law of Closure* reveals a psychological counterpart; it pertains to defining, refining, eliminating, and consolidating perception.[2] The study of reading, for example, has shown that if a group of people is presented with a paragraph that has one word blanked out, most people read the paragraph and automatically insert a word, then swear there was no blank spot. In the same manner, a person will interpret what is heard in keeping with his or her own thoughts, even though what is being said might mean something entirely different.

This magnifies to a point where we regard the human world as the essence of the universe rather than a part of it. People *anthropomorphize* reality by giving human traits to elements of nature, God, or anything else. The social world then becomes the principal navigational tool rather than orienting to the call of the great beyond. This effect of arranging perception limits the number of external emanations that can be tapped, which prevents everyone from becoming more aware. And so we collapse the sea of infinity in which we sail into something convenient, even trivial.

This also serves to reveal what happens when the unconscious begins to surface. The property of closure causes our conscious awareness to either disregard new perceptions or place them in a known category. The effect is the same: the conscious domain remains static. The good thing about this is that our energy bodies don't explode due to an overload of awareness rushing in. The downside is not recognizing more of our natural heritage. The barriers of perception are all forms of closure, with each barrier expressing closure in a different way. At the same time, growth to another level requires closing off obsolete prior behaviors.

The contrast between science and scientism serves to illumine the benefits and drawbacks of the open-close dynamic of awareness. Science is based on a rigorous method of inquiry with a continual push into the unknown. Scientism reflects consensual activities where thoughts about scientific knowledge are given more weight than the method that brought about the knowledge in the first place. Awareness and understanding from scientific endeavors change all the time, with new knowledge routinely replacing what has come before. Scientism surfaces when scientists no longer extend scientific considerations to all areas of inquiry and either remain locked in a previous model or try to force data into an inappropriate model; the door to true investigation then closes.

For example, a novel therapeutic agent that has been shown to effectively and safely treat disease may not pass laboratory analysis because the model being used to test efficacy relies on looking only at biological pathways used by the current class of drugs. But the new therapeutic agent might work differently than what has come before. If the requirements that the new drug must face before approval inherently discount their effects, the drug may never see the light of day. The evolution of models goes hand-in-hand with discovery.

In respect to bioenergetics, mystical experience, or a more extensive human anatomy, it is not that science is incapable of tackling the issues; it is that a sufficient number of scientists have not yet completely recognized new areas to explore. These areas are therefore often relegated to philosophy, the fringes of scientific endeavor, or the ranting of pop culture. The same applies to all behavior. Educators, for instance, can ask people to learn and accept the same, unchallenged norms or they can provide the essentials to enable people to actively learn, no matter how threatening this may seem to the teacher. What those requirements might be result from style and method. They are part of the artistic element of one's craft and are expressed as a given situation warrants.

In and of itself, the scientific method stands as an amazingly powerful tool. In essence, it represents objectivity. Optimally, scientific models provide a means for valuable determinations to account for new data and new revelations about the world. In practice, results are biased by what is currently held to be scientific. As interpretations directly hinge on cohesion, two people could read or observe the same data yet arrive at completely different meanings. Gathering information through the cornerstones of perception other than reason is not even considered. The method has to be applied before it yields results, and the type of results hinge on the level of skill—with the cooperation of learning and imagination defining the level.

For good and ill, closure is accentuated by group consensus, which lends mass and momentum. Simple rules of physics demonstrate that the inertia of a larger body makes it more difficult to change path. This forms the basis of a bioenergetic interpretation of why cultures often die; they are unable to change quickly enough to avoid natural disaster, war, atmospheric and weather conditions, or whatever else places them in jeopardy. Conversely, in his book *Integral Health,* physician Elliot Dacher points the way to a culture steeped in wisdom, one that takes advantage of what has been learned yet remains open to whatever waits. The result, he says, is human flourishing.[3]

While closure is required to consolidate gains of learning and for the application of knowledge, the trick is to remain open in the midst of tying off what is known. Imagination provides this relief. Overall, learning consists of a complex binary process of opening and closing awareness that leads to the integration of perceptions. You need to not only find value in your conscious, known world but also step into your unconscious, unknown world. The best models therefore incorporate not only the pieces of the picture in question but also openness to new information as well as require matching behavior. You then suspend the negative effects of closure and set the stage to make the unconscious more conscious.

FUNDAMENTALISM

When applied to groups, excessive closure equates with fundamentalism. Fundamentalism can be quiet or loud. It can easily take the form of professionals who refuse to hear new perspectives just because they think their position bestows the correct answer. A wrong medical diagnosis is then made or a bridge collapses. Or it can be a rabble-rouser inciting others to conform to some type of thought or behavior, leading scores of people who are caught in a current of emotion to follow a make-believe flag. No matter the context, the result of this form of closure is that misinformation is held as truth by group consciousness. This is where the individual must be able to stand alone. Navigating these travails forms an inherent part of the journey to self-actualization.

Whether a fundamentalist cohesion is based on intricacy of reason or emotion, the associated routines and rituals cement its unquestioned acceptance. We can think of this as a house of cohesion, with walls, windows, flooring, carpet, and so on. Various industries manufactured and distributed each element, particular cultural values spawned its architecture, and the building of it requires a number of skills. When all of this comes together in one construction, the complexity and power of the cohesion is immense. A person can get fascinated by logic and its interlocking structures to the degree that he loses sight of something beyond it. A person may come to accept the rote beliefs of a philosophy without taking time to measure its effects other than it offers participation within a group. Social acceptance is, after all, is one of our key motivators.[4]

At the heart of fundamentalism is common understanding, the very thing that leads to significant gains. Perhaps institutionalized thinking that calcifies thought and behavior marks a dividing line from more fluent behavior. It becomes the driving force that determines values rather than a template for encouraging learning. A point of view may make sense and thus no one wants to relinquish it; people become unwilling to entertain new states of consciousness, especially if doing so might make their current view obsolete. When this is backed by group consensus, the power magnifies. While collective knowledge can significantly add quality for the individual, the downside is that individuals surrender their autonomy to the group, forgetting that individual independence enables the group to flourish. Moreover, the bigger the impending changes to an established norm, the greater is the resistance to making the changes: the energy of inertia at work.

Political scientists refer to a *mobilization of bias* when organizations actively promote fundamentalist ideas by requiring a "non-decision" for people to remain in compliance with dogma.[5] In this type of setting people cannot stray from the fold through genuine inquiry or by entertaining answers that lie outside the organization's doctrine. This type of entrainment also applies to individuals who try to unduly influence others by using a prevailing bias, like race or gender, in order to restrict the flow of contradictory information. Unchecked, fundamentalism leads to tyranny and signifies estrangement from your core.

When individuals cement their allegiance to the group by moral self-righteousness, then others need to beware the tide of emotion that follows. The values comprising a fundamentalist stance help produce such responses. As neuroscientist and Nobel Laureate Gerald Edelman points out, "emotions are complex states arising from core interactions with value systems."[6] This complexity forms a potent cohesion, which then dominates the person rather than the person managing cohesion.

Any cohesive lifestyle has great power, enough to lead its adherents away from convention. Whether it is a cult, a corporation, an intentional community centered on shared values, or a metaphysical path, the adherents of any social group develop some version of a shared conditional energy field. In the same manner, participants within mainstream society develop a conditional field. In general, then, a gathering of like-minded people generates a force—sometimes for better, sometimes for worse.

The better aspect is that a group can usually explore aspects of the unknown and accumulate knowledge faster than one person alone. The worse aspect is that the shared understanding that results from these explorations may be misconstrued as being true reality. Whether this distortion comes from scientists, religious leaders, or philosophers, it indicates fundamentalism. Whenever there is an attempt to define, confine, or otherwise limit awareness—whenever a step is taken away from potential—that denotes fundamentalism.

Shamanism, like science or any other endeavor, finds itself subject to this same consideration. The vast accountability of the energy body model can provide a fast track to consciousness exploration or produce a swamp of knowledge from which you'll never escape. The philosophy itself contains remedy, though, and is found in using the craft as a boost to enter yet another realm.

A NATURAL ENERGY FIELD

It is important for individuals to give their best to others and to life. This can't be done in a fundamentalist context. When you cut yourself off from infinity, you diminish your relationship to life. Your best comes from new relationships based on opening to potential, collapsing that new awareness into a practical framework, and then making the collective more conscious. At the level of *being*—an effect of a natural field— your awareness paradoxically remains open, yet is sufficiently closed to enable you to lead an orderly life. Even grocery shopping requires order and therefore a degree of closure. But when the stream of consciousness closes too tightly, growth constricts.

From the perspective of energetic anatomy, all of this is quite natural. Humans have biologic closed electrical circuits. These are needed for the body to function. Humans also have open bioenergetic circuits that not only nourish the physical body but also connect us with other spheres of energy. From a quantum view, all energy connects at some level and therefore even closed circuitry is open and in some way influences and is influenced by other energies. The electrical circuitry in your home, for example, emits an electromagnetic field that in some way affects your environment and can be affected by the environment as during an electrical storm.

Fundamentalism may take hold at any stage of growth. Whether you are an apprentice or craftsperson, your energy field is conditional. It isn't until you break into the artisan stage that the influence of this type of energy is reduced. And even if you have groomed a natural energy field, you still need to beware of losing yourself in your personal thoughts about the world. A natural field permits extended participation with infinity; it doesn't guarantee it.

An example of achieving the correct balance of openness and structure can be seen in Maslow's attitude toward the term *ontopsychology,* which was coined to signify a new area of investigation relating to *being.* He expressed his hope that the new field was a true expansion of psychology, not an "ism" that would eventually turn into anti-science.[7] By that time in his life, he had grown beyond the field of humanistic psychology he fathered. He had become more interested in the spiritual dimension of human existence, spiritual in the sense of participation with creation and not necessarily having religious connotations.

The shift to a natural field represents an activation of *will* whereby the orientation to and sensing of life is more full-bodied. En route to this, new experience builds pressure within the energy body. This represents the potential for new conditions, new cohesions, and the possibility of integrating the new experiences. As these tumblers fall into place, as you integrate new awareness, revelations about the new cohe-

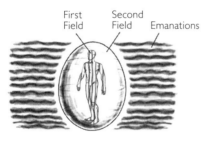

First Field   Second Field   Emanations

Fundamentalist Energy Field   Natural Energy Field

Figure 7.1.
A fundamentalist cohesion blocks awareness of the environment and inhibits learning. A natural field represents the balance and *flow* associated with *being.*

sion come to a conscious level. You need to continue measuring these insights in terms of core value. Assessment should not bring in superficial or grandiose concerns, both reflecting self-importance. In this manner, you continue awakening your energy body directly toward achieving the complete baseline of a natural field.

NEW AGE PHILOSOPHY

Fundamentalism can strike any person or any group, lay or professional. Earlier I singled out the practice of science because it is ingrained and influential in modern life, yet its internal politics are not that widely known. The same concerns of dogmatism also apply to shamanism. In a discussion of the pros and cons of fundamentalism, yet another force deserves recognition: the pop mysticism culture known as *New Age*. Over recent decades this movement has commanded significant attention, money, and resources. It has become an industry in its own right and continues to influence cultural values.

During the mid to late 1960s, the extent of this movement allowed the popular media to begin bringing information about metaphysical systems into greater view, leading to a general cultural awareness of chakras and meridians. Acupuncture has since been established as part of Western CAM, and chakras are now under scrutiny. The interest in these and other like-minded topics has not abated and the once recondite knowledge of ancient mysticisms continues to find expression in modern times.

The main thrust of the New Age movement, a renaissance of thought and experience, centers on awakening spirituality. It includes investigations of reincarnation, meditation, healing, and new relationships with God, just to name a few items on the agenda. Yet, much of this agenda has already been very well established for centuries in philosophies around the world. To a large degree the discoveries are incomplete reflections of pieces of metaphysical traditions. Perhaps what makes them new is the amount of attention given to them and the numbers of people who are involved. If this is true, the New Age movement could be considered a result of changes in the energy body's uniformity. As previously mentioned, the energy body may be evolving into a more spherical shape. If so, this would lend itself to more people perceiving a more holistic world. And holistic thinking is very much part of the New Age.

Like metaphysical philosophies, New Age perspectives are far-reaching and often touch every aspect of a person's life. Since in some ways New Age could be considered an umbrella for all metaphysical philosophies, it carries immense weight. However, this line of thought is still just another social arrangement, a conditional field based on an inherited set of assumptions about reality, rather than being an on-going reexamination of our lot as humans. While New Age thinking does provide some direction and offers ways to proceed, it is of finite form and therefore not the pure art of navigating infinity, as is the case with any doctrine.

Metaphysical philosophies deal with the underlying structures of reality, and New Age considerations often only skim the surface. Understanding the difference between occult and mystical makes all the difference in what is experienced. While this movement has provided the service of bringing more ideas to the light of day, New Age quickly gets old when the revelations of new ideas turn to dogma and cultish, occult behavior. People may defer to psychic prowess rather than something of deeper value, for example, reflecting a situation to watch out for as you explore any method for consciousness development. Whether your involvement is with the classic traditions or New Age pursuits, be careful, as you may think you've got it all straight when you really don't.

EXAMPLES OF FUNDAMENTALISM

When you talk the lingo of a system, and things start making sense, it can be very seductive. To avoid the pitfalls of fundamentalism, you need to accept the legitimacy of other points of view, especially if they conflict with yours. The universe is a wide-open place. Why confine it to your pet thoughts? If you let go and constantly challenge your assumptions, your thoughts and your world change.

To avoid getting caught in fundamentalism, it is also helpful to closely examine the precepts of any system. A closer look at some of the slogans and tips popular in traditional metaphysical philosophies and New Age movement can be very instructive.

The world is an illusion. Yes, it is an illusion in relation to other points of view. But using the model of cohesion and the assemblage point, we could also say that everything is real. Whenever cohesion formulates and an assemblage point position stabilizes, that makes something "real." Everything else becomes potential, real in its own domain but not necessarily an illusion. But any assemblage point position, whether for an individual or a group, is also an illusion when you compare it with infinite potential. Still, this thinking stems from an assemblage point position, which makes it real according to the rules that allowed the cohesion reflecting it to form.

There are no mistakes. This perspective definitely opens you up to potential, knowing that there is perfection in each and every event, but take a hard look. You've never made a true mistake? This doesn't mean you can't learn from your mistakes, and make something good out of them. But learning is limited when you think you never make a mistake as you give up a reference to further your life.

You create your own reality. This is a popular expression. But maybe the impact of this slogan has limits. It is a philosophical assumption based on a Western perspective of having free will; that is, it is an interpretation stemming from examining our actions based on a free-will model. It is not necessarily fact, even though we can see it working in our lives.

A slogan only holds sway if you use it consistently and take it seriously, not just when it's convenient. If you fully accept that you create your reality, you have to assume responsibility for everything in your life, including your neighbors and how they impact you. This doesn't mean you are responsible for your neighbors; it means you are responsible for having those neighbors in your life. In this manner, you unveil deeper levels of yourself. By going deeper and deeper, you come to your core; you get to a point where you no longer interpret or define the world, like saying "you create your own reality."

A counterpoint is that the pressure from cosmic emanations on our energy bodies causes our decisions. A decision occurs by acquiescing to a force that ultimately forms cohesion; maybe this is God's will, to use theological terminology. But since we've learned to develop reason over other modes of perception, we conjure up the perception that somehow we are the ones really making the decisions.

Earth is a school. There's no doubt that learning takes place in humans. Exactly what is learned may be open to question, but humans learn. In general, what is learned is more and more about the human condition, and not necessarily from a grand viewpoint. Therefore, saying, "Earth is a school" is projection based on the natural tendency to learn. In so doing, we hopefully make our environment a place of learning. But what life is, what it really is, and what it really is for, is a mystery dwelling in the depths of infinity. To view it otherwise locks the door to potential.

It was supposed to happen. Says who?

There's a reason for everything. Sure, you can find a reason for anything, but that doesn't mean that there *is* a reason for it. To have a reason for it, to find meaning, requires relating the experience to a specific logic. If this is done enough it builds a conditional energy field. One such field might lead you to reason that you are adept at mathematics because you have genetic makeup that lends itself to math. Another field might lead you to think you are adept at mathematics because you have good karma from a past life. Genetic expression then follows having good karma. This enhanced accountability is what makes New Age fundamentalism difficult to overcome. Having a wider perspective leads to the belief that you have the inside angle. An aspect of closure, humans attribute meaning and value to their thoughts about the content of the universe. This doesn't mean the attribution is correct.

We live in a world of duality. Yes, we do. Maybe this is because we have a two-sided horizontal brain: the right and left hemispheres. We project the innate tendencies of our hardwiring onto the external world: the world becomes dualistic because of the way the brain processes information. There is more to perception than it being dualistic, though.

The brain's structure may also make it clear why Toltecs say there are three energy fields. Remember that in addition to right and left partitioning, there is a three-level, vertical partitioning relating to physical, emotional, and abstract-mental functions. These vertical segments easily correspond to the first, second, and third energy fields. The association between the horizontal and vertical areas of the brain is what produces new models of reality, such as it being multidimensional. We then become more aware of whom we are and project that, rather than gain recognition of the way the universe actually is.

As you develop the stages of awakening a dualistic world of good and evil evolves into interpreting events as positive or negative. Eventually you see that your perception of the world is a state of mind.[8] The measurement behind this is that the definitions of good and evil result from one's ontological stage of awareness. The interpretations of good and evil then serve to hold that cohesion in place, self-validating the thinking behind it. This doesn't preclude the existence of a force that detrimentally influences behavior. As one expands cohesion, awareness of this tension takes on new meaning and offers new ability to handle it.

The Inquisition, genocide, or any of the atrocities in this day and age could be considered evil if the same standards are applied to them as are applied to a serial killer who beheads his or her victims. The person who feels revulsion over the serial killer may calmly accept the killing of thousands of people in a foreign land as legitimate, perhaps an expedient means to an end. The ethical guidelines for interpreting a given circumstance often result from what the group finds acceptable. The dualistic split may reflect a struggle among higher and lower regions of human consciousness, of self versus group, and of group versus group.

FREE WILL?

The concept of free will offers a good example of how an idea turns into dogmatic thinking, able to start arguments, if not wars, when people dig in too deeply with their viewpoints and build cosmologies around them. The mere ideas of whether the book of your life has already been printed and just waits for you to read it, or whether the narrative is yours to pen as you wish at any turn, are the matter of philosophical debate that often becomes the fodder of conflict. The differences about whether or not humans have free will illustrate the value of taking the time to look at other perspectives.

A major portion of many religions relates to this very point. Eastern philosophies are known to espouse the nonexistence of free will, whereas the Western mind-set contends that free will is part and parcel of human existence. Whichever viewpoint is valued, the perceptions relating to it are found in the capacity of humans to form subject-object relationships. Humans examine their condition and ask questions like, "If we have free will, what is its nature? How much choice do we have?" This question may be better stated as "Why don't we choose to act in ways that don't harm ourselves, others, or the environment—especially when we know our actions are causing harm?"

Notions pertaining to free will summon deeply rooted values of what it means to be human. This requires looking at individuals as unique, as being able to behave independently of the group. It carries that much meaning. In traditional Buddhist thought, free will doesn't exist because there is no self to have free will. Even some cognitive scientists hold fast to this view. On the other hand, free will is very much a part of Christian traditions. "Sin" is at times viewed as straying from the path, and *reconciliation* is placing oneself back in a proper relationship with God. Choice, then, or the ability to find redemption, derives from the thinking that we have options to select from, and the power to enact choice.[9]

Arriving at either understanding requires an intense effort of consolidating a number of seemingly disparate pieces of logic into a unified whole, a task no different from any other learning. The point here is that classic traditions expound particular points of view. That is both a blessing and curse.

Jung maintains that *will* implies having enough energy to act independently of instinct, yet the motivation of *will* is biological and therefore instinctual. From Maslow's perspective, free choice doesn't enter the picture until a person expresses self-actualizing behavior. His hierarchy of deficit and growth needs speaks directly to this.[10] If a person is governed by need, how much latitude for choice does he or she have?

As part of having no free will, we might regard our destiny as being already determined, and perhaps view all time as taking place within a single instant, with life being a magnificent play of perception of moving through time and space. At the same time, we could use this perspective to support free will in that self-determination is part of the nature of things. Both models enable expansion of awareness. The machinery of logic is just different. The resulting forms of consciousness and knowledge are different.

In his book, *Psychology of Religion,* scholar Paul Johnson argues that choice is evident when one is more conscious,[11] a position in line with Maslow's thinking. The energy body schematic with the interworkings of imagination and learning offers a look at what becoming conscious entails. This is supported with a right-left physical hemisphere model where integrating different functions of the brain leads to being more conscious.

From an energetic standpoint, though, inertia governs all of our behavior and free will corresponds with a sense of movement. Learning allows one to change inertia, but was the learning itself a product of inertia? Isn't most learning, at least in the early years of life, based solely on participating in a given reality? Free will, from this perspective, is just buying the only thing being sold. As you become more conscious, though, you may be able to manage the process. This could be evidence of free will or another by-product of inertia.

Belief in free will or no free will stems from one's cohesion, as each perspective represents an assemblage point position. The synthesis of the two ends of the free will/no free will continuum may not necessarily be a blending of models but the development of yet another model; the effect of a Hegelian dialectic where thesis and antithesis collide to create a new synthesis. In this example, the growth may be that of ontological intelligence—the full range of awareness—where the next answer, and the next choice, is found in the enactment of the next, higher order of logic.

According to the Toltec worldview, emanations carry commands. There is a command that humans must eat and another that humans must engage in self-reflection. How the commands are carried out, though, seems open to interpretation and decision-making. Choice then originates from completely surrendering yourself to an emanation in order to step outside of it.[12] By absorbing the energy of a certain level of consciousness, you open yourself to yet another influence. While you may lose a sense of choice in the new emanation, you've gained at least some freedom, and therefore some choice, from having become more conscious of the prior emanation.

The further you integrate the human world, meaning the more you command human-world emanations, the more you step into worlds beyond your current imagination; after all, we are multidimensional creatures living in a multidimensional creation. Choice then mirrors aligning with, or entraining to, particular emanations. All major religions and spiritual philosophies offer the possibility of this awareness regardless of whether or not it is related to energetics, or whether or not we have free will.

Both camps and everything in between can conjure up some pretty fancy footwork and we haven't even scratched the surface. One way or other, the belief you hold about the issue results from your entrainment to a line of thought, an emanation of intellectual energy. Not having free will supports behaving in line with the properties of energy where at a certain level all behavior has already been decided. Having free will offers a connection with energy fields that enable this thing called "choice."

Any way you look at it, it is all part of infinity's script. And within infinity, everything is occurring—including the legitimacy of all assumptions about infinity. It is at this point, says don Juan, that we are left with exercising only one alternative: the capacity to serenely face infinity as a result of being filled with awe at the unfathomable mystery we live in.[13]

MANAGING FUNDAMENTALISM

Fundamentalism is a powerful force of entrainment. This force can be perceived and transcended as part of ontological development. There's no doubt that the fundamentals—the essential basics—of a system serve to help liberate perception. They keep you heading toward your destination. It's only when you lose yourself in the fundamentals that you go astray. Here are some suggestions that may help you navigate infinity:

1. Don't use your knowledge as an excuse not to look at yourself.
2. Learn to *see,* as doing so suspends conditional fields and lets you directly examine energy fields. This provides the means to extend awareness beyond the known world. *Seeing* awakens the energy body. Chapter ten provides technique.
3. Shift your assemblage point regularly. Look at the world and act a little differently now and then. Stimulate your imagination. Fundamentalists try to maintain a certain perspective, and this means maintaining a particular assemblage point position.
4. Cultivate a bent for examination, for understanding. Toltecs have called this *sobriety* and hold that it automatically leads to a shift in the assemblage point.[14]
5. Challenge all of the assumptions that make up your worldview.
6. Don't let your love for the fundamentals turn you into a fundamentalist.
7. Don't confuse intellectual fluency with having the ability to do what it is you are talking about.
8. Realize that just because you have had an experience—like a

NDE—doesn't mean you know what it is or means in absolute terms.

9. Understand that groups go through the same process as individuals. Nothing is cast in stone and it takes time to weave perception from a baseline through altered states to another baseline. Individual consciousness and growth drives this process. Don't give unwarranted allegiance to a group.

10. Get comfortable with not knowing anything. Then open yourself to knowing. Repeat as needed.

Millions of people are being exposed to, and influenced by, fundamentalist thinking, be they scientists, politicians, religious zealots, hardcore New Agers, or whatever. When many people adopt a new pattern of thought, it results in a revolution. The communist, socialist, industrial, evangelical, and green movements are all examples, as is the Inquisition. At its face value, a revolution is neither good nor bad. The measure of its value is its effect on the consciousness and development of individuals and groups.

Yet, for the revolutionary transformation of freedom, even this power must be transcended. Supplanting one template of thought with another is not a recipe for complete evolution. All too often when people have authority in one field, they assume their knowledge transfers to others. In addition, people construct many interpretations of what they think is occurring rather than examine what is occurring.

If there were a technology that could accurately indicate how much of the energy body had become conscious, we would have a way to predict any person's level of fundamentalism or awakening. Seen from a behavioral psychological perspective, that would translate to hard data that could be used to predict behavior. From a transpersonal perspective, it would make the assessment of ontological development possible. We could then map practically any disorder and develop therapies, all based on the perspective that humans have objective, quantifiable energy bodies.

EVALUATING A PHILOSOPHY

Unless you are somehow gifted, to firmly move forward in learning you need a system that will offer you an enlarged worldview, channel markers to keep you on track, and how-to-do-it skills. This is exactly what metaphysical philosophies and science offer. The markers provided may be simple tips. For example, don Juan advised Castaneda not to become overconfident, as Toltec practices can be deadly. This is backed up with scientific research. Psychiatrist Arthur Deikman, in his landmark study of cult behavior, *The Wrong Way Home,* found that overconfidence leads to the demise of spiritual organizations as well as individuals.[15]

A philosophy provides a framework that can help you in the process of letting your current knowledge become obsolete as you develop a new set of perspectives. Part of the challenge requires you to remain true to a philosophy while also remaining true to yourself. In this light, a viable philosophy always has two features that indicate whether it's strong enough, and flexible enough, to get you to your core—the overriding consideration of developing your energy body.

The first indicator of a viable system is that it's non-exclusive. One part of this concerns access to ideas outside the system. That is, if you're a practicing Toltec and come across a Buddhist or Christian practice that helps you, you don't shun it because it isn't part of your primary path. You welcome and incorporate it into your life. The flip side of this is that ideas, practices, and procedures of a system are open to all. If they provide positive influence to a person or group, others should not be denied access.

Another facet of non-exclusivity focuses on whether practitioners follow the path they preach about. Deikman found that self-righteousness is a marked feature of cult members. You've found your way and that's that . . . often producing great suffering for those around you. Embarking on such a path may only lead into room after room of mirror images of yourself, or rather of the images you have of yourself. This is often accompanied by the attitude that group membership is the be-all and end-all; this is often taken to a level of criticizing if not ostracizing others.

The attitude that there is only one path and there are only a chosen few who may follow it provides another indication of cult behavior. Deikman found that devaluing outsiders firmly indicates cult activity.[16]

The second indicator of a viable system is that the philosophy clearly teaches that it is only a means to an end. It is to allow clarity for better assessment, not lock perception within its grand scheme. Author John Van Auken has observed that phenomena, or the imaginings of a worldview, can blind one to the greater realms of existence or can serve as a bridge to them.[17] Having fun with *psi,* OBEs, NDEs, and mystical experiences may open the way to a greater sense and vision of the world. On the other hand, these experiences may lead you to think that they *are* the world and to become so enthralled with your discoveries that you forget about further development.

A doctrine or system represents the articulation of craftsmanship. This becomes a group's baseline consciousness and like any other baseline the orientation, terminology, understanding, and skills change over time. Part of a high-value system is that it helps you continually expand your boundaries. For the individual or the collective, remaining at the level of craftsmanship invites fundamentalism. The path needs to point the way to artistry and, in so doing, connect you with infinity. Otherwise dogma and possibly cult behavior result.

In fundamentalism, instead of closure serving to support learning, the work of learning turns into acts of closure. As members of the flock, fundamentalists find meaning within group understanding. On the other hand, an artisan or master finds meaning by matching personal energies with pure potential, and then letting life unfold from there. This augmented awareness is then offered to the group for consideration, not compliance. From this relationship, each and every step of life means renewal, not repetition.

8

Building a
Creative Life

Creativity, or bringing something into being, results from weaving form and potential. Form is cohesion, a type of energy field. Potential is abstract energy, energy that has possibilities of realization but isn't there yet: perhaps a rarified type of form. Pure potential is completely abstract, the infinite creation, which contains everything but has no structure.

How these energies interact determines what you create—the imaginings of your life and world. Remember that whatever you experience results from your cohesion, or rather the capacity of your cohesion to perceive. Cohesion also determines how you continue to connect with potential, which influences what you experience as the energy body meets greater and more expansive emanations.

If you don't connect with potential, you circle within the conditional field you already have. This may keep you amused for a while, but you aren't going to grow very much. When you squarely face potential, you place your life on the line—each and every moment of it. This moves you from talk about life into a relationship with the world where you live to the hilt. The following perspectives serve to help you to orient to this edge and gauge how you build your life on it.

DISCOVERY

Part of creativity is discovery, which can take many forms. There is the brilliant flash of intuition, when all effort suddenly comes together to deliver an expanded knowing. This *Eureka!* mode of invention has been a mainstay since humans became conscious and curious.

Another form of discovery is serendipity, the seemingly accidental or chance discovery. When Alexander Fleming noticed that bacteria were not growing around the mold that had appeared on some unwashed culture plates he had casually left on his lab bench, he turned that observation into penicillin. Yet, as mathematics professor Steven Strogatz points out, serendipitous discoveries are not chance revelations. They occur because people are alertly looking for something; they "just happen to find something else." In his book *Sync: The Emerging Science of Spontaneous Order,* Strogatz entertainingly reveals processes of entrainment, resonance, and cooperation as being parts of a greater synchronicity occurring throughout life.[1]

There is also discovery as measured by the time-honored plodding of a disciplined mind as it wrestles with what is known, what it sees that doesn't fit convention, and eventually illuminates the unknown: that which waits behind a veil. Einstein remained on track for years as he developed the thinking that eventually led to his theory of relativity. The simple truth is that the heart of discovery contains many styles, these and others, and that each supports the others.

Discovery is regulated by models—small or large landscape views—which at once open and close perception. All of the different avenues of discovery are constructs that allow us to focus awareness in ways that deliver results. Even serendipity, where discovery-by-chance may seem random, needs the support of a context in which the discovery may take hold. Fleming, for example, had extensive scientific background that guided the application of his observation; penicillin didn't surface like a rabbit from a hat. At the same time, discovery also requires a suspension of what is thought to be true—a form of deautomatization—to allow imagination to come forth.

In one bioenergetic model, discovery hinges on how well a person aligns with the energy fields that contain what is awaiting discovery. This suggests that the thing being discovered already exists; awareness just needs to unfold into that realm. Put a different way, the inventor entrains to the discovery already existing in imagination, and then the inventor's skill in creativity determines the outcome.

Creativity hinges on the interplay of learning and imagination. For example, the wildly commercial success of the previously unknown "pet rock" was based on the known commodities of "pet" and "rock." Placing the two together was new but not foreign. Likewise, it took some time before the idea of a submarine became a concept worth developing, and then it took longer still to make it work.

Perception closes when data of a new and wider view is not recognized or is dismissed as irrelevant. The person advancing the ideas often suffers ridicule or worse by those who, for whatever reason, have a stake in the current scheme of things. Even in the midst of the technological development of undersea travel, in which supposedly foolish ideas became reality, the mere talk of something that could fly would have almost ensured a hard rebuff; the prevailing model regarded air travel as impossible and inhibited forward movement.

The process of discovery is like being part of a motion picture set that is so well designed that there lives an implicit assumption about its reality. Then the curtain lifts, revealing yet a new landscape and people say, "Oh, great, now we found the real world." This happens time and again as human knowledge increases, yet we are not taught that the curtain will rise once again to reveal yet another entirely new vista. Going backstage to observe what is really going on, rather than remaining focused on the special effects, is also at the heart of creativity.

INTELLIGENCE

A defining aspect of discovery is intelligence, resources you bring to bear on a situation, as well as the means with which you apply them. Intelligence is often presented as a score, an intelligence quotient, commonly known as *IQ.* In recent years, this has been challenged as being a very limited perspective on human capabilities. Some say the measurement of IQ is culturally biased, others say it focuses too much on intellectual capacities, and still others say it's just plain obsolete.

Research indicates that intelligence surfaces in many ways. Building on the rational and emotional intelligence considerations outlined in chapter three, we find that educator and cognitive scientist Howard Gardner provides evidence in his classic book, *Frames of Mind: The Theory of Multiple Intelligences,* that humans have within themselves a number of different intelligences. "Human beings," he says, "have evolved to exhibit several intelligences and not to draw variously on one flexible intelligence." Included among the intelligences that Gardner says we have are those of language, mathematics, music, the physical body, and social adeptness. He even suggests that there is a "spiritual intelligence."[2]

Intelligence can be defined as "the ability to meet and adapt to novel situations; the ability to utilize abstract concepts effectively; and the ability to grasp relationships and to learn quickly." Gardner finds intelligence to be the ability "to resolve genuine problems or difficulties." He adds, "possession of an intelligence is most accurately thought of as a *potential* [italics mine]."[3] Pure potential, then, is pure intelligence. It embodies all forms of intelligence, all waiting to be tapped in a variety of ways, to engender creativity.

Human intelligence is our ability to open to potential, to apply what is perceived, and to integrate the results. This profile may then be applied to whatever situation is at hand, whether it is working with mathematics, composing music, *seeing,* or dipping into social psychology. Since evolving the energy body relies on intersecting with emanations, with a greater potential of energy, with building new cohesions and then applying these results; intelligence may also be thought of as the ability to manage cohesion. Accordingly, plugging into potential is intelligent. Evolving through your energy body is intelligent. Bringing yourself to life is intelligent.

Discovery requires the vigorous application of intelligence, not just resting with innate ability. It hinges on allowing new insight, on bringing the unconscious to the light of day. It results from a solid relationship with learning that lasts a lifetime and is addressed further in chapter eleven.

ETHICS

A key aspect of intelligence is the ethic behind it. Ethics are governing principles of behavior: values, morals, rules. They may change over time and the considerations about ethical standards—including religious, cultural, professional, and personal values—are vast. Ethics also directly affect the quality and depth of coherence, as they are the measure of your orientation to core. In this manner, they influence the formation of your reality.

Ethics has become a well-developed line of inquiry with highly specialized divisions including *deontological,* or rules and principles, and *teleological,* or examination of behavior based on the purpose or end result. And new areas continue to emerge. *Human nature* ethical inquiry, for example, presupposes that behavior should be measured in line with how it affects personal development.[4] This not only means ethicists have developed an interest in the tenets associated with psychological well-being, but that the divisions represent the grooming of a profession's cohesion. Consistent with the development of models for self-actualization, this correlates with an evolution of ethics from social rules to the individual.

Individual and social ethics form foundations for intelligent, if not creative, behavior. There are no set answers; even centuries-old religious dogmas change. There are, though, bits and pieces to be considered in light of the energy body model, where ethics influence cohesion and represent growth toward core: the concept being to remove obstacles that prevent awareness of your natural condition. As food for thought, some considerations of an energy-based ethic follow.

Compassion

Compassion may be defined as "deep awareness of the suffering of another coupled with the wish to relieve it." Holding to this definition,

Toltecs may not have compassion. They may be able to empathize with or understand another's plight. They may be able to apply a lesson found in another's misfortune to their own lives, thereby avoiding the same trouble. They may render assistance. But they won't think that other people are powerless to the extent that they have to be coddled. They won't think the other person has to be changed, shown the light, or saved. The best of Toltecs have been born, says don Juan, from squalor. We all have the means to command our lives, he maintains, and so there is nothing to change in anyone. Yet shamans are often drawn to healing professions, and the desire to relieve suffering is clearly evident. The attitude associated with behavior, including nonattachment, might therefore be the defining element of compassion.[5]

The overall awareness of the person aiming to be compassionate, as well as having a grasp of the immediate situation, determines the effects. Compassion might be the salve that soothes and awakens or it might be just a personal power play to make someone conform. Being overly compassionate, for example, diminishes objectivity. The concern given to a situation can reduce your ability to assess the *meta*-problem. You have increased difficulty sensing the underlying problem causing the personal distress, rendering you unable to take effective action for a long-lasting remedy.

This is why some Toltecs strive not to care. This doesn't mean they are blasé or callous. And it certainly doesn't mean they lack gusto. It means that they strive for a level of objectivity to be able to act precisely and effectively. They are cultivating the keen indifference that will allow them to be successful. But it doesn't mean to be overbearing as don Juan says that balancing experience, wisdom, and knowledge requires kindness. Charles Tart says that conditions for "*effective* compassion" include having a range of personal experience, empathy that promotes objectivity, motivation to help, and the application of intelligence to resolve the suffering.[6]

Judgment

Judgment is a form of closure. It stems from interpretation and binds you to a particular emotional and mental disposition. Even at its best, judgment keeps you locked in the throes of fundamentalism. You may even want to physically attack others, starting a street fight or a war.

Judgment removes you from potential. It requires that you constantly justify your high-horse attitude, and requires you to work overtime to maintain that manner of self-reflection. What is ethical in one culture may not be in another. What is held sacred by some cultures may be heresy to others, even though people in both strive to do good deeds. Judgment can therefore be oppressive.

Being nonjudgmental doesn't negate discernment; the difference being judgment carries an emotional charge, a sense of condemnation, whereas discernment lends itself to objectivity. It also doesn't mean you aren't allowed to take steps to avoid difficulties or rectify injustices. It does mean giving freedom to the world to be as it is, which grants more reliability to your assessments of others and yourself, thereby giving you room to gain wider perspective. This stance permits the understanding that promotes positive change rather than ongoing strife. From yet another angle, a nonjudgmental attitude helps awaken your energy body. Stepping away from judgment provides more energy to handle the abstractions of the unknown as you ply them into your practical, known world.

Forgiveness

Forgiveness of the transgressions of self and others offers a release of the assemblage point, a release of a cohesion bound by judgment. But it doesn't mean being a whipping boy. It's a relaxation of tension that opens you to growth by ceasing to expend the energy required to maintain a non-forgiving attitude. Forgiveness abounds, but only after a shift in cohesion permitting a new relationship.

In *Why Forgive?* author Johann Christoph Arnold provides stories of the sojourns to forgiveness by various people that demonstrate why forgiveness has value. They clearly show that forgiveness enables us to free ourselves from the emotional debilitation of being tied down by bitterness, heal the emotional and physical disorders caused by the lack of forgiveness, and restore our primary relationship with God.[7]

In *The Power of Forgiveness,* a documentary by Martin Doblmeier, concepts put forward included forgiving oneself of transgressions as doing so leads to compassion and this may be a step before one can forgive others. The positive effects on health with forgiveness activating specific areas of the brain also have a place in the film, helping build a case that humans are biologically created to forgive. One interviewee is Azim Khamisa, a man whose son had been murdered. Trained in Sufism, Khamisa said forgiveness and compassion are "higher frequencies" whereas fear, hatred, and vindictiveness are of a lower order. In addition, the documentary brings to the fore that forgiveness connects you with the environment since you're no longer creating separation through condemnation.[8]

Power and Control

An effect of perceiving the world from subject-object relationships is objectifying the world, which sets the stage to view people and the world as objects subject to manipulation. It's an extension of closure. While we need to exploit the world to survive and prosper, we need to do so with care and balance as being part of the world. The manner in which you exercise control over yourself, others, and the environment, therefore, makes all the difference in your life.

The more control you have over your energy body, the more ability you have to actively mold your world. This is why control is one of the barriers to ontological development. It is difficult not to want to control your world; closure is innate. You may even want to be compassionate, to change things for the better, to relieve suffering, yet these can lead you to become a dictator. The effects of control on behavior can be very sneaky.

Business expertise and political skill, for example, expand the more a person learns and gains experience in those arenas. This makes the person more capable to enter positions of power. The capacity for power derives from being aware, more aware than the norm in a given situation. Other forms of awareness, such as *psi* and mystical experience, also provide evidence that increased awareness may be parlayed into holding sway over others as found in cults. How a person uses enhanced awareness directly impacts the personal connection with core. Distractions loom at every turn. Decisions represent the energy you have aligned with or wish to align; they indicate your cohesion. Some would say they represent who you *are.*

At the craftsmanship stage, when *will* is pulled from its dormancy, you can modify your circumstances by aligning with emanations of your choosing. The many forms of personal desire now tug at your sensibilities. As a preventive or corrective measure, don Juan says that it is a shame to align with the human world and forget that the assemblage point is a quality of being human, but it is even more of a loss to use this knowledge of the assemblage point for personal gain.[9]

Toltecs, says don Juan, are like anybody else pursuing a vocation. They can be good or bad. Since they've learned to move their assemblage points, they can easily injure others. But, he advises, we must move past ordinary considerations. We must be governed by morality and beauty. This involves the development of an ethic based on personal freedom rather than on the accumulation of power. Part of this ethic is the practice of impeccability, which automatically gives others their freedom as well. Don Juan says a person of knowledge—an artisan—would never under any circumstance harm another person.[10]

The guiding principle is that knowledge of the energy body is to be used to reach your core, not for control of any other type. Core is the essence of how you are created, and this release to a higher *will,* rather than to desire, delivers the principal characteristic of modern Toltec ethics. These teachings sprout from the energy body and highlight developing a natural relationship rather than having a conditioned relationship with the world. Creating a life based on expression of core is not considered personal desire. At each step, this measurement becomes an intricate and delicate balance.

In practice, you wouldn't *will* an outcome or even test the possibility of your ability to do so. And you wouldn't exploit others. When you work for a good life, any change that needs to come will come of its own accord by virtue of your ethic. By not using your resources for control, you can develop an exquisite relationship with the world. And, as don Juan says, there will come a time when you have all of your resources and abilities in check, and you will know when and how to use them. By then, you will have become the true artisan.[11]

Love

Love can be approached and defined in many ways. It can mean leaving things alone or taking action. It can be romantic or platonic, spousal or filial, tough or unconditional. It can be focused on a rock or into the depths of infinity.

Perhaps love is awareness itself, or perhaps it is the feeling of expansion. After all, when we fall in love we usually become more aware and feel as though we are stretching out. We are also more allowing, accepting. As a mode of expansion, love serves to allow a natural energy field.

Love forms an essential part of Christian theology. And love is at the center of Hindu Bhakti mysticism. Shamanic philosophy, which emphasizes deep understanding free from bias, also calls into play love, citing it as the only thing that offers joy and freedom. It carries so much weight it is something to be given freely to the world, to life, in the face of any circumstance.[12]

Don Juan says that Toltec seers *see* love as specific colors representing bandwidths within emanations, clusters that are part of what create different life forms. Even then, only one emanation is of the human domain.[13] Having a limited number of colors pertaining to one emanation doesn't support a worldview in which *everything* is love. In this instance, maybe the human aspect of the universe has been anthropomorphized to include everything. Perhaps the Toltec meaning needs to be recast. Yet if love is a form of energy, then perhaps the seers' determination is accurate. Different colors may represent different kinds of love, or it could be that love is a defining element of an entire bandwidth and one might then feel as though love is universal when aligning with an emanation. In any case, teachings on love are usually found in ethical systems. Whatever the orientation, love is a major component in living a conscious life.

Responsibility

His Holiness the Dalai Lama places each individual act in wide perspective. Two people sharing a well must be mindful of their actions in service to the other; each country needs to recognize that one faltering economy affects other economies around the world; and each driver needs to understand that the pollution of one car adds to the destruction of the entire environment.[14] Accepting the obvious means that each person carries immense responsibility for the self and the whole.

Quantum entanglement also speaks to interconnectedness, where the behavior of an object needs to be accounted for in terms of those objects in relation to it, and that objects may influence one another regardless of the distance between them. In other words, objects may be inextricably linked at a quantum level and to describe one requires understanding its counterpart. We can stretch this out to considering that all objects, everywhere, are connected in some manner. There is also thinking that the effects of entanglement may continue even after the physical link dissipates, such as when an object disintegrates or is destroyed.[15]

How this plays out is where arguments erupt. There is debate, for instance, as to the extent and influence of entanglement and what conditions need to exist for the intermingling to occur. Nuances of the argument rest with diligence of examination, with a clear sense of the lenses being used to investigate and interpret because the models used to investigate determine the results; they establish fences of assumptions regarding the nature of reality. With all camps providing petitions of evidence, characteristic of discovery (and perhaps with any line of thought) what is true today will change with time.

Yet even if quantum entanglement dynamics are found to be limited to precise circumstances, common usage of the term is allowing the concept of interconnectedness with others and the environment to gain a foothold in daily thinking, thereby reshaping other debates such as considerations of the human impact on global warming and of political intervention to prevent genocide. Over the ages, mysticisms have put forth the interconnectedness of all aspects of life as a formative tenet of their ethics, and now science is determining the validity of such a phenomenon even if it has yet to be extended beyond quantum mechanics.

Guidance for developing responsibility can be found in the body of ethics we use, be it religious or secular. Richard Sennett, in *The Corrosion of Character,* cites how the environment, zeroing in on the workplace, shapes personal responsibility. Often one ethic may be stated as part of the corporate culture but the forces within have a different effect, taking personal and societal tolls. He also cites a weakening of character in the modern workplace where people renounce accountability.[16]

Personal responsibility is where the rubber hits the road on the excursion toward infinity. It provides your immediate connection to your life and those about you. It produces the driving force of building a life. Responsibility, as an example of shamanic ethic, means that you are ready to die for your actions.[17] This is pretty crisp, clear, and clean. It falls to individual responsibility to summon those resources to reach core.

Character

The sum of all these attributes represents a person's character, or ethical strength. Character for Toltecs, as measured by *impeccability,* is the main ingredient of realizing the stages of awakening. Throughout Castaneda's books, don Juan delivers lessons on a complex style of character marked by saving energy, being deliberate and independent, and constantly stretching into the unknown. According to him, the backbone of a warrior is marked by humility and efficiency.[18]

Taoism holds fast to *virtue* or "uprightness." This is a perfect attainment of harmony based on the latent, innate power of the individual. Likewise, Maslow regards character as the deepest part of a person. He outlines five character attitudes and says changing any of them changes the person. These attitudes pertain to self, significant others, social groups, nature and physical reality, and, for some people, supernatural forces.[19]

A common aspect of these approaches is the quest to find and nurture your own innermost qualities. Whether you call it actualization, individuation, or virtue, the core value of each system is precisely that: core value. Ethical behavior emanates from each individual's core, from securing a relationship with the creative source of life rather than with social standing alone. Through finding your natural place in the world, you can better serve all.

ETHICAL MODELS

Models emerge directly from the collective consciousness, and some may say they are archetypal forms within the unconscious waiting to emerge into the light of day. For example, Jung offers a viewpoint whereby symbols with universal relevance exist in the collective unconscious. Archetypes are rarified forms rather than something ". . . stiffened into mere objects of belief." While personal unconsciousness is part of the collective unconsciousness, it only "rests upon a deeper layer."[20]

As we have access to the unconscious, bringing this into personal and collective consciousness is the work found in using imagination and learning. That is, the collective unconscious is universal human imagination, to use shamanic reference. The deliberate use of imagination allows personal and group consciousness to become more aware of the unconscious realms. This provides the opportunity to express the archetypes into our daily, conscious world.

Even if inspired by an individual, a model must have some type of relationship to the world outside the individual for it to have pragmatic use. Group consensus is an effect, or even a use, of collective awareness. At the same time, don Juan considers group agreements to be "skimming" as we forget our constructs are arbitrary arrangements and consider them to be reality itself.[21] This also applies to ethical standards.

There are ethical divisions between the major religions and within each one individually. When values clash, so do people. Wars have started over very simple things: the color of skin, the shape of eyes. These days, the topic of abortion often lends itself to a heated environment. Based on differing views, Right to Life activists have killed Right to Choose adherents. That is more than ironic. And mud-slinging, arm-waving, and epithet-calling galore can result from putting someone who thinks physician-assisted suicide is ethical in the same room as someone who doesn't.

There is also a growing ethic in some circles that holds high the value of non-interference. People may then avoid taking action in the attempt to let the entire world be free and to allow the infinite to be

just that. However, non-interference can be a horrid distortion of deautomatization in which anything is allowed to occur. All too often what
has been learned is cast aside. While the effects of global warming on
this finite planet may be just one experience of an infinite variety of
experiences of all creation, we need to be responsible creatures while we
are trying to be open.

What is the intrinsic human value of allowing genocide? Perhaps
non-interference reflects an innate recognition of the need to avoid
abuses of power but somehow is subverted into something else. Staying
locked open seems to be an exotic form of fundamentalism. These concerns make it clear that both the open and closed positions of consciousness are part of ethical conduct.

The Toltec model is a warrior ethic. Ethics are shaped by the perception that we are in a constant struggle. But the struggle isn't against
people; it is continuous engagement with the barriers that keep us from
freedom, from reaching core and, perchance, from traveling beyond the
human dimension.

GROUP CREATIVITY

Led by changes in individual consciousness, group consensus gradually
expands. What used to be solely in the realm of imagination is learned
en masse. Different, if not new, arrangements with reality occur all the
time. No matter the form, the arenas for creativity are immense.

A New Cycle

Don Juan divides the evolution of Toltec philosophy neatly into the old
and new cycles. The old cycle, which brewed for thousands of years, was
characterized by abuses of power, bizarre practices of bending human
cohesion into other life forms, and replete with obscure formulas and
incantations. He thought that these practices led to its destruction.[22]

Several hundred years ago, Toltecs were almost exterminated due
to warring, strife, and the Spanish Conquest of Mexico. Their intricate
reflection-projection blinded them to the impending environmental threat

of invading armies. "They didn't even see it coming," as the saying goes.

In the midst of devastation, the remnant of surviving shamans went underground and revamped their teachings. Observing that their prior behaviors had led to a dead-end, they developed an ethic in which the real purpose of their craft was to shift the assemblage point, and do so in a manner that promoted knowledge and freedom. In essence, the old cycle was based on bondage whereas the new cycle wished to exercise potential and, in so doing, revamp the basic options and behaviors concerned with being alive.[23]

One might argue it wasn't only the devastation brought about by European invaders on an indigenous culture that sparked a realignment of their ways but also the infusion of foreign consciousness that provided a new relationship to their world and to their consciousness. While the Toltec energy body map was quite detailed, perhaps even breaking new ground, their general intellectual sophistication may have been augmented by coming to terms with an occupation force, requiring some degree of cultural inclusion. Even though the native population outnumbered that of the invaders, the political and military might of the foreign armies established this external force as the dominant cultural influence.

This illustrates *assimilation,* where one group-consensus cohesion influences another to use a shamanic reference, and there is no reason why the Toltec endeavor should escape this aspect of adaptation as it applies to individual and group consciousness.[24] As a cohesional dynamic, assimilation relates to environmental entrainment and it affects thinking and other behaviors; therefore the interaction among cultures may have added a more abstract quality to Toltecs' considerations, which propelled their philosophy into new dimensions of understanding, leading to the birth of a modern cycle.

The new cycle reckoned that most of the difficulties faced by Toltec seers—old and new cycles alike—stemmed from self-reflection. This is demonstrated by comparing those who don't have self-restraint with those who seek practical goals. It is the latter group, maintains don Juan, who resolve the problem of self-reflection and what he refers to as self-importance.[25] This easily correlates with our current course of abuses of political and economic power and of environmental destruction.

It is also possible that those of old cycle were living up to their natural field. During that epoch uniformity of the energy body was oblong, limiting the range of cohesion. The options for behavior could only be expressed in specific directions. Stretching through the energy body for all the best reasons then produced dark aberrations rather than the more holistic, mystical orientation of the new cycle.

Characteristic of this inherent limitation, the old cycle didn't have a penchant for understanding, which is a signature of the new cycle. While Toltec inquiry is quite rigorous, it is markedly different from the standards of other modern disciplines. The accepted modes and means of perception alone highlight this variance. How the unconscious is brought to light, then, pertains to style as well as to the ethical standards surrounding these investigations.

A body of ethics is only as good as the orientation of those producing the ethic. If the ethos isn't derived from core values, the effect is estrangement from nature of which humans are part. With the historical reformation, the Toltec quest shifted from highly unusual and intricate cohesions designed for control to tempering cohesion in order to reach core, developing the artisan stage, and leaving the teachings en route to new avenues of freedom.

Toltecs are not the only people who have gone through dark times. The Christian Inquisition certainly carried out less-than-noble endeavors. In addition, a couple thousand years ago Taoists in China went through an evolution reminiscent of the Toltec experience. Prior to that time Taoists saw themselves as being ruled by a pantheon of gods and they sought temporal power. Over time, Taoism became more streamlined, instituting pragmatic pursuits such as being a force behind Traditional Chinese Medicine, and eventually developing into one of the major philosophies of our age.[26]

In our time, while the goal of acquiring temporal power remains pervasive we also face a different type of darkness: the potential threat of global warming. While scientific evidence indicating global warming continues to mount, in some circles controversy remains as to whether it is actually occurring as a result of human-made pollutants, whether it is a natural regularly occurring phenomenon, or whether it is actually occurring in the first place. For instance, investigators may legitimately question data obtained from weather monitoring stations that are in close proximity to commercial kitchen exhaust fans.

But debate is one thing; the obvious is another. So if we step aside from the argument itself, it seems plain enough that the mere act of reducing environmental toxins—no matter the reason—immediately creates a healthier environment. This commonsense harmony with the environment is a mainstay of traditional shamanic values.

Environment

Physicist Milo Wolff points out, "Every charged particle is part of the universe and the universe is part of each charged particle. This implies that each of us, including you and me, are connected together as part of the observable universe!" It has also become increasingly clear that inclusion of the environment is necessary to adequately define anatomy and physiology. Scientific studies, for example, show how conditions such as the degree of lighting affect biochemical reactions and behavior.[27]

In his groundbreaking book, *The Biology of Belief,* cell biologist and medical school professor Bruce Lipton provides a compelling case challenging current scientific thinking that genetics regulates cellular activity. Instead he holds that a cell's physical and energetic environment determine its life. Lipton also offers consideration that both of these models result from beliefs, not necessarily from what is actual.[28]

Our connectedness impacts virtually every aspect of our lives. How a group relates to others and to the world also determines the environment. Humans have populated Earth to an extent that our energies are now significantly influencing the cohesion of the planet. This is bioenergetics in motion, the relationship between organisms and the environment.

Self-reflection has an upside and downside regarding the environment. The downside is that projection-reflection blocks awareness; the upside is that it permits accurate assessment. Humans have done a magnificent job of carving out a niche that enhances survival and even allows for leisure time to play, travel, and contemplate. Yet this basic relationship causes difficulty. To sustain human life, we need to take the best of what we know and establish a new relationship—a symbiotic relationship—rather than continue as predators.

From an ethical perspective, global warming and an assortment of other environmental concerns are part and parcel of the issues confronting business. Site selection, emissions, deforestation/reforestation, renewable resources, and economic development are all part of the agenda. According to Michael Lerner, author of *Spirit Matters,* addressing corporate as well as individual and social responsibility for environmental concerns requires a spiritual assessment and direction. Lerner promotes a "globalization of spirit," where self-interest gives way to awareness and participation in a larger order.[29]

From a psychological view, Maslow points out that the environment of family and culture are absolute requirements for actualization. At the same time, autonomy is part of self-actualization, which results in less fear and anxiety as well as a greater ability to handle environmental situations like tragedy, stress, and deprivation. A greater independence that allows full individuality is realized but not, Maslow maintains, at the expense of the environment. The ability to act independently of the environment and to measure your steps by your own sense of responsibility is a defining attribute of psychological health.[30]

As articulated by Lipton, the field of *epigenetics* deals with how environment, perceptions, and beliefs affect genetic expression. This expression determines what proteins will be manufactured and how the body functions. In addition, in illuminating difficulties with experimenter bias—including how experiments are designed, conducted, and interpreted—researchers have recently cited quantum entanglement to explain how a model held by a person participating in an experiment is part of the environment and therefore a determinant of the experiment and its outcome.[31]

Biophysicist James Oschman points out that we live as part of multiple environments. From intracellular chemical communication to electromagnetic fields of power connected to extraterrestrial influences, we exist in a multitude of internal and external environments. Sound, light, and a variety of magnetic and electromagnetic fields are just part of this vast energetic landscape. It is also clear that this energetic environment affects physical health. Even a cursory look at weather changes and allergies reveals a causal connection between health and environment. Added to this, there is growing concern that human-made, energetic pollution disrupts the normal functions of the body.[32]

Overall, a holistic approach to health mandates an assessment of our relationship to our environment. Traditional Chinese Medicine is based on balancing the body with its environment. Homeopathy requires the practitioner to examine environmental factors that may cause, prolong, or maintain a disorder. And Valerie Hunt demonstrates how the environment affects the aura.[33] This is noteworthy as the aura reveals to some measure the condition of the whole person and often reflects one's state of health before the physical body manifests the positive or negative condition reflected in the aura. This means the aura can provide diagnostic measurement.

From a Toltec perspective, the energy body is *seen* as intimately connected with its environment. You are therefore part of all that is around you, seen and unseen. The alignment of outer and inner energies forms the basis of perception. When your perceptions change it is due to a change in relation to the environment. Expanding your alignments increases consciousness. This leads to tapping an ever-increasing order, resulting from accessing more emanations of energy.[34]

We are immersed in an infinite number of vibrations, says don Juan, and human perception is relegated to a specific region.[35] But collective consciousness expands as individuals continue to explore recondite areas of awareness and then express those findings within the whole. As a result, we may be stepping beyond what being human once meant as we awaken more of the energy body as a group.

Technology

An integral part of our environment, technology is a means to channel potential into practical use. No matter if technology consists of an ancient plow or a space shuttle, it represents a creative force that touches practically every aspect of our lives.

Technology is applied science. Well practiced, science grants adventures into the unknown and technology turns those endeavors into practical gains. Pharmaceutical drugs, for instance, represent technologies that result due to the hard-won findings of medical science. From tires to windows to engines and the means to make them, to the thinking behind it all, automobiles alone reflect how deeply technology pervades our lives.

In addition to the material and mechanical varieties, technology also includes cognitive forms. A working technology grows from a concept that is pulled out of the unknown and gains conscious footing; technology emerges from the human unconscious and the possibilities held within. Agreements formed in collective consciousness anchor it to reality. Our current line of technological development mimics heretofore science-fiction technologies. Reason is evolving and becoming more capable of handling out-of-this-world concepts. The notion of stepping on the face of the moon was once only found in an entertaining story. While it will take time for humans to build a flying saucer, teleportation of quantum matter has already become fact.[36] New scientific theories that alter the landscape of what is considered possible are rapidly emerging. Group consensus about reality will invariably change as well and, in time, children will be raised with an entirely new baseline state of consciousness.

As material technology is based in reason, it represents mental constructs emanating from personal and group projection. A metaphysical system offers techniques for not only implementing but intricately developing the worldview it espouses, where the emphasis is on innate ability to enhance awareness.[37] This can be seen in shamanic teachings, which render a mechanical, energetic view of human anatomy and physiology, as well as a means to manage these resources; they embody more than philosophy as they form a cognitive technology that places metaphysical theory into practice and experience.

Humans are assisted in their steps by a blend of material and cognitive technologies. Bioenergetic technology is an example of this; it reflects technological development based on a growing collective consciousness about energetic anatomy. Toltecs speed up their evolution by skilled use of imagination. As an aspect of their cognitive technology, the higher levels of imagination enable various time-travel modes of perception marked by out-of-body and near-death experiences.

Toltec abilities are derived, says don Juan, from *silent knowledge,* from awareness that is deep within us, at our very core, but outside the domain of reason's inventories.[38] Silent knowledge is a comprehensive knowing, a sense of natural order, a relationship with infinity. It indicates having at least a core orientation with advancement toward a natural energy field. Without necessarily knowing how or why, bits of the unknown are translated into conscious awareness. Accurate intuition in a novel situation is an example; you realize answers correlate with having actual knowledge of the environment. The main idea is that you're aware beyond your known references.

Like other stable perceptions, it is an assemblage point position. Don Juan adds that in our far-distant past, this was the natural condition of humans: that of behaving from silent knowledge. Then something occurred that created the ability to reason, and from that point we entered an evolutionary track concerned with objectifying our environment. The sense of being separate from the world was the beginning of objectivity and vice versa. This new relationship with the world magnified the perception of living in a material world, forming a pervasive technological worldview and culture.

Both material and cognitive applications of awareness are needed for humans to grow in modern life, both are created from group consensus, and both need tempering. Material technology is evolving rapidly and thereby producing a situation that its growth outpaces ethical considerations of how to use it. We have the means to quickly and completely destroy the inhabitability of our planet through warfare. For another example, manufacturing generally has not proficiently adjusted to the pollution it causes. We therefore need balance stemming from a well-formulated ethic that permits technological advances while restraining aberrant uses.

For reasons such as this, His Holiness the Dalai Lama argues that religion, which influences more people than does the more esoteric leanings of mysticism, remains relevant in modern society. And religion scholar Paul Johnson notes, "Religious behavior seeks the largest possible adjustment of life, for it is concerned about the ultimate relationships."[39]

By locking perception within a box reflecting its own abilities, technology may estrange the individual from recognizing native abilities. It may also continue to grow at a rate leading to more environmental destruction than benefit. And it may render futile the attempt to liberate a person or society from its grip. For his own field of bioethics, Leon R. Kass, author of *Life, Liberty and the Defense of Dignity,* argues for a more thorough examination of the discipline in order to develop a richer ethic. Bioethics, for instance, has grown from examinations of issues relating to death and dying while in a coma, to a range of topics such as transplants, stem cell research, and more.[40]

Acknowledged as one of the founders of bioethics, Professor James Drane argues in *More Humane Medicine* that the doctor-patient relationship has changed. Patients have different assumptions relating to physician authority and treatment has become fragmented. Free-market capitalism now has a major influence on the relationship. Drane points out that these and other factors require a return to the traditional foundations of medical ethics in order to restore the personal bond between the physician and the person who is ill.[41]

The growth of bioenergetics and transpersonal psychology may help produce an ethic for the development of consciousness. We would then have the power of a logically created system that paradoxically extends awareness beyond known limits. This would help develop reason to make sense of an ever-expanding order—stimulation that would enhance the quality of life for one and all.

Education

As a species, we need to take better care of educational systems and methods. It may be that a lack of relevance of what is being taught is adversely affecting the secondary school dropout rate. And the entire ethic of curriculum needs to be overhauled. Gearing the education of children toward helping a country compete globally may diminish creativity in a way as to have the opposite result. It may interfere, not only with self-actualization, but also may channel learning into arbitrarily predetermined categories often blocking new insights and therefore the ability to develop technologies.

As reference, there is style of learning, which takes into account ontological factors such as responsibility, innate drives and pace, and emotional intelligence. It also creates a solid and lasting relationship with learning. Initially developed by Benjamin Bloom, it is called "Mastery Learning," and emphasizes consolidating a step in learning a skill or subject before moving on to the next step, and that creating an appropriate environment for this is necessary. It is not rote learning, it is mastering the process of learning.[42]

Teachers, administrators, and institutions exert tremendous entrainment influences on how we view our world. The quality of instruction makes all the difference in what is learned and how one relates to learning. This makes it all the more meaningful for each person to assume responsibility for what is being learned and what to do about it. This allows one to offset poor instruction, if this is the case, and regain an edge for learning. Good instruction instills this attitude of personal responsibility; excellent teaching requires it.

CREATING YOUR LIFE BY LIVING A PATH WITH HEART

Now we get to the heart of building a quality life. In Toltec, Buddhist, and other traditions this has come to be known as living a path with heart. To fully engage life with abundant meaning, Jack Kornfield offers a range of perspectives and practices relating to inner transformation. Throughout his book, *A Path with Heart,* he provides insights on individual and group growth. For instance, he deals with self-knowledge, expanding awareness, altered states, ethics, and applying meditation to psychotherapy.[43]

Don Juan boiled down the process of creating a path with heart to using your death as a way to focus your involvements in life. The trick is to consult death in a way that it doesn't encumber, to use death as a tool to battle fear rather than be a morbid fixation. When making a decision, for example, make it in the light that it may well be your last act on Earth. From this perspective, there are no small or large decisions, just behaviors, which may be your last act on Earth. This helps bring to light the deepest drives and core values of a person.[44]

When you are suitably focused, the shamanic criteria for selecting the elements of your path are based on peace, strength, and joy. Once several pursuits have been initiated, you are on your path.[45] Rather than pursue money as a primary objective even though you really don't like the chase, for example, you involve yourself with something else. Viewed in the context of an energetic logic and ethic, having a large bank account is not errant, but going after money when it doesn't resonate with your core stultifies your growth. After several years of grooming your life based on peace, joy, and strength, you will have built a life with that foundation. It's not only a matter of living your life, but how you live it.

Other teachers suggest similar approaches to finding, expressing, and living core meaning. To penetrate the shrouds of awareness that interfere with developing a full and complete life, meditation and healing-technique teacher Stephen Levine also advises us to use death as a focus to bring ourselves to life. He advocates that this helps us live in a way as to "directly experience the moment-to-moment process that is our lives." And he also holds that it is fear that becomes the major impediment to this awareness.[46]

A leader of the positive psychology movement, Paul Pearsall points out the conditions of thriving include living a strong life, a deliberate life. He notes that peace and joy are aspects of flourishing. Like others, he advises, "Don't die until you've lived."[47] Reflecting increased investigations into metaphysics; positive psychology shares commonalities with classic traditions. Both find that awareness and flourishing go hand in hand, and both aptly highlight the common focus relating to personal and group development.

People usually derive meaning in their lives from group values rather than from within. Jung tells us that this makes individuation impossible, as the self is never developed, let alone lived. For individual imagination to become alive and functional, we need to be able to step away from the group. At the same time we are social creatures who derive value from participation with the group. The balance is to seek individuation while keeping an eye on what you can offer others. In this way, you learn to be yourself while being part of the group, which is a measure of self-actualization.

Personally and collectively, peace, joy, and strength characterize heightened consciousness. When these qualities manifest, the pieces of a path with heart—the activities you decided to pursue—provide the means to solidify other gains. A life formed in such a way will help you reintegrate your daily awareness after you've stepped into an altered state, for instance.

Whether or not you explore OBEs or other *psi* experiences, ontological growth automatically produces altered states of consciousness of the normal and paranormal by the simple fact of stretching into the unconscious, the unknown. How a person experiences this extension is often determined by training. A Toltec may have an OBE to better experience infinity while a Zen practitioner becomes more aware of infinity within a single breath.

Organizing and implementing expanded awareness within a Toltec, Zen, or other psychological path is the same, though, as it is part of the trajectory of gradually becoming more aware en route to creating a new baseline state of consciousness. While stylistic, creative paths share the common denominator of providing a practical means for stability along the way. Applied to the energy body, being skilled with altered states does mean you're just learning an unusual skill in relation to your normal life; you're engaging a process of reworking your life from the inside out. Everything changes.

Your path with heart is a way to begin working with cohesion. It balances the forces inside and out. This produces more awareness as your life awakens your core. Remember, all of the influences throughout your life shape cohesion, the determinant of your perceptions and behaviors. Finding out who you are, how you were created, is a matter of continual discovery. Living a path with heart offers a means to purposefully condition your energy body toward this end. This ongoing development is a solid step toward *being;* the consciousness Levine says allows us to "directly experience the moment-to-moment process that is our lives."

Perhaps we have stepped away from this life-bestowing relationship with the world because we have found too much security in the artificial stability consensual models provide. We continue to abandon the navigational rudder of silent knowledge and heightened consciousness as we surrender time and again to group consensus rather than to a higher, and possibly highest, creative power. Whether this is an effect of free will or whether we are following a time line of human evolution contained in a particular emanation that stands unchanged throughout eternity, the effect is the same. Either way, when we lose our sense of the greater possibilities of freedom that imagination bestows, we have no means to regain our natural heritage. The effect is a reduction in what we think can be done and what might actually be lived. Building a creative life entrains cohesion to a natural order, an arrangement emanating from infinity and found in the ever-present moment.

9

Living the Unfolding Moment

Life springs forth from the moment at hand. From this hinge, you can access any number of possibilities. Mathematically, we have the infinite points of connection a circle provides. Emerging scientific models suggest we have a number of alternative realities waiting to be tapped. Or perhaps the universe is inherently imagination. From any of these perspectives, experience forms from intent, entrainment, circumstance, and innate nature. By cultivating them, life—rather the perception of life—becomes exquisitely malleable. Anything can happen.

Being, the capstone of ontological development, is a precise state of awareness where creativity emanates from each and every instant. *Being* supersedes all models about it: whether the model is quantum physics or metaphysical cosmology, it falls to the wayside when you are in the moment. *Being* is a point from which you not only access infinity; you are infinity. You are fully living the unfolding moment.

BEING

In *Being and Time,* Martin Heidegger offers three basic suppositions needed to explore *being.* First, citing philosophical inquiry from Plato to Aristotle to Hegel, Heidegger regards *being* as the "most universal" concept and yet through centuries of investigation it has hardly been understood. Second, by nature it cannot be defined but this doesn't negate its meaning. Third, the quality of existence is self-evident. In each and every act, we use some aspect of *being*.[1]

Furthermore, he considers *being* as a "unitary phenomenon" and states that to study it we must define an ontological world that includes "being-in-the-world." With this grounding, Heidegger then declares that the new and significant relationship *being* offers enables us to transcend the worldly nature of life. He outlines *being* as requiring the understanding of oneness from the point of view of daily life as only then can we transcend this baseline state.[2]

First published in 1927, *Being and Time* resides firmly as part of the Western European philosophical tradition. Although we may not be any better off today in understanding something so paradoxical and so intrinsic to the human experience, over the past fifty years thanks to a growing awareness about various forms of mysticism (of which *being* is a principal component), the work of psychologists such as Jung and Maslow (which concerns fulfilling daily social needs to grow toward actualization), and now the advent of quantum physics (which reveals the intrinsic oneness of the universe), the nature of this phenomenon is getting a closer look.

Within the breadth of this work, *being* consists of maintaining a natural vibration, an ebb and flow between self and world, a grand harmony of energies within and without. In this exquisite state, you have a greater sense of self, a lightness of emotion, and a calm clarity that fills you with meaning. There is also a sense of oneness with all creation, and a feeling of having a personal place in the world. Paradoxically, this rhythm automatically carries with it the experience of nonattachment. The cosmos becomes impersonal.

Living in the moment characterizes *being,* and the moment at hand is the crossroads for potential and actualization. The moment is where life resides. Getting there and then staying there requires serious and disciplined effort, as *being* is the most sophisticated of all human behaviors.

Heightened Consciousness

Being may also be regarded as a constant state of heightened consciousness. It requires the synthesis of learning and imagination, a condition of artful living. Your first and second energy fields communicate and work together to give you a full-body sense of living. This provides your principal posture and orientation to navigate infinity.

The practice of heightened awareness takes you to more possibility, to being able to handle a variety of assemblage point positions. You now experience a continually expanding world of new options, perceptions, and abilities. As you travel deeper to core the intensity of your life increases; *psi* and mystical experiences spontaneously come into play as imagination gives entrance into myriad new dimensions.

In furthering our understanding of this awareness, Maslow has mapped out *B-cognition—being*-related cognition—in detail, assigning characteristics and values to a range of behaviors including problem solving, creativity, and peak experiences, whereas he relates *D-cognition* to deficit needs. Some of the traits of B-cognition are total attention, richer perceptions, an altered state of time and space, and positive experience. The attendant values include a sense of oneness, fairness, beauty, simplicity, and autonomy. B-cognition is a measure of self-actualization and the wellspring of creativity.[3]

While the wide-open consciousness of B-cognition supports growth-oriented behaviors, Maslow also presents it as having inherent dangers such as producing a lack of action, diminishing personal responsibility, and espousing too much tolerance. It therefore needs to be balanced in a way that practical daily requirements of livelihood may be enacted. Handling the downside of B-cognition is where a solid grounding in classical metaphysics adds immeasurable value. B-cognition then becomes a distinct class of behavior in that it contains the elements, goals, and results of a coherent, cognitive technology that impacts every aspect of our lives. We could call this behavior—the process of building and sustaining a purposeful awareness of the moment—*M-cognition, moment*-related cognition. It consists of endeavors in which you realize what is already inside you. It reflects all that goes into *metacognition,* the knowing and understanding of how it is that you come to know in the first place.[4]

In this manner, you may better come to know everything that goes into forming cohesion. To grasp this basis of perception, you need to address the mental, emotional, physical, and spiritual dimensions of individuals and groups. Added to this are the influences such as the multifaceted nature of time, culture, language, relationships, and so forth. Stepping beyond this detailed effort, you arrive at the direct sensing of cohesion, which stimulates *will*. With continued realization, you develop heightened consciousness, a direct avenue to *being*. It is then through this awareness that you navigate your daily life. By this time, you've reshaped your life, your world.

Core and Being

A firm connection with your core means *being*. Personality—the manner in which you express yourself—forms in the light of social considerations. You make your way through life trying to meet social needs, by aligning with group consensus. This has beneficial results; yet doing so may also estrange you from your individuality and from your core. B- and M-cognition skills are not yet well understood, even for individuals, so how can they be brought about en masse?

Personality is a facade, a veneer. However, strategies like a path with heart provide a means to match personality with core. When you behave from your core, or at least orient yourself to core, your personality then matches the deepest regions of yourself. As a result, you nurture a natural energy field; you enter into *being*.

Ontological Intelligence

Just to make a point, let's say that a person who is truly *being* represents the genius level of ontological intelligence. This necessitates orchestrating all aspects of the self. Each chakra needs to be awakened and in resonance with the others. Personality and core need to match. Individual and social requirements need to be in harmony. This is quite an accomplishment.

The awakening of this form of intelligence places you in the new, significant relationship to which Heidegger speaks. How you make sense of the world and how you continue to behave intelligently forms the new class of behavior aching for full examination. The study of mystical experience and other altered states provides guiding lights. Ontology is not just the study of the ways and means, the bits and pieces; it examines the whole of the person as measured by *being*. It also requires scrutiny of all connections with the environment—the being-in-the-world—and all other behaviors associated with what might be the epitome of living.

ELEMENTS OF BEING

Keeping in mind Heidegger's assertion that *being* is a unitary phenomenon and must be understood as such, here are aspects of that oneness:

1. You experience a sense of eternity within the present moment. All time seems to emanate and expand from the present. You can also witness time in different ways, such as linear, nonlinear, or simultaneous. This flexibility in perceiving time diminishes when the main focus of attention is not on the present.
2. Hand-in-hand with this sense of eternity is the sense that you want to pay immediate attention to whatever is occurring. You are in the midst of eternity and the present is just as good a place to be as any other; actually, it is the best place.
3. There is always the perception of newness. No matter how many times you travel along a certain route, there is always an impression that this is the first time you've passed that way.
4. You feel peaceful, relaxed. You might also feel a sense of well-being, from calm joy to ecstatic bliss.
5. You place the bulk of your attention on the environment and less on yourself. As you walk down a road, you pay more attention to the street, trees, people, what is happening in general, and less on your problems, concerns, joys, and other personal deliberations.

6. You feel a sense of rightness, of appropriateness. Everything in the universe is right and proceeding just fine. This might also be thought of as unconditional love.

7. You think less and use other faculties more. Thought removes us from experience (even the experience of thinking). The more we think and groom symbolic meaning, the more we extract our awareness from the essence of our lives. Putting an experience into words is not the experience; words represent the experience. Reason and thinking have value for developing certain kinds of knowledge, but they can limit us to the personality of reality and keep us from the direct experience that feeling, *seeing,* and imagination provide.

8. You feel more in touch with your core.

9. You feel confident. Your perception has a good, clean edge that enhances clarity.

10. You recognize that any reality you perceive is a reflection of yourself. You know that the way you deal with the world stems from the way you have trained your perception. This meta-cognition serves to reduce reflecting about the world in favor of heightened experience.

11. You have an innate sense of purpose. You feel meaning in your life.

12. You feel nonattached. You strive to do your best, but you are not tied to the results of your actions.

13. You feel balanced. Your physical and nonphysical energies work in harmony without the need to labor for balance.

14. You *are* and thus have less a need to know, at least in ordinary terms. You know you don't know what the world truly is, and that is just fine. You are comfortable with the magic of infinity . . . so fundamentalism doesn't take hold. You do keep tuned to further learning, though, as this revitalizes cohesion.

15. You are aware of multilevels of experience occurring simultaneously. The more you learn about a given procedure, the more likely you are to apply that knowledge. The more you apply

knowledge, the more you will innovate, or arrive at new applications. While in a state of *being,* learning, application, and innovation take place automatically. You generate effective solutions without the usual effort expended on this kind of task. These levels of experience work automatically as part of a natural, spontaneous order within your life.

This list could go on. But even trying to describe *being* by listing attributes may be somewhat foolhardy, because it is a state of consciousness beyond description. If you are in it, overanalysis will almost surely take you back out of it. But by knowing what to look for, you can begin to align your perception in the direction of this experience. In a nutshell, *being* consists of a continual, direct connection between self and world. It results from consciously awakening, the deliberate effort that leads to the natural condition of being fully conscious of being conscious.

BECOMING

Maslow maintains that self-actualization is everything that a person can become, an ultimate achievement. But we can't see what we can become because we are dominated by whatever need pulls at us.[5] *Becoming* necessitates constant venturing into the unknown. It suggests the ability to move toward, or maintain, *being,* to move with life's experiences by saturating yourself in each moment and, at the same time, by completely letting go of each moment. It is an unfolding. The conditions of your life emanate from that instant. Viewed in this way, learning is *becoming* and vice versa.

Maslow asserts that "*being* and *becoming* are not contradictory or mutually exclusive" and that both are rewarding.[6] Both require simultaneously connecting with potential and allowing that connection to give rise to actuality. Maintaining *being* requires constant *becoming* and constant *becoming* takes you to *being.* Neither is static, excessively closed, or dogmatic. The two arise from a continual dance with learning and imagination, with potential, and with infinity. In this dance you entertain possibilities and move toward those that resonate with core. But if you identify too much with these goals, you will once again pin perception to the definition, to the thoughts, rather than to the experience. That prevents you from awakening completely, removing you from the very energy of the venture. You then succumb to closure, which blocks *becoming*.

As you awaken your energy body, you automatically activate latent capacities of perception. Developing these gives rise to factors that are similar to those found in *becoming* and *being*. For example, don Juan says that *seeing* is the greatest accomplishment of an artisan because *seeing* places you at the doorstep of mastery. Yet a person can lose oneself in the intricacies of what is being *seen*. The person may become less objective and more obsessed, ending the robust ontological development of the energy body. The immediate consequence is that the person fixates the assemblage point rather than coming to terms with its nature, its relativity. This is a key point, he says, in understanding the inherent properties of perception.[7]

The skill is to remain unbiased in order to allow *seeing* to reveal more of what humans and the world are. This is possible only through *becoming*. It is the descriptions of reality that ensnarl us, states don Juan. If we remain unbiased and free as we learn, we stand a chance of complete awakening.[8]

Physicist Roger Jones helps place this in another context. He notes that Newtonian science contended that there is a clearly defined, objective world that exists independently of observation. With the advent of quantum physics, the role of the observer came into consideration, as did the notion that what is being observed can't be separated from the observer; by the very nature of quantum theory the observer and that which is being observed are entangled.[9] The consciousness of the observer directly influences what is being observed. The point here is that when measured against infinity there is no ultimate accounting for what is perceived, no encapsulating it. A new model, as measured by a new assemblage point position, will always emerge as we get better at perceiving infinity.

Flow

A main characteristic of *being* is *flow* and *flow* aptly characterizes *becoming.* Psychologist Mihaly Csikszentmihalyi explores this in his book *Flow: The Psychology of Optimal Experience.* He says that joy, creativity, and total involvement with life are all aspects of *flow,* and comprise conditions of optimal experience. Furthermore, Daniel Goleman says that being able to enter *flow* is ". . . emotional intelligence at its best; *flow* [italics mine] represents perhaps the ultimate in harnessing the emotions in the service of performance and learning."[10]

Accordingly, deliberately entering *flow* is not a haphazard, farfetched proposition. It challenges you to jettison everything that holds you back, and then catapult your awareness into regions that remain unimaginable for most. *Flow* occurs from adeptly navigating potential. A degree of abandon fosters it. You have to push forward. Relaxation is also needed. Even in strenuous athletic activity, relaxation is a main ingredient for optimal performance.[11] Developing a natural energy field also requires relaxation. Energy cannot circulate when constrained. A natural energy field has no ordinary definition; you don't have to maintain it by force. Residing in a natural field maintains *flow.* And this works hand-in-hand with heightened consciousness.

Timing

As Heidegger maintains, time offers the possibility of moving forward, of *becoming.*[12] *Being* results from residing in the continuously developing moment and for this timing carries the day. Timing in this sense means you have keen awareness of your place in the world and how to effectively navigate your path through daily life. An unnatural pace blocks imagination and learning, and thus *becoming,* and therefore you need to discover your natural pace in all activities; it's not like you have to behave only one way. Emotional intelligence establishes a strong step in discovering your innate timing. Too many thoughts about the world and you lose your sense of the world. This refined balance with the world automatically leads to peak experiences. Timing, then, stems from awareness of the moment, allows you to connect directly with the world, and promotes quality of life.

Another effect of timing is experiencing a shift from reviewing time to looking into the face of on-coming time, another element of *being*. Usually, we view time as linear, aligning our perception in a manner that we view time moving from the past to the present to the future. To make a decision, we call upon past experiences and project that information into the future, thinking the stability and predictability of the future is held together by events of the past. While this rings true to some extent, it produces self-fulfilling prophecy by weaning out potential; especially potential that doesn't immediately connect with our known world. Life then unfolds by the conditions we give it. We also see continuity in another's behavior based on our experiences with them, and then get disgruntled if their behavior doesn't fit our expectations. As we hold the order of our world to a linear progression of time, it becomes a major force affecting our perception. We forget it is a convenient arrangement to help us make sense of our experiences, and lose ourselves thinking it is the only way the world works.

To face time, you maneuver your cohesion to a new coherence, a new assemblage point position. You face upriver, so to speak, to witness the origins of time. This has the effect of enabling you to hook onto potential, to nonlinear time that spreads in many directions. This helps manage *flow*. However, time and *flow* may be viewed as entirely separate dynamics. *Flow* results from achieving a solid alignment with an emanation and then feeling the resonance of energies, whereas time and timing are the measurement of this action.

To have proper timing, you need to gain masterful control of your energy body, which involves a highly refined balance with the world. Proficiency with timing therefore rests in the artisan stage.[13] As an artisan, you can step away from the familiar and bring potential into play through *becoming-being*. To make a good go of it, your instincts must be sharp. You have to sense how to behave in the given moment and from this awareness have your livelihood provided for; in other words, from the moment you automatically lay the groundwork for what will be needed in the future. To derive concrete value from *being*, it has to facilitate and augment survival.

Timing allows cohesion to adjust naturally and helps you remain aware of core, causing more of the energy body to awaken. Thinking then reflects *becoming* rather than functioning as mechanical and static projection-reflection. Feeling turns into a measurement for timing, thereby enhancing emotional intelligence. Valerie Hunt's "mind field organizer" of emotions then allows for the formation of new cohesions. In the shamanic framework, we can relate the capacity of mind to the overall energy body and the organization of mind to cohesion. Completing the loop, thinking then *flows,* or *becomes,* from this emotion-based organization of perception. This entire endeavor brings about awareness of *will,* the epicenter of the cornerstones and the ballast for the entire energy body.

WILL AND INTENT

If we really can't talk about *being,* then why is there all this talk? First, it is the nature of humans to reflect and project, to examine their conditions and figure out the possibilities. To manage this, modern Toltecs learn to reason their way out of reason. Part of their emerging style is to make leaving reason in service of developing the whole of the organism an entirely reasonable proposition, in which reason gradually gives way to *will.* This is the proverbial slippery slope, as reason also likes to have its way, so to speak, and fixate attention. Excessive closure and fundamentalism often result from well-crafted rational arguments. Like other aspects of ontological growth, the balance between reason and *will* requires deftness. The way to learn any ontological skill is to actively engage it, to discover for yourself what it takes to bring you to life.

Will is the governing force of cohesion and a determinant of the location of the assemblage point.[14] To awaken *will,* you have to step outside of your thoughts . . . all of them. At the same time, you tap capacities of yourself that provide all of the sense that thinking provides, plus more. You can't cut off your thoughts and hope everything will come out just fine. If you arbitrarily leave thinking behind without another form of guidance, you will find yourself without means on a stormy sea. The stages of growth act as channel markers to allow you to gradually, steadily, and surely form a new relation with the world. To load the chances in favor of success, your venture must be conscious, not random.

As the basic force of cohesion, *will* is a primary means to shift cohesion. *Will* always performs this function; however, for most, *will* remains latent, doing its work without conscious awareness, which results in a diminution of potential. In the Toltec model, sustained *being* presupposes having activated *will* and having done so while oriented toward a natural field. It is quite possible to activate *will* but remain in the craftsmanship stage as *will* permits many conditional energy fields, some of which prevent further growth.

The mirroring quality of perception results from the reflective properties of the energy body's membrane, the spherical-like boundary of uniformity. In normal circumstance, the mirrors bounce back to you the self-made images of your inventory. The problem is that we get lost in our own reflections. We don't even know that *will* and the energy body form part of our anatomy as it was never introduced into our inventory. There was not a mirror so labeled to reflect it. The shamanic inventory kept it alive and therefore deserving of this recognition. In actuality, there are no mirrors. It is only a way to illustrate the mechanics of perception; specifically, the reflection that occurs throughout cohesion and at all levels. Bioenergetically, the perception of reality results from the coherence among all pieces of your inventory. The better connected the logic holding it all together, no matter if it is of the first or second fields, the clearer your picture as coherence reflects this harmony and a more integrated cohesion forms.

Disharmony, or lack of coherence, may express itself as near- or far-sightedness, to illustrate by common reference. If you're nearsighted, you won't establish a positive connection with the environment and your considerations will be highly self-reflective. Far-sightedness means you don't have a viable personal relationship with the environment, as you are too responsive to the entrainment influences of the world. You are "out there" rather than in your body. Either way, you don't have a felt sense of your energy body and how it connects to and harmonizes with the environment. Arousing *will* begins an orientation for balance within and without.

When you develop this spherical quality of perception, you may perceive a greater environment outside the membrane, which facilitates connecting with a broader range of emanations. Continuing this exploration, you begin to glimpse the third energy field. Infinity resides in each of the three fields. It's a matter of continual development as to how far you enter and explore them. The first and second fields are within and without the energy body while the third field is exclusively outside the human emanation. However, you can have a relationship with all three.

To get to the artisan stage requires placing an emphasis on reaching unbounded potential as represented by the third field. The artisan has grown beyond ordinary and nonordinary considerations, beyond the first-field behaviors of consensus society and the second-field activities of the shamans. The artisan has also eliminated self-reflection. But even if you're not an artisan, balancing with the three fields to whatever degree possible minimizes projection and optimizes timing. In addition, as you focus your awareness toward the third field, you more skillfully navigate the barriers of perception.

The transition to *will* occurs with shifts in your baseline state of consciousness, especially when targeting the stages of development. While bringing *will* out of dormancy, it is common to have altered states that cause glitches in your behavior. Your memory might not seem as sharp. Or you may stumble for words when you're usually eloquent, for instance. During a business meeting, you may experience interruptions in your thinking as imagination abruptly commands your attention. This is normal as talking is an indirect function whereas *will* places you in the immediacy of the moment, and thus you're engaging in a radical shift in your relationship with life.

Over time you'll get a better grip on such nuances. As *will* activates, for instance, your speech emanates from your entire body rather than from mental formulation. Put another way, by using *will* speech may originate from imagination, feeling, or *seeing* as a response to your internal or external environments. Instead of being an expression of subject-object relations, talking results from your entire self and is guided by intent. You may hear others talking but rather than go through your normal mental deciphering, the talking translates to awareness through feeling as it assesses the words and provides meaning. As you learn talk and listen from the body rather than from the brain it unfolds into a new, daily-life pursuit. It's a different cognitive style.

A permanent baseline shift toward *will* occurs when you are able to place the accent of your daily life on feeling and imagination. Rather than go through the day referencing what you have learned, you sense the fuller energies of the world by giving precedence to your emotional intelligence and imagination. From this, you allow learning and thinking to come and go like the ebb and flow of the tides. Your life takes on a dreamlike quality reflecting heightened consciousness. An activated *will* places you in a cosmological inspired stream of events, as it were, whereas before your life was governed by convention. You stay focused and grounded, though, by intent.

Intent consists of the deliberate focusing of *will*.[15] *Will* is unbridled energy, whereas intent is the harnessing of that energy. For example, *becoming* is developed through consciously applying intent for that result and intent guides the uses and results of imagination. Intention doesn't exist solely for these purposes, though. It is a natural ability affecting all spheres of life that is beginning to receive rigorous examination. As mentioned in chapter two, intent is under scientific scrutiny as a determinant in remote healing.

Csikszentmihalyi also says that consciousness is "intentionally ordered information."[16] "Order" includes all kinds of organization, not just verbal information. It both reflects and results from a stable cohesion of any magnitude. This type of awareness exists as a result of thinking combined with anything that enhances cognition, yet it is not thought itself. It exists in its own realm, a precursor to enacting all forms of behavior. It is also the natural world. Oceans contain order, as do jungles, as does the universe. How humans perceive that order is another matter. To supplant the order of an ordinary cohesion for that of *being* requires extended, intentional effort as you enter into the natural order.

Csikszentmihalyi continues by saying that intention is the force that maintains order.[17] We thereby have the stable intent of *being* and the intent of movement found in *becoming.* By relaxing into this pair, and by remaining vigilant to the work, you bring both to life. You *become* conscious. In so doing, you bring yourself to life in a most remarkable and intelligent manner. Humans generally entrain to the intents passed down unquestioned over generations. We then assume a fundamentalist posture as we live our lives by rote, and limit our options to those given us through status quo teaching. The group consensus of the era reinforces this as it informs us of our reality. In contrast, if you have the ability to manage your life, to produce positive experiences, to keep growing in leaps and bounds, and all the while have your awareness flooded with life each and every moment, then you are an intelligent human *being.*

Will allows possibility. Managing this is where intent comes in. It keeps cohesion focused, keeps awareness ordered, and maintains your daily requirements for life. It also allows you to access new order, new cohesions. By the time you get to a natural field, you are well beyond ordinary meaning. For, as don Juan says, his *will* keeps him alive regardless of his personal choice, or regardless of anything he thinks or *sees* about the world.[18] Having stepped into imagination to that degree, he has become a living part of all creation.

NAVIGATING INFINITY

The stages of personal development are steps to awaken the energy body. *Being* is an effect of taking these steps, a derivative of long and arduous work. The active ingredient of *being* is found in *becoming,* the motion of creativity. Sustaining *being* requires a precise life.

In the film *Apollo 13* astronauts returning from the moon had a disabled spacecraft. Based on the true story of NASA's Apollo 13 trek into space, the film depicts oxygen tanks rupturing, electrical systems failing, and the astronauts truly put to the test. In order to reenter Earth's atmosphere safely, they had to navigate their craft within a paper-thin margin. If they had failed they would have bounced off Earth's atmosphere like a billiard ball, to be sent hurling through space to meet their certain doom. Likewise, sailing the seas of infinity requires navigating a razor-thin margin. The odds are staggering, but don Juan and others have hit the mark. Why not you?

To do so, you need to be in *flow* as this is the measure of your personal relationship with the greater environment. To stay in *flow,* you have to let go. When you let go, you open yourself to many different influences. Timing plays a critical role in helping you stay focused. You then retain purpose of mind and manner. You must have your bearings as the heart and mind required to navigate infinity require discipline. In addition to your general ontological development, there are a variety of navigational tools.

Cognition

Cognitive guidance arises from the influences that produce awareness and govern our behavior. Most often, this is seated in mental activity. As previously mentioned, however, remember that emotional intelligence enhances reason. Goleman points out another side where reason balances emotions. For instance, he says that uncontrolled anger results from a lack of cognitive guidance. He says it's an inability to control base-level emotions through the application of reason. He also indicates that many of our emotional memories that have evolved over thousands of years may be out of date, ". . . especially in the fluid social world we humans inhabit."[19] If so, these emotional guideposts produce behaviors that haven't kept pace with the world we've built. As a result, we're out of touch and out of balance.

Thought focuses energy as do emotions, rendering the intermeshing of emotion and reason an avenue along the stages of awakening. Goleman points out that thought is a major influence in determining which emotions are experienced.[20] In addition, thought is sufficiently powerful in that it creates entire worldviews, entire realities. But, again, these are intellectual constructions. The meaning of cognition, and so cognitive guidance, needs to be stretched out to cover any mode of perception that promotes awareness, understanding, and knowledge. As emotions organize perception, they need to be understood as a part of cognition, along with the other cornerstones, chakras, and anything else that increases consciousness and learning. Cognition, therefore, intimately intertwines with ontological intelligence.

In this light, metaphysical systems are cognitive technologies. These philosophies contain worldviews and techniques that bring the worldviews to life. These systems can help you learn *becoming,* which then allows your thoughts and feelings to enter more expansive orders of awareness. But a metaphysical guidance system that accounts for so much can be quite intimidating. A good system can account for anything you experience. The problem, then, is that you might lose yourself in the gyroscope and not sail the ocean in front of you. To avoid this danger, a good guidance system teaches you self-guidance, not dogma. A viable system offers exactly this: a form of guidance, not a completely accurate picture of reality. When you aim your intent, the guidance it provides keeps you on track. You then develop your own guidance system. You learn how to think, feel, and *see* for yourself, which transforms outer guidance into inner guidance. When you learn this, you are on your way to activating *will,* which delivers even more powerful forms of guidance. In terms of cognition, you are substantially more aware.

Instinct and Intuition

Another form of guidance is rendered by the often-subtle perceptions of instinct and intuition. The difference between them is that instinct is "any natural and apparently innate drive or motivation," whereas intuition is "immediate understanding, knowledge, or awareness derived neither from perception nor reasoning."[21] Instinct is often considered a more biologic response and intuition a general awareness. Both result from a direct connection with the environment. In each case, your capacity to respond to the guidance makes all the difference. For instance, insight may result from a burst of energy and yet the revelation may be weak and have no lasting value regardless of the degree of euphoria accompanying it. This is different from the intense but "quiet" information made conscious during a mystical experience. As with everything else in your life, the task is to pay attention and come to your own terms, claim your own knowledge.

In the bestselling book *Blink,* Jerome Malcolm says that experience educates intuition and instinct. There is no question that experience educates instinct, especially when instinct is often considered an effect of conditioned responses. Habituated behavior formed in part from eons of evolution based on self-in-relation-to-environment awareness. Organisms generally have the innate capacity to learn from current situations and exhibit new instinctual behaviors. The imperative to survive provides the incentive to learn, to develop new responses, and to pass this along to offspring for continued modification.[22]

On the other hand, it may be that experience allows the person to accept the awareness; that is, the person permits the information to become conscious based on having an established sense of it. Behaving in new ways makes the energy body glow, says don Juan.[23] In other words, experience expands the conscious field. Repetitive behavior forms cohesion. A scientific correlate is that behavior and experience affect neural pathways. With an increase in the types of behaviors, or a repetition of specific behaviors, more of the brain is activated.[24] Correlations between brain functions and cohesion make brain physiology a useful reference for the study of the energy body and vice versa.

Healer Carolyn Myss uses intuition to diagnose physical disorders. Her skills stretch to being able to apply them nonlocally, with great physical distance separating her and the subject. And Einstein found that there is no logical path to the elementary laws of physics; arriving at them was a function of intuition. Don Juan maintains that intuition is totally accurate unless the information is clouded by personal considerations. This assertion is backed by psychological research demonstrating that intuition can be highly accurate, but prejudice and fear can lead one in the wrong direction.[25]

Intuition often delivers awareness that transcends all the information available by facts. Even though you may not have a reason for holding a point of view, it might be the more enhanced perspective leading to a wiser decision. It often requires years of experience to know whether intuition-related impulses arise from habit or genuine guidance, with difference being the maintenance of a conditional field or orienting toward a natural field.

The effective use of instinct and intuition provides the guidance to remain in the moment. A person who is *being* doesn't think, at least in exclusively mental terms. That person remains in touch with a greater sense of order provided by the complete energy body, and this is fed to consciousness by instinct and intuition. Well-developed implementation of these innate capacities reflects a marked degree of proficiency with silent knowledge, and this type of relation with the world turns learning into art.

Experts

Whether you need new plumbing or a surgical operation, advice from experts may save the day. This type of guidance is especially valuable when you either cannot clearly discern your way or you follow poor inner guidance. Within the stockroom of mirrors, there are plenty of false images and echoes. Often these distortions result from excessive personal desire, unethical power plays, fear, or worry. External reference points can offer good feedback to enable you to test and measure inner guidance. An expert may deliberately help you to orient yourself, or at least provide a sounding board so you can work through the problem. Experts can help you to break through the projective effects of conditional fields that shape your perception.

Other sides of turning to experts show that we have a marked tendency to look outside ourselves for answers, blindly follow authority, and relinquish personal responsibility: the epitome of warped guidance. To counteract this tendency and help you to stay true to your path, it is good to remember that, whatever their specialty, experts abide by their models. After all, that's where their expertise comes from. But there are times when experts know so much they have forgotten the basics. Lack of touch with the fundamentals may even lead to fundamentalism.

In his critically acclaimed book, *How Doctors Think,* physician Jerome Groopman explains that doctors may make incorrect diagnoses due to "attribution errors," where diagnosis is based on stereotypes. When a diagnosis stems from this form of projection, it may lead to the patient receiving the wrong treatment. Similarly, Shunryu Suzuki tells us, "In beginner's mind there are many possibilities; in expert's mind there are few." The Zen student is encouraged to reclaim his or her "original mind," which equates with consciousness that is neither closed nor full. It is empty yet attentive. It is assured and peaceful.[26] This teacher sounds like Maslow describing B-cognition.

Environmental Indications

New weather patterns, melting glaciers, and disappearing species are examples of the world providing guidance. Guidance derived from environmental conditions of one sort or another has long been honored. In his landmark book, *The Origins of Consciousness in the Breakdown of the Bicameral Mind,* Julian Jaynes outlines several forms of guidance based on divination. From the arrangement of sticks on a floor to the swirl of oil, to various forms of omens, humans have always sought to make sense out of their world by looking directly at it, or rather *seeing* into it.[27]

Toltecs have developed a sophisticated manner of reading omens by forming a language based on symbols that permits communication between oneself and the world.[28] Specific colors, for example, carry precise meaning. That meaning is conveyed when a certain color appears, especially if it manifests in an out-of-the-ordinary manner. For example, if to you the color orange means danger and you're considering whether or not to walk down a street and a nearby orange car honks, the communication—the guidance—is to not walk that street. The siren of a police car provides guidance and in a general fashion so do the laws governing specific behaviors. Certainly a road hazard sign is an environmental indication worth heeding.

The way in which this type of communication has formed is similar if not identical to the manner in which written, cultural languages develop. The use of environmental indications relates to how cohesion has formed. The meaning and value ascribed to them is a step-by-step process of connecting with the environment and making internal adjustments. Changes in cellular behavior are a sign something is happening in a scientific experiment, and this is the version of reality most of us participate in. The accurate use of omens highlights one aspect of having developed an equally legitimate, albeit different, shamanic reality. There's no reason why you can't access both.

At the level of *being,* the necessities of personal navigation take on even more delicate distinctions. A natural field requires you to step beyond conditional fields of science or shamanism to participate fully with the environment. Whatever occurs in your life is part of a pattern, new or old. The pattern may be unfolding or a remnant of that which is passing. The key is to pay attention. The means of navigation, from intuition to personal omens to rules of the road, are then learned as you progress along your path.

Meditation and Prayer

Another form of guidance unfolds from meditation and prayer. It comes from listening to what bubbles forth from your consciousness, either from just being aware or by asking a question that, in a sonarlike manner, results in some form of revelation. Sometimes meditation and prayer are difficult to separate into discrete functions. Other times, they are driven by specific religious or psychological techniques. Psychologist Charles Tart refers to meditation as "practices intended to change the quality or state of consciousness of your mind." Prayer, he maintains, "is effective insofar as there is a 'supernatural' or nonordinary order of Being or beings who might respond to it."[29]

Meditation has been scientifically shown to affect emotions in a positive way and in some studies meditators reported a higher level of contentment than non-meditators. And prayer has been shown to promote healing, whether the patient is nearby or at a distance from the healer.[30] Both meditation and prayer use intent but in different ways.

Meditative guidance can be the more passive while prayer the more active. In both cases, the quality of guidance stems from how well one is focused on, or attentive to, the abyss of infinity. How well you allow something beyond personal considerations to occur determines the results.

Path with Heart

With all the energies swirling about, you need focus to get on in the world. You need a rudder. This is where the path with heart plays a significant role. In the previous chapter, the guideline given for this path centered on participating in those areas of life that provide peace, joy, and strength. The objective is a life with meaning, ownership of the one book that is yours in an infinite library. In the more expansive pursuit of personal development, a path with heart plays other critical roles.

A path formed in this way also orients you to core, your natural intent. As a result, your life closes off in natural ways. You can't do everything, which means the items you select automatically perform the learning functions of closure while simultaneously remaining open. You augment your life rather than force it to conform to rules that don't match your sensibilities. The elements of your path—livelihood, family, profession, and so on—are not the real deal. *Living* your life in relation to these elements is the vital act. The lesson is learning who you are and how to parlay that into a good life. A path with heart represents a way of navigating infinity.

As you form a natural energy field, you automatically align with and experience events resonating with your core, matching your nature. You don't have to be everything to everyone. You don't need to know everything. You can have biases and incorrect assumptions. Your energy body is a spark of infinity not the entirety of it, resulting in inherent limits to awareness and knowledge as well as the breadth of wonder. You just have to be your complete, natural self.

This orientation also helps you find your personal timing, your individual relation with yourself, those about you, and the greater world. Your sense of connectedness with all areas of your life enhances your passion. Timing then enables you to sustain *being*. The circle of infinity forms yet again as *being* enhances your connectedness with the wide-open world and with your personal path. The more you find your path, the better your timing. By the time you reach the artisan stage, your timing demonstrates moment-to-moment precision.

Reflecting your growth, the elements of your path change over time. Knowing that any path might end, or that you might step off a path at any moment, helps to center you in the moment and to prevent you from thinking about how your life should unfold. While you can't do everything, you can learn to *become* and *be* as you let your life unfold naturally. Don Juan says that this results from proficient *seeing* and is marked by the capacity to seemingly vanish while remaining totally present, to become nothing while *becoming* everything.[31]

With pure learning, what you see today is different from what you observed yesterday or will tomorrow. The entire universe is *becoming,* and conditional fields blind us to that awareness. By orienting yourself to core, the circumstances of your life occur of their own accord. You then find your own place in the world, and gracefully live it.

Becoming-being contains the atmosphere of ongoing renewal, of continual discovery. It is a radical reformation of your baseline state of consciousness characterized by a natural field: awareness that has been there all along but is discovered only in the moment. It also reflects complete entrainment to your personal emanation. This enables you to consolidate your life, including setting the stage for the future while remaining steadfastly in the present. Managing your life so that you tune yourself to this requires developing the many facets of body knowledge.

Body Knowledge

In some way, the shape or form of all guidance hinges on body knowledge, learning all of your innate capacities. Each navigational tool requires paying attention to what the body senses, and to how you relate to any given event. By using your entire body—your entire anatomy—you gain the ability to connect intimately with the world. Doing so is more athletic than academic.

Body knowledge reflects a silent-knowledge understanding of

cohesion and its connection with a multidimensional environment. Generating it consists of a shift in the assemblage point that brings about immediate awareness of circumstance rather than reflecting on it. The degree to which you can step beyond self-reflective processes to allow a greater awareness to come forth marks the development of body knowledge.

In their book, *The Body Has a Mind of Its Own,* science writers Sandra Blakeslee and Matthew Blakeslee point out the nature of human perception as consisting of *interoception* and *exteroception,* or the quality of consciousness to constantly map changing conditions within and without the body. By relating these to specific areas of the brain, they maintain that internal mapping generates homeodynamics or the regulation of internal conditions. External mapping connects awareness of your body to your environment and vice versa. These processes help connect the body and brain, what they refer to as body and mind. No matter one's definition of mind, their work demonstrates that connecting aspects within self and self with the environment provides ". . . the foundation for emotional intelligence."[32]

As a brief summary of shamanic-related process, full body knowledge is governed by *will* and directed by intent. Developing and maintaining *being* centers on body knowledge. It is a natural effect of continually shifting potential into realization, of staying in touch with infinity and allowing that connection to pull the best out of you. The cornerstones of perception are all functioning, and each mode of perception is joined into a unified whole, making it possible for you to have a unique relation with the world. Your path with heart provides an avenue to this level of realization. Your life will then evolve to something beyond your current imagination. This directly pertains to cohesional intelligence as the awareness the body provides hinges on the functioning of the energy body.

M-Cognition and Transpersonal Bioenergetics

M-cognition—which covers muscle to mystical aspects of mind—represents body knowledge at its finest, a practical utilization of an extended human anatomy. It also illuminates an orientation to *becoming-being.* A person who has achieved *being* has awakened his or her energy body, and has probably used the specialized procedures of a specific metaphysical, psychological, or religious tradition. If this type of cognition were accepted and encouraged as a matter of group consensus, it would mark a radical transformation in the current human baseline state of consciousness. As don Juan says, when a person is aware, such as from the disciplined edge of awareness *being* instills, no external forms of guidance are needed as one is fully capable of navigating infinity by one's own resources.[33]

This is where M-cognition deserves further research and illumination as it concerns the development, process, and daily practice of ongoing *being,* thereby incorporating everything that goes into grooming and deliberately maintaining this behavior. For this book, coining this term serves as an exercise in imagination and hopefully helps you come closer to understanding *being.* The same applies to transpersonal bioenergetics. This term carries the necessity to tackle the same subject from a multidisciplinary approach. A wider, more detailed map of the environment needs to come forth, not only for a general orientation to life, but to make better sense of the energy body: how it is created, what sustains it. M-cognition establishes a reference for this quest.

While the terms may not stick, they highlight examining the human condition from other angles. Perhaps expanding what is currently known about B-cognition and transpersonal psychology satisfies this purpose without any fancy footwork of added terminology. That's fine, as the ability to *be* should be the focus, not contrived nuances. Consolidating all of these perspectives into a map that enables a greater understanding of human consciousness and the world we live in is the work of hand and heart. A first step is that of gaining awareness that these options exist in the first place. Then coming to terms with this requires the development of the appropriate cognitive tools and abilities. This prepares you to embark on the grandest of adventures, a voyage into the unknown navigated by your conscious participation with infinity.

10

Energy Management Skills

The following techniques apply to everyone regardless of your chosen path. They disrupt habitual behavior, rearrange how you look at the world, and liberate perception. They are part of the technological gears that enable the management of cohesion.

These skills destabilize conditional fields in a way as to enable the energy body to become more conscious. Many resources shedding light on these types of skills are readily available, including those referenced throughout this book. Further exploration depends solely on your motivation to seek answers using your own resources. Doing so is requisite for anyone aiming to claim the resources of their energy body.

DEAUTOMATIZATION

The essence of deautomatization is allowing dormant abilities to awaken by suspending the day-to-day consciousness of that which is known. This is accomplished by minimizing projection. The style of an exercise is subordinate to raw exertion coupled with the intent to fully engage the process, the learning. This is a *nonpatterning* process whereby you deliberately interfere with closure, with the tendency to create patterns of perception, a procedure don Juan calls *not-doing*.[1]

While closure facilitates learning, deautomatization prevents the formation of rigid patterns. A key to managing the deleterious effects of fundamentalism, for instance, is to accept particular teachings while simultaneously letting them go in order to allow new relationships to emerge. For this, you need to add the ingredients of personal responsibility, independent thinking and feeling, nonattachment, fluidity, constantly challenging assumptions about reality, minimizing self-reflection, and utilizing everything else that a workable philosophy provides, including leaving the philosophy behind. This is how you allow the energy of infinity to feed your awareness.

The core of deautomatization requires remaining unbiased or unfettered by interpretations, including those arising from models of reality. You don't assume the implicit facts of models, be they small or large, are unquestionable. Reality once espoused a flat world, and subsequently that all the pieces of the world are not connected. Copernicus and quantum physics, respectively, dissolved those views. It is a mistake to think that new worldviews won't emerge.

A significant advantage of this concept-free state is granting you the ability to break the boundaries of your normal way of viewing and interacting with the world. You can also reconcile opposites to find balance in the midst of the pushes and pulls of differing values and standards. You then have new options, behaviors, and problem-solving capacities. Maslow's B-cognition deals directly with this, including the inherent difficulties it presents as outlined in the previous chapter.

Practicing feeling and developing emotional intelligence, which go hand in hand, offer substantial means to reorient your stance in this world, a principal effect of deautomatization. One way to focus on feeling is to pay attention kinesthetically, to pay attention to the sensations in your muscles and physical body in general. The perspectives that follow are also in this category of managing awareness.

Self-Reflection
Self-reflection results from internal dialogue, the incessant verbiage about the world being one way or another. While it builds cohesion, it may also

lock your assemblage point into place. And what you think about the world may, or may not, be true. Whatever the case, self-reflection creates a force that influences your energy body. Tart holds that our internal dialogue continually reinforces group consensus and that "it absorbs such a large amount of our attention/awareness energy that we have little of that energy available for other processes."[2]

Stopping this internal chatter is a major way to step out of conditional fields. When you are taught to talk, says don Juan, you are taught to dull yourself. The day-in and day-out references to the same things reduce the flow of energy between you and the environment. At the same time, he states that the more fluid and varied your internal dialogue is, the more resilient you are.[3] This is part of reasoning yourself out of reason and into a more expanded participation with the world. By the artisan stage, you are living within a more comprehensive order than is provided by reason.

Furthermore, an artisan doesn't think, at least in ordinary terms.[4] The stockroom mirrors have been well cleansed, minimizing projection. There's only the immediacy of the moment to be lived, the *being* of it. It is by getting out of your self-reflection that you bring about body knowledge and heightened consciousness. Rather than ordinary mental or emotional considerations, the reflection needed for *being* consists of navigating intensity of experience.

All deautomatization skills help you step outside your thoughts. As an exercise, stopping self-reflection allows the environment—from the general conditions of your life to the greater cosmological expanse—to have greater influence. Don Juan prescribes a meditative walk for this.[5]

As an example of this procedure:

1. Walk with your hands in an unusual position that does not attract attention. The novelty directs energy away from the ordinary pattern of attention created by your usual way of walking. If you hold your hands in a dramatically unusual position, you have to contend with other people sending their energies toward you as they wonder what you're doing.

2. Direct your vision toward the horizon. If you are in a hill or

mountain environment, steadily look ten to forty feet in front of you. If you look twenty feet away, for instance, continue looking twenty feet away as you walk.

3. Unfocus your eyes, allowing your peripheral vision to absorb as much as possible.

4. Listen to and smell the environment. Feel your surroundings. You're trying to get out of your thoughts and into your body.

5. Walk at a normal pace, or slower than your normal pace.

6. For safety, walk where you don't have to contend with traffic or other obstacles. Otherwise, you're thinking about navigating rather than interrupting your thinking.

7. Once you gain competency with turning off your flow of thoughts, you can do this by intending it.

Feeling

Feeling equates with deautomatization. It counters projection. You can talk about what you're feeling, about the relation between thought and feeling, but overall doing so sheds little light on this cornerstone as experience delivers body knowledge. To begin getting a handle on feeling:

1. Don't interpret events. Accept them at face value. This form of nonpatterning means you feel them out rather than think them through. Stopping your internal dialogue is an effective bridge for this.

2. What do you feel about specific issues: politics, relationships of one kind or another, the film you just saw?

3. Now ask yourself how you feel about these. "What" and "how" are two different functions.

4. Observe yourself responding emotionally to events throughout your daily life. Objectively assess these reactions.

5. Use feeling rather than thoughts for assessment. Listen with your heart when someone speaks rather than entrain to their words. Go behind the scenes to let yourself become aware of motivation, of complete experience.

Intent

Focusing energy toward something carries effects. From prayerful direction of healing energy to a woman lifting a car off a child to perceiving precise psychic information, intent changes circumstance. It is the primary means of managing cohesion. At the same time, intent may not be conscious. It may result from enculturation, training, or other entrainment influences, and so you have an intent exerting influence, and determining your life, without conscious recognition. To traverse the stages of awakening, you need to command intent, form it into a steady stream of energy, and thereby establish *unbending intent.* Unbending intent shifts the assemblage point; it forms cohesion.

Intent is also the fabric of silent knowledge as it carries the commands that sustain all aspects of creation.[6] In relation to personal intent, you can intend something to happen in order to fulfill a wish or desire. However, artisans back away from the drive for control so they may participate fully with the emanation that sustains them. Within an emanation is intent, the hinge of silent knowledge. By latching onto cosmological intent, you enter that stream of energy. In other words, we usually regard professionals as giving their all to their chosen path, to the intent of their profession. From an ontological perspective, artisans give themselves to creation. Conscious participation with your emanation—your core intent—includes navigating this awareness as ongoing immersion in the natural order of your life, a process of "surfing" *flow* that automatically guides you to *becoming-being.*

To gain a sense of functional intent (the kind you need to direct your life in a positive manner), participate in the following process. As sports rely on physical-body intelligence, this activity helps establish a full-body relationship with intent, thereby increasing understanding. For this example, the end result is to accurately shoot a basketball. To realize beneficial results, establish the corresponding intent.

1. Gather all the characteristics of basketball into a bundle: imagine handling the ball, passing, dribbling, and shooting.
2. Imagine standing in front of a basket as though you are shooting free throws from the foul line. Place your awareness inside the

hoop, gauge the distance and force required to project the ball to the basket, and then imagine and feel the ball drop through the net for a clean score. Take a few shots.

3. Gather the sense of all of this into a distinct focus. As you do, you will realize you've stepped away from thought into a more complete relationship with the action. Your thoughts, feelings, and behavior combine to form a single motion based on the intent of shooting hoops.

4. From your beginning perspective, you're on automatic and your guidance for behavior comes from your focus of running or dribbling or shooting. Each behavior carries a specific intent. Combined, they produce "basketball" intent. From an energy body viewpoint, you are managing cohesion.

You can sense the intent of your personal emanation by rotating in a circle while standing in the same spot, then feeling the strongest direction. This is a natural intent, not a contrived version based on desire and self-reflection. This is also a good exercise to develop intuition and may be applied to problem solving. For instance, imagine various scenarios related to a specific problem and while doing so feel which one has the strongest resonance and strength as a path. Objective rendering requires keen discernment of desires, goals, orientation, and the like as you sift through your feelings.

Entrainment and Resistance

In order to be conscious of how cohesions form, you need to be aware of the basic maneuvers of opening to, and closing off, their determining influences. Depending on the situation, both processes yield benefits and drawbacks. By actively entraining your perception, such as forming a path with heart, you accept and move with particular energies. With resistance, you block a condition or circumstance from gaining sway. You may completely step away from a seductive influence or resist it in a way so as to study it. You might examine personal and professional peer pressures in this manner, for instance.

Blind refusal to acknowledge a circumstance is a negative form of entrainment rather than resistance, as this keeps a conditional field locked in place and therefore behavior associated with that field is automatic, habitual. Deautomatization suspends these types of behaviors. Faith in a divine order or being, on the other hand, entrains you to a higher level of participation with the world. Don Juan referred to this combination of being open and/or closed as being accessible or inaccessible and he encouraged inaccessibility to human-made order and accessibility to Spirit, meaning developing core awareness and a conscious connection with infinity.[7]

He also thought that worry entrained perception in an unproductive manner. When you lose your bearings and become too centered in what circumstances may portend or what others may think about you, you entrain to group consciousness rather than stay focused on self-actualization. In this light, worry is succumbing rather than creating. This neatly contrasts with constructive reflection where you contemplate and consider rather than develop hard-and-fast interpretations, an activity Goleman finds helpful to enhance emotional intelligence.[8]

The balance of these perspectives is found in maintaining your own sense of self and choosing that with which you wish to align. It requires personal responsibility and an orientation toward growth. It forms the center point of how you connect with the world.

Balance

The more your cohesion shifts, the more your world becomes fluid, and may even seem unstable from time to time, especially during transitions between cohesions. Altered states, including spontaneous *psi,* mystical experiences, and all sorts of nonsensical things might happen. To deal with this, you must continually adjust and adapt. This is where balance comes in, a combination of patience, awareness, perseverance, and fluidity—not to mention the timing involved of knowing where you want to go, what your priorities are, and what you intend to do along the way.

A core ingredient of balance is being grounded. This means you have your own life, your own solid sense of yourself. The path with heart offers this ability. But it also means you are experiencing a complete flow of energy. Charles Tart advocates balanced development of the body, intellect, and emotions.[9] Each influences the others.

Release and Recharge

You cannot develop new cohesions when holding on to the old. James Oschman references energetic signatures of trauma, and maintains that they are resolvable. And Reiki teachings acknowledge habitual patterns that are unconsciously maintained and the need to resolve these emotional structures.[10]

In general, you need to refresh your energy body just as you would take a shower to cleanse your physical body. Moreover, assimilation and elimination of energy is required as much as with physical-body processes. In Toltec literature, a principal means to do this is through the *recapitulation*.[11] This consists of methodically reviewing, releasing, and recharging your energies. By providing a means to review everything that forms, and has formed, your cohesion, the overriding maneuver of this technique is allowing core energy to surface.

Recapitulation exercises allow you to let go of cohesion automatically, so you may then let go of worry, discomfort, and that argument you just had. It is a form of forgiveness, considering that you can't change cohesion, and therefore your behavior, unless you let go of the old cohesion to make room for the new. *Becoming-being* is also a state of ongoing release in that it requires letting go of the good things in life as well. You don't turn your back on them; you let go of the moment that contained them. A path with heart sets the stage to allow good moments to keep occurring.

Paying attention to the breath is often the initial reference point for the recapitulation no matter the method. In Zen, for instance, breath is the doorway that connects inner and outer and acts as a centering point for meditation. In addition, adherents of Tantric Yoga use their breath as a fulcrum to consciously move energy through the body as well as to release and remove blockages of energy in a similar manner as outlined here.[12]

Tart says that prayer is also recapitulation. As you remind your-self of your knowledge and intention, he indicates that its effectiveness hinges on the amount of consciousness brought to the exercise.[13] These examples lend credence to the thought that a central feature of mysti-cisms is that they all focus on the universal human condition, but how they do so is stylistic.

A shamanic variation of the recapitulation utilizing breath follows:

1. Place your chin near your right shoulder. Now move it in a smooth, sweeping motion to your left shoulder. Then back to your right shoulder.

2. Adding another piece, as you repeat step 1 inhale through your nose as you sweep from right to left, and exhale through your mouth as you sweep from left to right, and then return your head to a relaxed position looking straight ahead as you exhale. That is the simple mechanics of it. Begin again with your chin near your right shoulder.

3. Now as you inhale, intend your breath to pull in the energy of the event, person, or feeling under examination. Feel yourself connect with your subject of study, and then use your breath as a bridge to bring that energy into your body. To get a sense of this, pick a minor event that is still somewhat troubling to you.

4. As you tap your memories, work from the items surrounding the event, to the people involved, to your feelings.

5. Let your body do the work. Your part is to engage the exercise and, above all, *intend* the recapitulation: the review, release, and recharge. If you feel your head wants to move in a different rhythm or direction, that's fine. Let your body be in charge, not these directions.

6. Immerse yourself in your memories without indulging. Allow yourself to fully relive the event. If your images or thoughts move to a different subject, allow this to occur.

7. Now it's time to yield to the energy. Let it work within you so you may enter all the crevices you have forgotten. Your body

does this of its own accord; there's no need to force the issue.

8. Allow the energy to dissipate of its own accord. This facilitates realigning your energy fields.

9. Get in the habit of reviewing and releasing anywhere, anytime. Even in the middle of a business conference, you can unobtrusively make one or two breathing sweeps and release energy that spontaneously surfaced. You also find that your intent sets the recapitulation process in motion whether or not you perform the breathing sweeps. What matters most is intending the recapitulation, not the specific manner of doing so. You may then feel energy moving and releasing anytime, anywhere. When proficiency in recapitulation has been developed, it is possible to gather the full sense of the process, eliminate the steps, and then just apply intent for the same results.

Relaxation

After dismissing the positive claims of meditators about meditation, physician Herbert Benson eventually decided to at least take a look. He then clinically observed "striking physiologic changes" in meditators that included lowered heart rate, metabolic rate, and breathing rate. The connections between meditative relaxation and good health were obvious and Benson went on to write his best-selling book, *The Relaxation Response,* which has remained an important work for over thirty years. In recent years, additional studies show that relaxation contributes to conditions for *flow,* and that this promotes health.[14]

Tart points out that relaxation promotes meditation and meditation enhances relaxation. He goes on to say that one set of psychological structures may prevent another from functioning. For instance, relaxation could help a person minimize physical pain but the pain might be too overwhelming to allow relaxation.[15] In application, cohesion is a psychological structure. With a disorder such as pain, relaxation might interfere with how cohesion binds and the coherence producing the pain then dissipates. But if the pain is too overwhelming, then the combination of a recapitulation exercise and relaxation might prove helpful. The recapitulation could weaken the coherence of pain, and then relaxation could step in to allow the resolution of tension, thereby minimizing or removing the pain.

Energy psychologist Gallo backs up this general principle by indicating that when trying to remove trauma, relaxation lessens anxiety and encourages healing.[16] Relaxation, then, allows energy to shift and new awareness to surface. It promotes natural timing and makes you generally more competent.

Decisions

Decisions can place you in relationship with a new emanation and modify your cohesion. They reorient your focus and therefore how you connect with the environment as they act to form new baselines of cohesion. A decision also reflects implementing cohesion. Not wavering from a decision strengthens cohesion. Unchangeable decisions, says don Juan, groom unbending intent. He advocates not changing a decision unless it is by another decision. He removes equivocation. He also advises us to make decisions free from fear or ambition. In short, he uses character to build the energy body's resources. Whether decisions are based on deficit or growth needs, or whether or not free will exists, the basis for decision-making is awareness and responsibility. He also doesn't look back, which promotes *becoming*.[17]

Nonattachment

Nonattachment brings to bear a different relationship with the world; it is not severance from anything. It offers a way to understand life, maintains Suzuki. It is when too much emphasis is placed on something that difficulties stemming from attachment become evident.[18]

Tart says that nonattachment is "learning to 'look neutrally' on *whatever* happens, learning to pay full attention to stimuli and reactions but not to identify with them." He adds that while nonattachment helps the machinery of the mind run better, there may be difficulties. One is that when a person seems unaffected he or she might really be uptight, reflecting a lack of neutrality. The other problem occurs when the person has had no practice with new situations and so acts inappropriately.[19] The remedy for both of these is more experience with an eye toward growth and improvement.

Nonattachment augments *becoming,* as you feel and think freely. Don Juan says that a person who is nonattached has only one thing: the power of decisions. When this is added to awareness of death, he continues, it leads to a life of efficiency and gusto.[20] The thing to do when you act inappropriately is to not fret and to regain your nonattachment. This is another form of deautomatization. Suggestions to begin learning this skill include:

1. Recognize that you are fully connected with the world and are responsible for your actions.
2. Strive to remain calm and unfettered during any situation. Frequent meditations may help.
3. Participate in group activities without regard for how you are perceived by the group. This doesn't mean to act foolish, but if you should behave contrary to the group's protocols, let any criticism or accolade slide away from you. A goal is to become less reactive to condemnation or praise in order to stay in touch with your own resources. And when you do unwittingly react, don't worry about it. Nonattachment helps you hold your center and to absorb experience with the least bias.
4. Remain aware that you are developing nonattachment and patiently let that awareness provide the lessons. You set into motion the lessons needed simply by intending them. Your awareness then carries the day.

Habituation

Self-reflection is often habituated thinking, in which awareness remains focused on the same options. The routine of habits forms and cements cohesion. This works positively as in performing all the habits to be professional at work, or instituting a new set of habits that enhance personal growth. At the same time, habits may lock perception in place.

Neurologist Donald Calne cites habituation as the oldest form of learning.[21] Repetition is a primary education tool. But to add to the skill of learning and to form new cohesions, you must hold what is known in abeyance in order to determine its current value.

A way to do this is to alter your routines. This could be as simple as reversing the way you put on your belt, or what time you have lunch. What is needed is disrupting influences to shake up cohesion. Remember, new behaviors stimulate both coherence and neural pathways.

In general, deautomatization supplies the lubricant to rearrange habits, to drop some of the old ones and generate new ones. Letting go of expectations of results and practicing new modes of perception both facilitate and are facilitated by deautomatization. *Dishabituation*— altering the routines that bind cohesion and restrict neural pathway formation—disorients cohesion, loosening it in order to re-form. This also supplies an antidote to fundamentalism. Otherwise, your life becomes a stereotype rather than the vital force it should be.

The formation of reality is an effect of habituation; a result of extended cultural *conditioning* whereby we entrain our resources to social standards. Behaviorism, the first force of psychology and often considered to be the most scientific of the four major branches, reveals the power of conditioning in shaping individual and group perception and behavior. Our modern world has been shaped by constant reference to the findings and values of science, for example. Entering shamanic realms utilizes the same process of conditioning by removing some values and behaviors and instituting others. With sufficient behavior corresponding to these habits, a new world comes into view. Being able to observe this natural process is a significant step toward managing it, and there's no better place to start than by self-examination.

Self-Observation

The mystic Gurdjieff thought that "seeing oneself" was part of self-remembering, remembering all the things that are a part of you, even if not yet recognized. This sense of self is a catalyst for self-knowledge, and yet it doesn't mean you really know yourself.[22] Not knowing yourself can be a good thing in that you continually allow new facets of yourself to surface.

Context—anything that applies to a situation—supports self-observation. You have structure with which to gauge your actions. Even if it is just in reference to personal desire, context provides a sense of order for what you are observing. This might be as simple as examining your motivations.

Self-observation also fosters objectivity and is at the heart of meta-cognition. Tart holds that we often fail to make a clear distinction between observer, observation, and observing the observer, yet he points out that the latter is contained in many meditative disciplines. He also advises the development of discriminative awareness by consciously attending to mental processes in a manner so as to separate input from reaction.[23] By paying attention to your thoughts, for instance, you stand a better chance of not blindly following them. And by observing your actions, you can step away from rote, conditioned behavior.

The skill of self-observation is therefore that of being conscious of being conscious. The capacity to do this increases corresponding with a decrease in projection-reflection. The more you observe, the less you reflect, and vice versa. As Tart mentions, though, some type of self-referencing is necessary to observe these effects. Furthermore, an inability to self-observe ensures discord. As Professor B. Allan Wallace informs us in his book *The Taboo of Subjectivity,* self-monitoring is a fundamental element of human intelligence and well-being, and that a loss of this may lead to unproductive behavior.[24]

In addition to self-understanding, self-observation allows for course corrections, to be able to assess how your behavior matches what is occurring. You need to *see* your behavior to change it. To facilitate this:

1. Imagine watching yourself from a vantage of a few feet away as though you were having an OBE and watching yourself.
2. Watch yourself without judging or censoring your behavior. Try not to identify with any roles. Just allow yourself to *be.*

3. Assess which behaviors provide energy and which don't; which provide peace, strength, and joy and which don't.

4. Study how you interpret events and what relation these have to the stages of awakening.

5. Observe events at face value. For instance, if you see someone walking on the other side of a brick wall, you don't see a person walking. More likely, you just witness a head moving along the top of the wall. This is the "Fair Witness" skill as depicted in Robert Heinlein's classic work of science fiction, *Stranger in a Strange Land,* where a class of trained professionals report only what is directly observable.[25] The idea is to circumvent excessive closure and not fill in the blanks even though they make sense. Don't permit imagination to overly influence interpretation.

MANAGING MODELS

Even when you encounter opposing thoughts, there is always a stable middle ground. Opposites such as external-internal, thesis-antithesis, and predator-prey, are better handled by knowing how to manage the models from which they originate. Thinking you have free will or not stems from interpreting an event based on personal conditioning, the nature of your cohesion, and usually stems from cultural cosmologies. The perception of free will may be rooted in the brain's mechanisms, with the sensation of choice being created in memory, as there is evidence that electrical impulses signal an intention to act before a person is conscious of a decision being made.[26]

Western philosophies tend to come down on the side of having free will, whereas Eastern systems are often comfortable with proposing that we don't have free will. Holding your attention in between these opposing concepts produces more awareness of the events themselves. You become more aware of experience rather than being more aware of an interpretation about the experience. This is the tightrope of life as well as the remedy to fundamentalism.

The following deautomatization meditation helps deliver awareness to an in-between point, a place of no tension between opposing points of view. Experiencing balance between two contrary ideas provides direct knowledge that concepts are the building stones of reality, that realities can exist independently of one another, and that it is possible to derive value from not continually referring, and deferring, to a specific model.

Free Perception

Humans have long struggled with oppositions such as believing we have complete free will or that we have none, with seeing ourselves as co-creators of reality or just observers of that which already is, and thinking that there is no future or that the future is already fixed. If you have deep-seated beliefs regarding any of these concepts, temporarily suspend your beliefs and play for a moment in another sandbox. If you have difficulty forming an image or perception of any step, pick a thought or object that somehow relates to the step. I also suggest familiarizing yourself with all of the following steps prior to proceeding.

1. Visualize, feel, or otherwise perceive a sphere of energy representing the joy of having free will. Immerse yourself in this sphere and allow it to fill your entire being. Your decisions are yours. You have the natural freedom to make your own choices.

2. Place this energy aside for the moment and perceive an energy sphere representing the magnificence of not having free will. You are part and parcel of a divine order and you realize how intimately you are connected with the divine as you perform as an actor on a stage. Your part has already been given to you. Have fun with it.

3. Place both energies before you, equal in distance on each side of the center of your perception. Place your attention in between these energies. Find the balance point—the free perception point—where you are in harmony and feel no tension between the two energies.

4. Leaving that awareness, visualize, feel, or otherwise perceive a sphere of energy representing the brilliance of co-creating your reality. Through give-and-take, you interact with the entire cosmos and your reality is molded.

5. Placing this awareness momentarily aside, perceive an energy sphere representing the power of gradually becoming aware of that which already exists. Movement through time and space exists only as an exercise in perception. All time resides in the present and moving through space is the movement of mind. Everything always was and always will be. As you increase your awareness and travel through what we call time, you gradually become aware of that which already was, is, and always will be.

6. Bring both of these energies to the fore of your awareness. Go in between them to the free perception point. Allow whatever perceptions that occur to occur.

7. Leaving that awareness, in your own way perceive a sphere of energy representing that there is no future. The future manifests only as a result of what happens in the present. And the present is the present. "Future" is only a thought.

8. Place this energy aside for the moment and perceive an energy sphere representing the future as already existing. Rather than causing an event to happen as a result of your thoughts, you have those thoughts because the event has already occurred. All your actions are preordained. You travel through your feelings to the place where they have already happened. We are all catching up to find out what is already there.

9. Place both energies before you and place your attention in between them at the free perception point. Notice any and all results.

10. Using your imagination, form a triangle. The three points of the triangle represent the free perception points of steps 3, 6, and 9.

11. Inside, at the center of the triangle, find the free perception point, the place of no tension.

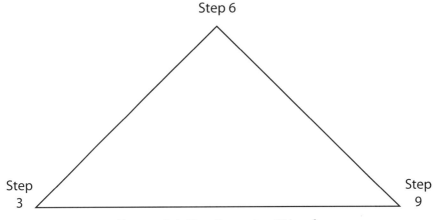

Figure 10.1. Free Perception Triangle

12. At the free perception point notice a speck of white light. Approach the white light, which grows larger, more brilliant. Place your attention at the threshold of the light.

13. Hold the question "What do I need to learn most at this very moment?" in your consciousness. Then feel free to ask anything you wish, like "What would be a good learning task?"

14. Leap into the white light. As you do, release your question and allow it to flow away from you into the light. Allow the answer to return in its own time by any means of perception.

15. Remain in the light as long as you wish. Return when you wish.

A	Balance	B
free will	free perception	no free will
co-creator	free perception	aware of that which is
no future	free perception	future already exists

Each of these elements is a type of cohesion, a certain assemblage point position. Notice that the concepts of column A and column B are logically consistent. Not only is one secular and the other religiously oriented, being a co-creator with the divine follows the thought that you have free will and that you can use your *will* and intent to build your world. In the same manner, becoming aware of that which already is follows from having no free will and that the future is fixed in place. You can add to the elements in each column as long as all of the elements of a column remain consistent and can be logically related to each other.

When a sufficient number of elements have been brought together, you have a model, perhaps an entire philosophy and maybe a full-fledged reality. Use the exercise to step in between science and shamanism, for example, with science representing a world built through reason and shamanism a world formed through cohesion. By doing so, you won't be bound by either yet may enjoy the fruits of each. The constellations of thought resulting from these approaches to life influence perception, which influences behavior, which influences experience. Experience then self-validates the respective philosophy, which produces a loop where perception and experience are already determined.

Finding the free perception point and using it to move the assemblage point is one of the more valuable results of commanding this skill. When perception is not hemmed into a point of view, it has greater freedom to move. This cleansing action may also be used as a deliberate step toward mastering imagination as this exercise represents stepping beyond the ordinary into what might be. In this manner, the ability to manage models provides a path for discovery.

Seeing

Seeing is cutting straight into streams of energy. It often carries a visual sense associated with perceiving different forms of light, but is not itself visual in the normal sense. As it requires using the entire body, this type of awareness makes sense from kinesthetic and intuitive channels. It consists of a shift in cohesion that establishes a relationship with the environment that activates this cornerstone. For this, you need to be mindful of your connection with the world and allow a type of communion to move you beyond normal perception.

Seeing may be unique to a person in the way information becomes conscious. The structure of light may vary while the meaning remains constant, for example. Two people could *see* differently but arrive at sim-

ilar conclusions. There seems to be common features as well. An interesting anomaly, for instance, is that when a person *sees* during daylight,
the environment becomes darker, and conversely a dark environment
becomes lighter. Completely *seeing* another person's energy body often
translates as perceiving packages of luminosity. The energy body might
appear as an oblong ball of light, and the surrounding world comprised
of long strands of intense yet softly glowing strands of light.

A preliminary to *seeing* is gazing, or opening up. The Free Perception
exercise is a good place to start. The following steps, here described in
relation to *seeing,* can be used to develop any mode of perception. It is
a deautomatization exercise that permits the energies forming cohesion
to circulate more freely and allow new perceptions to surface to a conscious level.

1. Relax. Try to be nonattached to anything you perceive. Let go.
2. Establish your intent to gaze.
3. Don't focus on the world as you normally might. Don't pick out
   an object then look or stare at it. Let your eyes go "soft," unfo-
   cused, but with a steady gaze. Your sight may be directed toward
   a specific object, but you simultaneously expand your vision to
   the full periphery.
4. Feel your body merge with the world. Remain centered within
   your body as you connect with the external world. Feel the flow
   of energy.
5. Gazing at shadows is very relaxing. You can use virtually any
   shadow to gaze at. To elevate the level of skill, form a full pattern of shadows in the same manner you would create a tree
   out of branches and leaves. Instead of attending to the normal
   features of leaves, branches, and so forth, you construct the tree
   from the shadows within it.
6. If you *see* a haze or rain of light, a thin film of energy, or what
   looks like swirling dots, let them be. Don't focus on them or
   you will pull back your prior cohesion and refocus automatically
   on the ordinary, physical world. You'll restore your normal habit

of viewing the world. The light is the energy world breaking into your awareness; you are *seeing*. Later, when you gain more experience, you will be able to focus on that energy and it won't disappear. You will then be able to expand that world. But until you train your eyes, and your body, your old habits of perception will rule. Later, you'll have a new set of habits and can tap the world of energy anytime, anywhere.

Seeing automatically removes the influences of models. What you do with your experiences—how you interpret them—remains quite another matter. You might end up building elaborate models that have no lasting effect other than halting your growth. When *seeing* occurs, let go of habits, including those found in models, in order to take your skills of orchestrating various energies to the next level.

As with any learning, experience modifies your awareness in such a manner that you can make more sense of what is *seen* as you have more relation to it. At the same time, *seeing* removes you from preconceptions and accelerates learning. A gifted novice can *see* into a business problem, a scientific investigation, or the workings of the most advanced philosophical discipline. What is done with that awareness is yet another matter. A novice and master are both subject to the same learning dynamics; however, implementation of what is *seen* hinges on cohesion being developed to a corresponding level in order to act on the awareness. This is what the master has mastered.

Imagination

We live in the fabric of imagination, our portion of infinity. We experience its multifaceted landscapes and express this in terms of what we have learned. One way to work with imagination is through dreams, these being the stuff of imagination; in essence, they are one and the same. The following suggestions may help orient you.

1. When you recognize you are dreaming (either during sleep or day-dreaming), drop your awareness into your gut. Odds are you'll find yourself centered in your head as you chatter on about everything.

2. As you enter the region of *will,* feel yourself tracking the dream images. Set the objective of stabilizing this visual stream into a storyline, into a consistent dream environment. The procedure for this consists of simultaneously paying attention to yourself and the dream with the intent of participating inside the dream. This is more an athletic maneuver than an intellectual problem.

3. One of the more imposing obstacles to entering imagination is self-reflection. When the dream begins to shape up, you may reference the past, future, anxieties, joys, or what have you. After all, doing so is habitual. But here it is more than a distraction as you need to face into time, face forward into the emerging experience in order to fully participate inside the dream.

4. Experiment. Find exercises and maneuvers that work for you. These come of their own accord by paying attention to the entire experience—all aspects of what is occurring within you and of imagination. To give you an idea:

   a. As outlined in chapter four, meditate until you enter blackness.

   b. Then intend a shift into imagination. For instance, imagine you're walking down a street in a foreign country, dressed in native garb. From inside the dream, position yourself in back of yourself. Hang back so you can watch yourself walking down the street. Keeping focused on the goal of entering imagination builds unbending intent.

   c. Imagine that energy bodies begin to rain from the heavens. An energy body falls a little distance away but directly in front of you. Inside this energy body is a version of you, dressed as you are, and looking straight at you.

   d. Place your attention inside the version of you that is walking down the street. Transfer your attention to the version of you that is inside the energy body, and then perceive the dream from that vantage.

   e. Use this imaginative play to get a sense of transitions so you may surface inside the dream itself.

5. During these shifts, especially if you fully enter the dream, you may find yourself in a high-energy, high-potential zone where anything can happen. It is as though your assemblage point is free falling. Until cohesion stabilizes, you remain susceptible to any entrainment influence. The slightest fluctuation of thought or feeling can end or redefine the dream.

6. You may also feel movement, from floating to high-speed travel. Allow these sensations. Breathe easy and stay relaxed. You want the transition to begin and to end with your awareness inside the dream. With practice, you'll figure our how to regulate speed, just like learning to walk or run.

7. You may also experience a range of sounds and vibrations. It may even feel as though a train is rushing past your doorstep or a tornado is crashing through your room. This is normal. Let the fright go and move on.

8. Surf the transition. To ride the wave you have to navigate it on its terms, all the while remaining centered within and focused on entering imagination.

9. Initially, your focus was to enter a dream. At some point, aim for another goal in order to apply your new ability. For instance, when inside imagination gaze at the dreamscape in order to *see*. You're in heightened consciousness and this provides the where-withal to become more proficient with your abilities. From within imagination, you'll find *seeing* easier, keener, and more productive.

Imagination allows you to break free of conditioning to enjoy new models, new arrangements with your life. *Seeing* permits you to cut through to the essence of something, anything. Feeling offers an efficient means of guidance. Combined they intensify experience and boost learning. The use of these cornerstones and skills allows you to manage your energy body and chart new paths. They are the basics that may be applied to any stage of development allowing you to step through doorways of learning time and again.

11

The Heartbeat
of Learning

Regardless of your stage of development, having the basics of learning under your belt is essential in order to consciously awaken. As characterized by working through altered states to discrete altered states to a new baseline, each shift in cohesion represents learning. The more awareness you have integrated, the more you have learned. The greater you plug into the environment, the more awareness you have. And in an infinite world, there is always more.

The heartbeat of learning consists of continually expanding into imagination and then contracting that awareness into practical application. All of the imagination and learning perspectives in this book serve to help you regulate your energy body to permit this form of accelerated learning. As with anything else, you can keep developing these and other techniques to elevate your level of ability.

COMPONENTS OF LEARNING

The following section provides an overview of a few key aspects of effective learning. They are meant to enhance understanding of cohesional dynamics as they build on the known world while taking into consideration

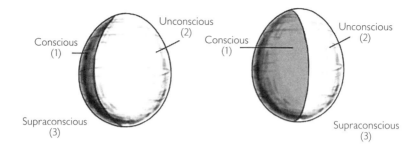

Figure 11.1. Energy Body Learning

From a shamanic perspective, learning and imagination provide a rhythmic process of increasing the known and reducing the unknown portions of the energy body. Understanding that there is an aspect of existence that can never be known—the unknowable—serves to keep the arteries between learning and imagination open and vital.

venturing into the unknown. Skills and processes referenced in the previous chapters promote the development of each these behaviors.

Memory

In daily use, we relate to memory as consciously recollecting the past. Examining how this occurs, scientific investigation has defined memory as ". . . the way the brain is affected by experience and then subsequently alters its future responses." Memory therefore creates a hinge to look at how past events affect future behaviors. In like manner, don Juan holds that our experience of the world is based on memory.[1] Reality, then, both personal and consensus, is constructed in part from a stream of associated memories that create a pattern, a view of the world. There needs to be continuity of learned relationships in order to make a leap from past events to figuring future responses, and the options for this behavior stem from what has meaning, value, and relevance as these are the forces that collect memories.

In a brain model, continuity of perception results from the formation of neural networks. Repetition of experience and the internal narrative that cements the meaning of experience stabilize these pathways, producing long-term memory. A wide range of associations occur during correlating certain letters to form a word, for example, to how bio-chemical activity gives rise to cellular interactions and pathways. Nobel Laureate Eric Kandel says this process requires an anatomical change, rendering a more lasting and complex network.[2]

This hardwired network changes as the web of memory changes and vice versa. It may expand due to new experiences or dissipate from lack of use. Having more contexts from which to derive meaning from new experiences adds to how the brain adapts. Part of this *neuroplasticity,* says psychiatrist Norman Doige, comes about as the abilities and func-tions of memory change as a person grows older. Children's memory carries different qualities than those of adults, for example.[3] One might speculate that these types of variances are also found among the stages of awakening, with each new stage reflective of a more enhanced neural network or energetic coherence.

Another portion of these mechanics is that a person can use the same plastic quality of the brain to unlearn their continuity by remov-ing associations that lock memories in place. Remove a piece of the interlocking aspects of an event that gave rise to a memory and the neu-ral network dissipates, thereby changing or eliminating the memory. Likewise, if you can summon a sufficient number of associations, you can restore the entire memory.

In this manner, you can also reshape mind. Just as memory reflects your repetitive behaviors and internal narrative, which give meaning to experience, it conditions perception as to what forms your inventory. Mind is therefore structured in the same manner as neural networks. It then fol-lows that the nature of the network indicates the way mind has been con-ditioned. Perhaps inventories and neural networks are mirror images.

Possibly even more indicative of the flexibility of memory, imagina-tion can be used to intentionally make changes in the pathways and determine new memories, a purposeful remodeling of networks. This doesn't mean you changed the event that placed the experience-memory in your neural network; it means you have a new *perceived* relationship with the continuity of experience, which then alters your narrative, your stream of thoughts about your life. In practice, for instance, you may rearrange facts to establish a new past-to-future continuity and in so doing give yourself a chance to respond more intelligently. Applying this to reality, a consensus view of the world results from people sharing a similar network, and this has the effect of reinforcing specific pathways of perception. Change the network sufficiently and you change reality. It's a matter of how potential and actual interact. This is a bit of the metaphysics behind the formation of what is deemed to be "real."

In addition, a person's affective style influences memory. Candace Pert maintains that emotion is a means of activating a neural circuit through-out the entire body.[4] Therefore your emotional stance helps form memory by developing your narrative, the resulting associations, and then the con-tinuity of your reality. Meditation and relaxation promote emotional flu-ency and therefore the ability to access other states of consciousness.

This brings us back to the location of memory. Most researchers rel-egate memory to the brain. Reflecting their whole-body approach, Toltec shamans ascribe to a different model and so place it in various places throughout the body. Through centuries of examining memory through *seeing,* they reached consensus that the brain registers, not determines, what takes place in the physical and energy bodies. Memories associ-ated with specific parts of the body then stimulate certain areas of the brain. Scientific considerations supporting this shamanic perspective are beginning to take root. For example, in addition to Pert's findings, by relating memory to the extracellular matrix the entirety of the body is involved with memory.[5]

As Kandel mentions, it is scientifically accepted that different types of memory are relegated to different regions of the brain. For example, peak experiences suspend and stimulate specific brain functions. Also of interest is the Blakeslee's presentation of a brain-map model where memories initiating behavior of learned muscle responses emanate from brain maps. While the map represents functions, the brain remains the controlling focus. Yet another consideration Lipton puts forth is the emerging evidence indicating that cells use their own style of memory for intelligent decisions to help ensure their survival.[6] It is as though each model, scientific and shamanic, mirrors the other yet with first cause originating either in the brain or the body. After all, since each approach forms and is formed by memory, each has entrained to a different narrative and continuity. Taking in all of this, shamans could simply be wrong, or perhaps science has not yet developed a model that permits different insight. And perhaps factual only relates to a model, not necessarily to an actual condition.

These models are also similar in terms of the formation of neural networks and cohesion. Experience combined with repetition of narrative creates energetic structures in the brain or in the energy body and the ability to remodel networks or cohesion seems evident. From a biophysics perspective, it is possible that shamans first measure the behavior of energy and how that translates to anatomy and physiology whereas scientists usually seek first cause by studying physiology.

In that neural networks and cohesion form in similar manner and have similar effects, they provide useful models to study each other. A network becomes permanent, for instance, the more you develop a certain skill or viewpoint. This also reflects a cohesional shift: the more extensive and interrelated coherence, the more extensive the baseline. The more memory networks you have, the more you step toward a new stage of awakening. In each model, the breadth and depth of the respective network marks the difference among individual abilities as well as overall ontological condition, or total-life focus.

In addition, Tart addresses the phenomenon of *state-specific memory*.[7] Experiences in ASCs or d-ASCs, for example, illustrate this as you must return to the constellation of perception associated with an altered state in order to remember it. To bring the event to a conscious working memory, you need sufficient repetition of the memory, which enables it to be easily referenced as you've formed the required neural networks.

Looking at this from the energy body, remembering means you have returned your assemblage point to the place associated with the experience; you have shifted cohesion to the coherence storing the memory. This applies to ordinary and state-specific memory. For instance, you may not remember having had an altered state until your cohesion expands to where it fully incorporates the experience associated with the memory, until you have the wherewithal to manage your ASC and place it in a new baseline. For all types of memory, the recapitulation provides the intent to consciously remember in order to review and release the energetic fixations.[8]

Shamanism also puts forth quite another reference, another set of associations, for the relationship between memory and experience. In terms of multidimensional reality, a new memory could mean you've actually jumped realities into another stream of experience. Your memory changed because in this new continuity the event didn't occur in the same manner as it did in your prior memory. The event is materially different and is part of a continuity matching your new memory. Another way of saying this is that you latched onto a different emanation. When you have either memory, it is because you have aligned with the energy emanation that carries the respective experience.[9] *Seeing* provides a means to assess the nature of emanations as it allows direct perception of the flow of energy. From this point, managing memory takes on new features. Tapping different emanations may produce memories of other dimensions, of heretofore unconscious healing practices that are naturally embedded in the energy body, or of a long-forgotten event brought forward in time by the recapitulation.

Just as there are various forms of intelligence, there are aptitudes relating to memory. These often influence one's choice of professional path as it connects to natural ability, meaning, value, and relevance. One person might have excellent recall of textbook instruction, while another is fluent with science fiction concepts, and yet another adept with remembering nuances of people. One person's bent of memory might lead to a synthesis of aspects of time that accounts for teleportation to how *psi* functions to speed of cellular communication, while another person invents a fuel-saving automobile engine, while yet another person produces Broadway plays.

From this brief overview, it is evident that memory plays various roles in our lives and affects learning in ways far beyond the single act of recalling the past. What, then, can be done to work with memory as applied to your energy body? The following techniques offer a guideline. If needed, please refer to previous sections of this book where they are presented in more detail.

1. In general, deautomatization suspends associations and perhaps complete neural or cohesional networks. Depending on the specific technique, certain areas of the brain and energy body may be activated or held in abeyance. This allows you to deliberately intend changes to bring about a range of behaviors such as changing a specific memory to how you use memory to entering new meanings about memory.

2. Stopping your internal dialogue is ideal for interrupting your narrative. Upon examination, you'll discover you have a storyline for all your activities. If you continually carry around everything you find meaningful, you limit learning. Step into fresh, open, unbiased perception from time to time. This is the center of *being*.

3. To lessen the hold memories have on your cohesion and on your neural networks, recapitulate the events forming your life. During the recapitulation you deliberately recall events, and often events long forgotten unexpectedly return to conscious memory. The exercise then allows you to discharge the energy holding together the cohesion without losing the memory or learning.

4. To encourage a new set of relationships, meaning, and continuity forge your path with heart.

5. Rigidly holding onto memories inhibits new awareness. This narrative prevents formation of new pathways, new cohesions. Dishabituation provides for new experience and new energetic structures to form. When you base future behavior solely on past events, you block imagination and the ability to respond to the world in new ways. In this manner, memory can be managed rather than allowing it to remove the remembrance that we are part of infinity and live in a multidimensional world.

Intelligence

In his book, *The Genius Within,* neurosurgeon Frank Vertosick places intelligence beyond commonplace memory, saying it is ". . . the general ability to store past experience and to use that acquired knowledge to solve future problems."[10] In *How the Mind Works,* cognitive science professor Steven Pinker presents it as ". . . the ability to attain goals in the face of obstacles by means of decisions based on rational (truth-obeying) rules."[11] Both orientations pose a range of questions: How do we define a goal? Is intelligence a biological imperative or an aesthetic decision? What is rational? Is it intellectual alone or can we also apply it to obeying rules through the use of intuition or *seeing*? And what is the method for determining "truth"?

Vertosick points out that some bacteria possess intelligence since they defeat antibiotics as they surge forward and evolve into highly resistant strains. They don't use mental intelligence; chemistry has been their language for millions of years producing a highly successful way of solving their life-threatening problem of antibiotics. There has to be some form of "truth-obeying" rules on which the bacteria base their form of decisions.[12]

From a similar principle, animals overcome obstacles to successfully migrate or to alertly watch over their own kind as they take shifts in eating and acting as sentry. According to the definition of mind presented earlier, animals don't possess mind as they don't self-reflect in such a manner as to create inventories. They abide by a natural intelligence that is not rational in the ordinary use of the term, yet is rational as they behave in line with some type of truth-obeying rules that can be highly intelligent. Both bacteria and animals act rationally in that their behavior works, not that it reflects intellectual logic. To therefore relegate intelligence to intellectual properties removes humans from the environment, diminishes awareness, and estranges us from the greater order of life.

As often considered, intelligence also pertains to fluency of insight regarding the prevailing model, be it of a laboratory experiment or a worldview. There are different facets to this. For instance, the ability to form detailed constructs from an already established model is beneficial. Doing so reflects a standard view of the role and value of memory. A person might then provide a more elaborate, scientific picture of cellular behavior. There also exists the ability to take existing pieces of a model, or different models, and develop new context and applications, which indicates creativity and learning. At the same time, relegating rote recall of facts, no matter how sophisticated, as being a pinnacle of intelligence undercuts efforts to extend consciousness into new areas as it enhances the status quo rather than extending awareness into imagination to foster leaps of learning.

In addition, speed of processing information is often hooked to defining intelligence, as with IQ measurement where this is reflected in the score. In resolving a crisis, speed helps. This may translate to life or death. Rapid learning is a sight to behold. But speed is also relative to the method being applied to achieving a goal, and quickness doesn't always equate with the ability to produce optimum response. For instance, a person may process information so quickly, he or she misses data that should be included but is not part of their inventory. The degree of objectivity summoned also plays a role in the quality of their perceptions.

Or, for another example, one person could come up with an excellent solution in two minutes only to be trumped by another person who has meditated for ten hours and then delivers an answer that formed suddenly, without mental deliberation, in the instant prior to ending meditation. Yet another person could philosophically ponder and, by relating the situation to a wide range of possibilities derived from experience and memory, come up with the most intelligent answer. Furthermore, acting too quickly may produce detrimental consequences such as from inadequately measuring ethics or not fully determining the long-ranging effects on the environment of a technological invention. Speed might solidify an ignorant response and reflect lack of intelligence.

At the same time, as speed of processing can apply to any form of intelligence, it does stand as a legitimate measure. But what is being measured and to what end? What expresses more intelligence: speed of mental processing or speed in utilizing imagination? Processing therefore needs to be based on natural ability of the whole person. Forced speed, an arbitrary requirement to perform quickly ingrained in many cultures, prevents *being,* which represents a natural relationship with the world and carries its own timing. Owning up to and abiding by an innate trait is intelligent behavior and shouldn't be tagged solely to speed. We need, then, to question the viability and value of measuring intelligence rather than allowing it to unfold. How this relates to an individual's style of what information is processed and in what order are part of the consideration. This brings to bear ontological intelligence, which finds expression though a path with heart. If limiting definitions cause us to overlook something vital to our well-being, individually or collectively, then it isn't intelligent behavior.

Having said this, speed of learning is essential to navigate the stages of awakening, to actually find yourself in the artisan's domain before you run out of time in life. Perhaps time and the ability to manage time, including personal timing, should be examined as a distinct form of human intelligence. To refine ontological timing, you might decide to alter your normal rate of walking. For some, it may also seem like you're not processing events quickly enough to keep up with others and you may be viewed as embracing a diminution of intelligence. Fear of being ostracized may then add pressure to conform, resulting in estrangement from self.

In addition, timing is principally measured by feeling, which again brings to bear emotional intelligence. Using Valerie Hunt's consideration that emotions organize the mind, then a person who is not as fast with mental processing as another but quite adept with emotional processing of information—something that is not generally measured in contemporary life—should, in these terms, be the more intelligent. From this angle, the intellect only processes a portion of what emotional intelligence is capable of processing. This notion alone reshapes how we would view intelligence.

Another type of intelligence to consider placing in textbooks is *multidimensional,* or the ability to relate many dimensions to each other and simultaneously to the problem at hand. You may also think of this as spherical, or full-bodied, intelligence, characterized by the ability to synthesize seemingly disparate pieces of information. The Free Perception exercise in the previous chapter serves as an example of weighing opposite concepts to arrive at new insight. Developing this ability might require venturing into other dimensions as doing so provides experience for enhancing memory and a wider perspective to assess problems and goals. You might then process and synthesize information better, if not faster, to arrive at an imaginative solution.

Doige says novel environments trigger *neurogenesis,* or rejuvenation of the brain.[13] By exploring areas of perception and consciousness other than those of consensus reality, you stimulate not only your energy body but also neural pathways, which augments ability. This is another indication that cohesion and neural networks correspond and may influence each other. Through stimulation both can rebuild and even expand, and the manner in which this occurs illustrates how one model helps make sense of the other.

As with any form of intelligence, it's all for the better if someone has intellectual prowess. But is it being used to awaken the entire energy body or just a narrow range of functions? As with Tart's view of memory, intelligence needs to be assessed as a state-specific phenomenon, something that cannot be a one-size-fits-all approach. Intelligence, like other behaviors, functions from cohesion. The ability to manage cohesion changes the landscape of intelligence, of potential, of possibility. Doing so indicates the ability to learn, perhaps the defining aspect of intelligence.

From an energy body perspective, the basis of intelligence is cohesion, the general determinant of awareness and problem-solving ability. Cohesion forms through learning and imagination, and thus the degree of awareness relates to the breadth and depth of cohesion. The nature of cohesion also corresponds with problem-solving ability. Through understanding and managing the intelligence of the energy body, you awaken multiple intelligences such as those outlined here and in chapter eight, with all of these influences combining to enhance ontological intelligence.

Cohesional intelligence spins these considerations anew; new doors to discovery abound. All said and done, awakening your energy body leads to your natural intelligences, including the best way to implement them—keeping in mind that the way you use what you have also relates to intelligence. The cumulative effect of employing these intelligences is that of bringing yourself further to life, allowing your potential to be realized, and enabling you to experience a deeper, more meaningful life.

A few perspectives for grooming intelligence include:

1. Use memory for reference, not for strict maintenance of your reality. Memory provides a foundation for continuity and continuity hardwires memory. A fixed continuity means you've a conditional energy field and the aim is to work through such fields to a natural field of *being*. At this point, continuity takes on completely different meaning.

2. Experience, experience, experience . . . as many aspects of life as you can. As outlined above, experience feeds your brain, energy body, and all of their systems.

3. Relate your experiences to each other and to others' experiences. Draw diagrams of these relationships if doing so makes this more effective.

4. Study energy body mechanics. Learn the ins and outs of cohesion as all forms of intelligence are governed by their respective cohesions.

5. Try to sense connecting with the environment and the related rate of processing information based on being focused in your thoughts and head or in your feelings and entire body.

6. Don't be concerned with looking completely ignorant on a regular basis. Allow yourself time to absorb and process information without feeling you have to appear "in the know." Over time, this contributes to expanding your cohesion and knowledge.

Objectivity

Objectivity provides both ballast and rudder for inquiry. It centers you, enabling a means to better navigate your life. It is also an effect of learning. As professionals learn more about their specialty, for example, their objectivity is enhanced as they obtain a wider angle with which to measure. This could lead to fundamentalism, though, as you might settle into the wider picture and unwittingly get lost by constantly cross-referencing the same thoughts and feelings, thereby preventing further exploration and learning. Objectivity requires mental and emotional intelligence devoid of reactivity caused by excessive allegiance to a specific cohesion.

The same applies to consciousness development: the more you develop ontologically, the more objective you are about life in general. You deal with situations as they are, rather than what you imagine or want them to be; you bring potential to what is actual rather than ignore the actual. Then again, you stand to lose yourself in your imaginative adventures, as real as they might appear, and never enjoy the grander scheme brought about by awakening your core to infinity. This is the difference between a life lived in terms of social dictates, or lived in line with the way you were created.

In dealing with these ins and outs, objectivity provides a significant influence in forming cohesion as it reflects the need for accuracy in building an inventory. With diligence, and the secure relationships among data provided by logic, cohesion's baseline incorporates core awareness. Projection and reflection are thereby minimized, and ethical balance and overall harmony automatically begin to enter consciousness and behavior.

As Tart points out, a great discovery of our time is that what seems to be objective observation actually reflects the biases of the experimenter. Science, often considered a bastion of objectivity, is a social enterprise. It yields to logic from group consensus. This presents both blessing and curse. The nature of it requires that scientific data be available to the group, especially to qualified investigators who assess and respond. When an experiment can be replicated time and again, the group accepts the results and we have another benchmark to measure novel studies.[14] And so knowledge moves forward.

The downside is that new data is often expertly refuted as it doesn't fit with established models. While the cooperative nature of research supports objectivity, it is easy to get lost in current knowledge as it becomes interpretation based on what is thought to be possible and is therefore not at all objective. In a study of creativity, for example, psychiatrist Nancy Andreasen points out that while observations may be objective, the results may be subjective.[15] A conclusion from arranging facts in a certain order might not be objective; it might result from biased memory or personal desire.

Illustrating this energetic, there is a contingent of people who propose the earth is hollow, possibly providing an inhabitable environment. Contradicted by all measures of modern investigation, this thinking has been relegated to pseudoscience.[16] Looking at this from another angle, the proponents of this theory might be sensing that the backdrop of the physical world is not comprised of physical matter but of energy. Without having context for this form of sensing, their perceptions of an extradimensional environment gave rise to an interpretation that the physical earth is hollow. That is, while they extended their awareness and sensed something different (the absence of solid earth), their interpretation could have been influenced by a lack of context, a diminished awareness of cornerstones and quantum physics, for instance. The initial perceptions may be objective; the interpretation is not. Their perceptions legitimately stand to extend the current worldview, but then fall into disrepute due to the interpretations. The seed of knowledge never bore fruit.

William Byers, author of *How Mathematicians Think,* makes an interesting case that further illuminates this dynamic. He says that while logic provides stability and common reference, math transcends logic. It exists beyond a collection of answers and *requires* [italics mine] a subjective component. This leads to *understanding* [italics his]. Understanding requires intuition. This sets the stage for the logic that stabilizes a point of view to fall to the wayside if intuition contradicts factual conclusions. This ambiguity, states Byers, opens the door to imagination, revealing ". . . the nature of reality itself, or at least the manner in which the human mind interacts with the natural world." Therefore, objectivity is at once a necessary determinant for accumulating knowledge and also a mirage.[17]

In measuring reality, all interpretations are skewed to the reflections of human perception and limited by anatomy. Uniformity and cohesion determine the range of potential, for instance, yet add measure to the existing picture of our anatomy. Professor Wallace tells us that when exploring consciousness we need to ". . . identify the metaphysical doctrine that underlies and structures virtually all contemporary scientific research." The foundation of this doctrine, he says, is that of scientific materialism, which, in part, consists of objectivism, reductionism, and closure. Therefore, while scientific knowledge and objective knowledge are often synonymous, the results of such inquiry reveal "rules of the game," not necessarily absolute truth.[18]

The complexity of this book results from bringing to bear several disciplines to a common focus. It serves as an example of the detail and intricacy of energy body processes. There are many influences that go into building cohesion and we are not conscious of the vast majority. We then unwittingly behave from significant bias as we bend our perceptions of the world to suit ourselves.

Understanding the labyrinth of objectivity engenders the ability to employ it. Applying objectivity to this work, for instance, we need to view the energy body as simultaneously independent of the environment but also enmeshed within, and governed by, it. The energy body can move about and assess situations through subject-object relationships, yet it exists firmly as integral with the environment. Managing this internal-external referencing offers challenges. Projection and reflection rear up at any time, desires cast one against the rocky shore, and accurate orientation often seems out of reach.

Metaphysical philosophies constructively use such forces of perception. By understanding that the energy body intimately connects with the world, for example, the perception of separateness that non-attachment instills contributes to balanced objectivity. This presents the high side of forming subject-object relationships. With these systems, you may consciously enter environments conducive to learning. The stages of awakening provide an outline of what to look for, a path with heart offers stability, and timing generates the grace to navigate your circumstances. You then obtain the widest, most accurate viewpoint, experience a greater world, and hopefully live a better life. How is this not intelligent?

Listening

Listening provides a key ingredient for any aspect of learning. If you're constantly telling yourself what the world is like, you can't listen to another line of thought. Effective listening instills openness without prejudice. You allow interpretations to come to your awareness naturally rather than engage ongoing formulation. A fundamentalist acts and talks as an expert, yet doesn't acquire new information. Cohesion then remains not only conditional but also static.

Daniel Goleman provides categories of listening such as *defensive* and *active.* Often listening takes on a defensive quality, such as exhibited during an argument, and so nothing is gained and often much is lost as one conditional field collides with another and the people involved hear only what they want to hear. Goleman considers empathy—hearing the feelings behind the words—to be the "most powerful form of defensive listening." He cites active listening as being when one person provides feedback to the other and then listens anew in an effort not to make assumptions or jump to conclusions, and thereby garner at least a measure of objectivity.[19]

In broad application, to listen means to "pay attention."[20] In this light, listening is a deautomatization procedure that utilizes as many modes of perception as possible. For example, to *see*—listening to energy—awareness must be open in order to connect with the world free of bias; otherwise, *seeing* remains latent. Meditation is also listening, as is the general use of intuition, and as is feeling the intent that carries words spoken or written.

Self-guidance

If learning necessitates stepping outside consensus, then relying on your own resources is imperative. Without doing so, you remain within group cohesion, which dampens imagination. To navigate life and learning, self-guidance stems from impressions, feelings, visions, and physical sensations that let you know what is going on. Just like learning a written language, you can develop a rich means of communication. To help you begin:

1. Initially, find a time and place where you'll be uninterrupted. As you develop self-guidance, apply it to situations where you will be interrupted and where you use it in group environments.

2. Feel for any sensations in your body: tingling, pressure, pain. Place your attention in that area. Allow the sensation to expand within your full attention. Within your awareness, perceive what represents, why it is there.

3. Use as many forms of communication as possible to "hear" the answer. You might perceive images, sounds, or kinesthetic sensations.

4. Throughout the day, assess your feelings. While you're out for a walk, you might feel like heading in a certain direction. While talking with your partner, you might feel like doing something in particular. This may also help facilitate brainstorming sessions at work.

5. Play with these thoughts, feelings, and images. Notice if symbols intuitively mean something to you. Try them out as guidance by using them as environmental indications.

6. Study and test your guidance. In time, you'll learn what to trust. In essence, sure-footed internal guidance comes from silent knowledge.

Silent Knowledge

Silent knowledge results from connecting with and *seeing* energy fields, not through reason and talking. It originates from forging a link with intent.[21] Emanations embody intent, which means intent ranges from the personal to the cosmological. There are those that bring individual energy bodies to life and those that create universes.

We all have silent knowledge, says don Juan, a complete knowledge of our condition. He adds that once a person learns of this possibility, it is a matter of awakening to it, of removing the natural barriers to this birthright.[22] Practices and procedures such as outlined in this book, and those presented in other traditions, are sleight-of-hand techniques to help usher you to silent knowledge. They serve as necessary artifices to achieve a completely different relationship with yourself and the environment. This new awareness can't be outlined as it is a matter of silent knowledge, and represents your individual pattern of energy and how that connects with and expresses itself among all the other energies.

Managing *flow* requires this form of awareness. *Flow* feels like a stream of energy running through you. Try to cling to it and it disappears. Allow it freedom and it guides you toward fulfilling your nature. The sensing of this rarified energy intensifies the more you connect with core. From this orientation, you learn quietly and abundantly.

You groom silent knowledge through exploring the cornerstones, intent, and new relationships with the world. You learn to approach life from a different reference, that of innate ability rather than deferring to a description of the world. Potential abounds. Taking this to a professional level requires employing the same energy management skills that placed you on the threshold of silent knowledge. Applying yourself is a matter of personal responsibility. The basics of energy management provide the foundation for such a quest.

A Learning Posture

Here is a summary of behaviors that promote learning. Combined they offer a posture to help you walk attentively and purposefully throughout the course of a day, no matter the environment.

Maintain cool effort. Don't bash your head into walls. Don't try to force the world into compliance with your wishes. Learn what the world *is*. Don't arbitrarily work according to another person's timetable. Have a little fun finding out the natural rhythms of your life. Then relax, be patient, and let your energy body breathe. Learn to love to learn. Have a "romance with knowledge," as don Juan puts it.[23]

Exercise a high level of inquiry. Stay open and flexible. Keep asking questions. Don't settle for an answer when your body yearns for more. Look at the evidence, at what occurred, at what is . . . not what others say is so. Use all of your experience and let your knowledge be rendered obsolete when appropriate. Use all the deautomatization skills you can at any time you can. As philosopher Arthur Schopenhauer says, "The contemplation and observation of everything *actual,* as soon as it presents something new to the observer, is more instructive than all reading and hearing about it."[24]

Sustain the pursuit of objectivity. By applying the lessons of cohesion, we know that anything we perceive is simultaneously real and illusory: real from its own vantage point, illusory (potential) from another assemblage point position. We have objectively-defined anatomical hardware, yet the experience it provides is subjective. Quantum theory tells us that results are influenced by the observer, which makes everything subjective. At the same time, this awareness indicates objectivity. You might say objectivity is what keeps you from lying to yourself. It is what allows you to accurately observe and assess yourself, others, and the world. Interpret events based on a commitment for accuracy rather than on personal desire.

Acknowledge complete responsibility. Do so for all your behavior, for all that you perceive, and for everything that results from your inquiries and adventures. Claim what you know in a way that accents continued learning. Rather than constantly emphasize, "I know," exercise the open switch to listen and observe without losing sense with what you do know, where you're going, and how it all fits.

Cultivate ever-expanding context. Effective learning requires having context with which to apply experience. You can partake of an exquisitely rich learning environment yet not be able to take advantage of it, as you don't know what it represents or what to do with it. *Seeing* without knowing of this mode of perception provides an example. Odds are that most people will dismiss spontaneous *seeing* as an anomaly since they don't have context regarding it, and so the experience may be relegated to a state-specific memory. In this instance, context includes such things as knowing of the cornerstones, how they work, their range of perception, how they relate to exploring the world at large, and then all of these specifically focused on *seeing.* The same applies to ordinary situations. Could a cowboy of the 1800s know what to do with an automobile, or could a person never exposed to information technology know what a computer represents, let alone what to do with it? Context also represents a conditional field and therefore learning carries the added ingredient of the continual expansion of cohesion and context.

Learn for mastery. Prepare yourself to take your learning into new areas, some of which may cause unwelcome comments from those who consider themselves authorities. Balance and relax within and without. Minimize reflection and projection. Release any hold the new cohesion has on you to avoid fundamentalism and continue learning. The more cornerstones you use, the more information you have to ply into expanding cohesions. The more you listen and remain open to learning, the more skill you employ. Learning in such a manner harnesses an intentional process involving ever-expanding abilities.

This posture relates directly to an energy body posture. When you try to determine your life by reason alone, you warp cohesional energies. Thought is but a fraction of the resources available to assess learning and life. At the same time, a similar dynamic may occur when you've activated *will,* meaning you have learned to engage life with your complete energy body. If you try to command your life with *will,* you again distort internal energies as well as your relationship with the world. A viable posture is to center yourself in openness and then direct your specific actions with intent, a posture leading to *being.* This grants you the ability to pay attention to the moment, remain open to new information, and yet remain sufficiently closed to sustain focus and accomplish your goals.

LEARNING PROJECTS

Forging a path with heart offers one way to make sure that what you learn provides purpose and meaning. Hooking your path to stages of awakening promotes ontological intelligence. A way to augment your path with heart is through learning projects. They help you stimulate and manage your resources and accelerate your learning as you explore imagination. As a result, you're constantly stepping into the unknown while grounding yourself in daily life. Repetitive behaviors aimed toward a goal gather unbending intent, increase awareness of your inventory, and consciously develop new cohesions. Learning tasks that are well integrated with your path with heart take you to core.

Learning projects help you dive into your energy body, to intellectually and energetically explore. A good learning project requires that you actively imagine an imagining while in imagination, to manufacture a specific situation or activity in your imagination that you may return to when you wish. For instance, you may enter imagination to explore the nature of perception, to write a book, to develop architectural blueprints, to use your heightened awareness to perceive the subtle energies of plants in order to gain knowledge of their healing properties, or anything modest or grand that takes you deeper into learning. The task also requires learning how to return time and again to the subject you are studying. You therefore stimulate and stabilize imagination. And then in a traditional shamanic maneuver, you apply your knowledge in your daily, waking world. You therefore engage the psychological process of heading from a baseline state of consciousness through altered and discrete altered states en route to a new baseline.

Learning projects are a way to use deautomatization, imagination, personal responsibility, intent, and all other techniques in a positive way. By constant focus on a goal, unbending intent allows you to enter new domains of consciousness, which in turn produce new imaginings. Once you complete a task, you will have learned the mechanics of cohesion. For a project to propel you to the next level, it has to be far-fetched, something beyond your current sense of what is practical or even doable, and it has to awaken imagination and solidify learning. It is your path forward because a learning task is not simply a matter of using the cornerstones; it requires using the entire craft for the overriding purpose of ontological development. This growth provides for a keener focus on the task.

To decide on a task, use your imagination to determine an ability that you have interest in acquiring, and one that is also well beyond your current abilities.

Meditate while holding your purpose at the center of your awareness, and then allow yourself to become even more aware. An unexpected idea may come to you, something that you had no interest in before. Your task may seem odd. At first, don't worry about the task being right or wrong. The central consideration is to work with the resources of your extended anatomy. Over time, examine what the project requires for ethical balance within you and with the world. Like learning other skills, you'll become more proficient the more you practice. Don't consider what you'll think about after the course of your project. Optimally, you will have developed your cohesion to another level and any thoughts about what that might entail are projection and only serve to keep you pinned to your current conditional field.

As with almost any endeavor, put your mind to the task and make it happen. Step-by-step exercises may provide guidance, but are only buffers; in themselves, they don't provide the means for success. Once you get a feel for learning projects, they will take you to unforeseen places. By eventually giving your imagining practical application, you bridge imagination and learning. Then the expanse of energy found in potential takes shape in a workable, realizable format in your daily life. This expands the first energy field and reduces the second, rousing more of the energy body to consciousness.

In high school, my English teachers thought I was hopeless, and I passed my classes by the skin of my teeth. I was thoroughly disenchanted with writing because of this experience, but not because I necessarily lacked an innate drive to write. I was just not allowed to approach it other than via dogmatic rules. I accepted the writing task don Juan gave me out of respect for him, and I later considered it advantageous to earn a degree in journalism to help fulfill the task. The other part of the task required that I actually learn what I would write about. Guided by don Juan, during the many years of outlining and applying the techniques found in Castaneda's books, I also worked on the wordsmith part of my nature; writing became something that now contributes to my livelihood. I eventually completed my project by publishing two books (under the name Ken Eagle Feather) that provide a shamanic orientation to the properties of the first and second energy fields, respectively.

For another example, as Castaneda didn't consider himself a writer don Juan gave him the task of *seeing* his books already written while dreaming in the deeper levels of imagination. It thereby became an ontological development project rather than a literary exercise. Did he use dreaming to find an archetypical form of shamanic teachings? The question and all that it conveys point to another area for research.

Castaneda's teammates had projects requiring them to gain proficiency with altered states of consciousness to learn healing, carpentry, and providing solutions to human predicaments and problems.[25] They discovered that, in performing these tasks, individual consciousness meets and exceeds the baseline state of consciousness for both individuals and groups. As with learning projects in general, this consisted of interplay between imagination and learning. In general, the next phase of a task is to give back to the group; perhaps a person becomes a healer rather than just studying about it. Professional skill then continues to develop the more one learns.

Such examples are not limited to those under don Juan's wing. Norbert Classen, author of *Das Wissen der Tolteken* (The Knowledge of the Toltecs), uses energy body processes to hunt meteorites that have fallen to earth. He gazes at stones until he becomes saturated with their energy. The stones then appear in his dreaming. From that point, he learns new things as he *sees* other aspects of the stones. He then transports these qualities of perception to his "other side," the consciousness characterized by waking life. Going back and forth, he eventually dreams of new stones and where to find them. While Classen uses this method to track meteorites, he advises the process is not limited to finding stones as it may be applied to finding pretty much anything.[26]

A person with another bent of nature might hunt meteorites through diligent research and voraciously read about space, asteroids, classification systems, the locations of where they are found, and then after finding a meteorite provide all the reasons why it was at a certain location. Both people found the rock in different ways: one directly, the other indirectly. Any explanation for why the stone was at a location is based on the consensus of those who study such phenomena as well as the consensus of those who use a specific method. The deautomatization of it is that the meteorite was at a specific location. It was found using a particular process. And that's that.

When you finish your task, another will claim your allegiance. As before, it will require that you enter arenas of consciousness that reside beyond your learning and imagination. From years of following a path with heart, though, the ability to proceed will fall into place. This doesn't mean you've arrived on easy street. The ongoing necessity to rigorously study subjects that were once, and in large measure remain, beyond your grasp will remain abundantly apparent. The obstacles will be the same as before, although seemingly higher and wider. But to not give it a go is unthinkable. Outward success or failure is irrelevant, although success kindles more fun.

These projects greatly facilitate learning how to manage your energetic resources. When coupled with an objective like ontological development, they add to the overall inertia of managing cohesion. You are not using the task just to learn a particular subject; you are using it to grow as a complete person. A learning project moves you firmly toward the next level of growth: an apprentice-level project provides the means to step into craftsmanship, and a craftsmanship task ushers you to artistry.

The worse case scenario is that learning projects keep you from becoming dull, lackadaisical, bored, and resting too comfortably within your current cohesion. In short, they offer robust stimulation of your energy body and point you in a direction that renews your sense of life. This alone is worth the ride.

Epilogue

We can use the findings from diverse disciplines such as processes of neural networks, influences of epigenetics, dynamics of states of consciousness, procedures for self-actualization, and properties of physics to illustrate the energy body because these seemingly disparate subjects are all functions of cohesion, the part of our energetic anatomy where the meta-cognition that gives rise to each of them takes place. While there is interaction among all systems comprising human anatomy and awareness, cohesion as governed by energy body mechanics is the common basis of perception and behavior. At the same time, these specialties can help shed greater light, in a faster way, on the nature of cohesion.

The shamanic view of the energy body doesn't obviate anything; it only serves to enhance and expand. It opens new avenues of inquiry for what may be brought into our world. In bringing to bear an extended human anatomy, it reveals increased capacities of consciousness and behavior that have been there all along. By mapping the properties of cohesion, we gain a better understanding of perception and our place in the world. Through personal application, this opens the book of your life, and not just to a page or chapter.

The quest to explore and use the energy body provides sustenance and renewal to all areas of life, its effects are that entrenched in human affairs. Even so, at every turn something or someone signals halt. It's easy to close the book and forget about it, and so close off awareness, meaning, and your sojourn. Difficulties here and there along your path may actually be insurmountable but, free will or not, that awaits discovery. Overcoming external obstacles is not the final test of success anyway as there is a greater, more profound meaning of life and living it, the very heart of it.

It is in the nature of our era that we need to build a deeper relationship with our world. Our survival may depend on it; just take a good look around. For this pursuit, science and shamanism stand best to assist and illuminate when used in concert. They both accelerate learning and have recognized value in all corners of the globe, and combined could offer new options and means to gain balance among individuals, groups, and environment.

Such a journey requires achieving new levels of imagination and learning. We need new navigational maps, and those of ancient and modern making could serve us well. From science and technology to ethics to education, if not across the spectrum of human endeavors, this undertaking stands to awaken immense potential. This pursuit is the same for each of us, for as adults we must assume responsibility and chart the course, and all the while remember that even as children we sensed a life of abounding potential, perhaps, even, of touching infinity. . . .

Notes

CHAPTER 1.
SHAMANISM FOR THE AGE OF SCIENCE

1. Under the name Ken Eagle Feather, I have written *Traveling with Power* (Charlottesville, Va.: Hampton Roads Publishing, 1992); *A Toltec Path* (Charlottesville, Va.: Hampton Roads, 1995), re-titled *On the Toltec Path* and re-released as a tenth-anniversary edition (Rochester, Vt.: Inner Traditions/Bear & Co., 2006); *Tracking Freedom* (Charlottesville, Va.: Hampton Roads, 1998); *The Dream of Vixen Tor* (Charlottesville, Va.: Tracker One Studios, 2001); and *Toltec Dreaming* (Rochester, Vt.: Inner Traditions/Bear & Co., 2007).

2. Carlos Castaneda, *The Teachings of Don Juan: A Yaqui Way of Knowledge* (New York: Simon & Schuster, 1968).

3. UCLA Department of Anthropology, e-mail correspondence, October 5, 2005.

4. Carlos Castaneda, *The Fire from Within* (New York: Simon & Schuster, 1984), 49.

5. Gerald Piel, *The Age of Science: What Scientists Learned in the Twentieth Century* (New York: Basic Books, 2001).

6. His Holiness the Dalai Lama, *The Universe in a Single Atom: The Convergence of Science and Spirituality* (New York: Morgan Road Books, 2005).

7. Susan Blackmore, *Consciousness: An Introduction* (Oxford: Oxford University Press, 2004), 2.

8. Ibid., 14; Barbara Platek, "The Good Red Road," *The Sun* (April 2005): 5–12; and Houston Smith, *The World's Religions* (New York: HarperCollins, 1991), 380.

9. Sidney Spencer, *Mysticism in World Religion* (Gloucester, Mass.: Peter Smith, 1971), 9–17; and Paul Radin, "Monotheism among American Indians," Dennis Tedlock and Barbara Tedlock, eds., *Teachings from the American Earth: Indian Religion and Philosophy* (New York: Liveright, 1975), 219–47.

CHAPTER 2. A WORLD OF ENERGY

1. Portions of this chapter were first published as "Bioenergetics: A New Science of Healing," *Shift: At the Frontiers of Consciousness* no. 10 (March–May 2006): 11–13, 34.

2. *American Heritage College Dictionary,* 3rd ed. (Boston: Houghton Mifflin Company, 2000), 139.

3. Alexander Lowen, *Bioenergetics* (New York: Penguin Arkana, 1994), and Fred P. Gallo, *Energy Psychology: Explorations at the Interface of Energy, Cognition, Behavior, and Health* (Boca Raton, Fla.: CRC Press, 1999).

4. James Oschman, *Energy Medicine: The Scientific Basis* (Edinburgh, Scotland: Churchill Livingston Press, 2000), 232.

5. Ted J. Kaptchuk, *The Web That Has No Weaver: Understanding Chinese Medicine* (Chicago: Contemporary Books, 2000), 14.

6. Chakra, http://en.wikipedia.org, August 27, 2008; and Libby Barnett and Maggie Chambers with Susan Davidson, *Reiki Energy Medicine* (Rochester, Vt.: Healing Arts Press, 1996), 20–21.

7. Samuel Hahnemann, Wenda Brewster O'Reilly, ed., *Organon of the Medical Art* (Palo Alto, Calif.: Birdcage Books, 1996), 4, 235–37.

8. Paracelsus Clinic website, www.paracelsus.ch, July 15, 2007.

9. "The Royal Rife Story," www.rifehealth.com, September 30, 2006.

10. Clark A. Manning and Louis J. Vanrenen, *Bioenergetic Medicines East and West: Acupuncture and Homeopathy* (Berkeley, Calif.: North Atlantic Books, 1988), 9.

11. "Energy Medicine: An Overview," *Backgrounder,* National Center for Complementary and Alternative Medicine, March 2007.

12. Oschman, *Energy Medicine,* 76–79; Hong-Chang Yang, Jau-Han Chen, Shu-Yun Wang, Chin-Hao Chen, Jen-Tzong Jeng, Ji-Cheng Chen, Chiu-Hsien Wu, Shu-Hsien Liao, and Herng-Er Horng, "Superconducting Quantum Interference Device: The Most Sensitive Detector of Magnetic Flux," *Tamkang Journal of Science and Engineering* 6, no. 1 (2003): 9–18; and Takenaka Corporation website, www.takenaka.co.jp/takenaka_e/techno/19_sldrm/19_sldrm.htm, August 16, 2007.

13. Dr. Korotkov Co. website, www.korotkov.org, August 18, 2007.

14. PIP Bio Imaging website, www.pipbiofieldimaging.com, September 12, 2007; The Centre for Biofield Sciences website, www.biofieldsciences.com, September 15, 2007; and presentation by Brian Dailey, MD, at a conference sponsored by The Institute for Therapeutic Discovery, September 8, 2007.

15. University of Colorado at Colorado Springs website, www.uccs.edu/rjones, August 1, 2005.

16. As of the writing of this book, I was employed by The Institute for Therapeutic

Discovery (www.tiftd.org) and Beech Tree Labs, Inc. (www.beechtreelabs
.com).

17. Larry Dossey, *Reinventing Medicine: Beyond Mind-Body to a New Era of
Healing* (New York: HarperCollins, 1999), 27, 58–59; and Marilyn Schlitz
and William Braud, "Distant Intentionality and Healing: Assessing the Evidence," *Alternative Therapies* 3, no. 6 (November 1997): 62–73.

18. James Oschman, "Energy and the Healing Response," *Journal of Bodywork
and Movement Therapies* 9 (2005): 3–15.

19. Oschman, *Energy Medicine,* 11.

20. James Oschman, e-mail correspondence, May 19, 2005, and June 11, 2005.

21. Milo Wolff, e-mail correspondence, October 14 and 15, 2005.

22. Institute of Transpersonal Psychology website, www.itp.edu, October 2, 2005.

23. Stuart R. Hameroff, Alfred W. Kaszniak, and Alwyn C. Scott, eds., *Toward
a Science of Consciousness: The Tucson Discussions and Debates* (Cambridge,
Mass.: The MIT Press, 1996, 1998, 1999); and Philip David Zelazo, Morris
Moscovtich, and Evan Thompson, eds., *The Cambridge Handbook of Consciousness* (New York: Cambridge University Press, 2007).

24. Abraham H. Maslow, *Toward a Psychology of Being,* 3rd ed. (New York: John
Wiley & Sons, 1999), 85; and Paul Pearsall, *The Beethoven Factor: The New
Positive Psychology of Hardiness, Happiness, Healing, and Hope* (Charlottes-
ville, Va.: Hampton Roads Publishing Co., 2003), 203–19.

25. Andrew M. Colman, *A Dictionary of Psychology* (Oxford: Oxford University
Press, 2001), 739; and Moti Ben-Ari, *Just a Theory: Exploring the Nature of
Science* (Amherst, N.Y.: Prometheus Books, 2005), 24.

26. Published by Simon & Schuster and its imprint Washington Square Press,
Carlos Castaneda wrote *The Teachings of Don Juan* (1968), *A Separate Real-
ity* (1971), *Journey to Ixtlan* (1972), *Tales of Power* (1974), *The Second Ring of
Power* (1977), *The Eagles Gift* (1981), *The Fire from Within* (1984), and *The
Power of Silence* (1987). HarperCollins then published *The Art of Dreaming*
(1993) and *The Active Side of Infinity* (1998).

27. Violet S. de Laslo, ed., R. F. C. Hull, trans., *The Basic Writings of C. G. Jung*
(Princeton, N.J.: Princeton University Press, 1990), 147–48.

28. Maslow, *Psychology of Being,* 20, 32.

29. A. R. Lacey, *A Dictionary of Philosophy* (New York: Barnes & Noble Books,
1996), 205; and Dagobert Runes, *Dictionary of Philosophy* (Totowa, N.J.:
Littlefield, Adams, and Co., 1980), 219.

30. Colman, *Dictionary of Psychology*, 443–44, 600; and Sally P. Springer and
Georg Deutsch, *Left Brain, Right Brain,* 4th ed. (New York: W. H. Freeman
and Co., 1993), 272; and Richard M. Restak, *The Brain: The Last Frontier*
(New York: Warner Books, 1979), 49–71.

31. Carlos Castaneda, *The Power of Silence* (New York: Washington Square Press, 1987), 155–90.
32. Tom Weber, "Life Altering," *UMaine Today* (March/April 2008): 11–13.

CHAPTER 3. ANATOMY OF THE ENERGY BODY

1. Oschman, *Energy Medicine,* 74, 206, 209.
2. Paul Davies, "The New Physics: a synthesis," in Paul Davies, ed. *The New Physics* (Cambridge: Cambridge University Press, 1989), 1–6.
3. Robert M. Berne, Matthew N. Levy, Bruce M. Koeppen, and Bruce A. Stanton, eds., *Physiology,* 4th ed. (St. Louis: Mosby, 1998), 653.
4. James Austin, *Zen and the Brain: Toward an Understanding of Meditation and Consciousness* (Cambridge, Mass.: MIT Press, 1999), 83–88; Bruce Lipton, *The Biology of Belief* (Santa Rosa, Calif.: Elite Books, 2005), 163–65; and Blackmore, *Consciousness,* 246–48.
5. Robert O. Becker and Gary Selden, *The Body Electric: Electromagnetism and the Foundation of Life* (New York: William Morrow, 1985); and Oschman, *Energy Medicine,* 61.
6. International Association for Biologically Closed Circuits website, www.iabc.readywebsites.com, September 22, 2006.
7. World Health Organization, *Standard Acupuncture Nomenclature,* 2nd ed. (WHO Regional Office, Manila, 1993).
8. Kaptchuk, *Web,* 41–74.
9. Ibid., 75–104.
10. Presentation on Functional Magnetic Resonance Imaging studies conducted by Joie Jones, Professor of Radiological Sciences, University of California, Irvine, and subsequent conversation, November 2008.
11. Caroline Myss, *Anatomy of the Spirit: The Seven Stages of Power and Healing* (New York: Harmony Books, 1996), 69.
12. Nadi (yoga), http://en.wikipedia.org, December 14, 2007.
13. Milo Wolff, e-mail correspondence, October 14, 2005.
14. Castaneda, *The Fire from Within,* 50.
15. Christopher J. Conselice, "The Universe's Invisible Hand," *Scientific American* (February 2007): 35–41; and Timothy Clifton and Pedro G. Ferreira, "Does Dark Energy Really Exist?" *Scientific American* (April 2009): 48–55.
16. James Oschman, e-mail correspondence, September 10, 2005.
17. Barbara Ann Brennan, *Hands of Light: A Guide to Healing Through the Human Energy Field* (New York: Bantam, 1987); and personal observations.
18. Rollin McCraty, *The Energetic Heart: Bioelectromagnetic Interactions Within and Between People* (Boulder Creek, Calif.: Institute of Heartmath, 2003), 3–6.

19. Castaneda, *The Fire from Within,* 157–59.
20. Ibid., 108; and Castaneda, *The Power of Silence,* xv–xvi.
21. Jon Whale, *The Catalyst of Power: The Assemblage Point of Man* (Findhorn, Scotland: Findhorn Press, 2001).
22. Castaneda, *The Power of Silence,* 6–7.
23. Ibid., 166, 244; Blackmore, *Consciousness,* 13; and Runes, *Dictionary of Philosophy,* 198.
24. Castaneda, *The Fire from Within,* 83.
25. Castaneda, *Tales of Power,* 95–96.
26. Oschman, *Energy Medicine,* 29.
27. Daniel Goleman, *Emotional Intelligence* (New York: Bantam Books, 1995), 83–86, 136–38.
28. Valerie V. Hunt, *Infinite Mind: Science of the Human Vibrations of Consciousness* (Malibu, Calif.: Malibu Publishing, 1996), 104–31; Antonio Damasio, *The Feeling of What Happens: Body and Emotion in the Making of Consciousness* (New York: Harcourt Brace and Company, 1999), 41; Candace Pert, *Molecules of Emotion* (New York: Scribner, 1997); and Candace Pert, "Molecules and Choice," *Shift: At the Frontiers of Consciousness* (September–November 2004): 21.
29. Castaneda, *Tales of Power,* 95.
30. Arthur Schopenhauer, E. F. J. Payne, ed., *The World as Will and Representation,* Vol. 1, 2 (New York: Dover Publications, 1969).
31. IBS Research Update website, www.ibs-research-update.org.uk, September 22, 2006.
32. De Laslo, *Basic Writings,* 41–43.
33. Ibid., 56.
34. Ibid., 59.
35. Ibid., 43, 57, 140.
36. Ibid., 59, 122.
37. Castaneda, *The Fire from Within,* xiii.

CHAPTER 4. THE FORMATION OF REALITY

1. Entrainment references, http://en.wikipedia.org, October 2, 2006.
2. Irving M. Copi, *Introduction to Logic,* 6th edition (New York: Macmillan, 1982), 99–105.
3. Damasio, *Feeling of What Happens,* 308; and Castaneda, *The Fire from Within,* 176, 213.
4. The Quotations Page website, www.quotationspage.com, December 10, 2006.
5. Castaneda, *The Art of Dreaming,* 22; and Eagle Feather, *Toltec Dreaming,* 94.

6. Colman, *Dictionary of Psychology,* 404.

7. Glen O. Gabbard and Stuart Twemlow, *With the Eyes of the Mind: An Empirical Analysis of Out-of-Body States* (New York: Praeger, 1984), 150.

8. Castaneda, *The Art of Dreaming,* 142.

9. Robert Monroe, *Journeys Out of the Body* (New York: Doubleday, 1971).

10. Eagle Feather, *Toltec Dreaming,* 44; and Joseph McMoneagle, *Mind Trek: Exploring Consciousness, Time, and Space through Remote Viewing* (Charlottesville, Va.: Hampton Roads Publishing Co., 1997), 15.

11. Arnold Mindell, *Dreaming While Awake: Techniques for 24-Hour Lucid Dreaming* (Charlottesville, Va.: Hampton Roads Publishing Co., 2000), 6.

12. Maslow, *Psychology of Being,* 85.

13. De Laslo, *Basic Writings,* 148; and Abraham H. Maslow, *Maslow on Management* (New York: John Wiley & Sons, 1998), xx.

14. Gerber, *Vibrational Medicine,* 17.

15. Catherine Arnst, "Biotech, Finally," *BusinessWeek* (June 13, 2005): 30.

16. Henry Petroski, *Design Paradigms: Case Histories of Error and Judgment in Engineering* (Cambridge, UK: Cambridge University Press, 1994), 1–2.

17. Lionel R. Milgrom, "Entanglement, Knowledge, and Their Possible Effects on the Outcomes of Blinded Trials of Homeopathic Provings," *The Journal of Alternative and Complementary Medicine* 12, no. 3 (2006): 271–79.

18. Oschman, *Energy Medicine,* 154.

19. Thomas S. Kuhn, *The Structure of Scientific Revolutions,* 3rd ed. (Chicago: University of Chicago Press, 1996), 77–82.

CHAPTER 5. EXPANDING THE BOUNDARIES

1. Charles T. Tart, *States of Consciousness* (Lincoln, Neb.: http://iUniverse.com, Inc., 2000), 5–9.

2. Blackmore, *Consciousness,* 248.

3. Castaneda, *The Fire from Within,* 23.

4. Maslow, *Psychology of Being,* 31–33, 170–75.

5. Castaneda, *The Fire from Within,* 50.

6. Seymour H. Mauskopf and Michael R. McVaugh, *The Elusive Science: Origins of Experimental Psychical Research* (Baltimore, Md.: The Johns Hopkins University Press, 1980), 5, 169; and Charles T. Tart, *Open Mind, Discriminating Mind: Reflections on Human Possibilities* (Lincoln, Neb.: http://iUniverse.com, Inc., 2000), 61, 76–82, 85.

7. Mauskopf and McVaugh, *Elusive Science,* 3, 13.

8. Gabbard and Twemlow, *Eyes of the Mind,* 15–23.

9. Joseph McMoneagle, *Memoirs of a Psychic Spy: The Remarkable Life of U.S. Government Remote Viewer 001* (Charlottesville, Va.: Hampton Roads Pub-

lishing Co., 2006), xi–xii; and personal conversations with Joseph McMoneagle and a client during 2005–2006.

10. Brian Greene, *The Fabric of the Cosmos: Space, Time, and the Texture of Reality* (New York: Alfred A. Knopf, 2005), 11–12.

11. Philip C. Almond, *Mystical Experience and Religious Doctrine: An Investigation of the Study of Mysticism in World Religions* (Berlin: Mouton Publishers, 1982), 122–23.

12. Fritjof Capra, *The Tao of Physics: An Exploration of the Parallels between Modern Physics and Eastern Mysticism* (Boston: Shambhala, 2000), 52–54.

13. Hunt, *Infinite Mind,* 163.

14. William James, *The Varieties of Religious Experience* (New York: New American Library, 1958), 292–94; and Maslow, *Psychology of Being,* 93–106.

15. Runes, *Dictionary of Philosophy,* 203; and Spencer, *Mysticism in World Religion,* 213–17, 176–86, 305.

16. P. D. Ouspensky, *The Fourth Way* (New York: Vintage Books, 1971), 97–104.

17. Charles T. Tart, ed., *Altered States of Consciousness,* rev. ed. (New York: HarperSanFrancisco, 1990), 581–99.

18. Jack Kornfield, *A Path with Heart: A Guide through the Perils and Promises of Spiritual Life* (New York: Bantam Books, 1993), 120–22.

19. Almond, *Mystical Experience,* 69–91.

20. Leah Buturain, "Materializing the Mystery: Body Imagery in Catholic Visual Culture," presented at the Luce Colloquium, Fuller Seminar, February 16, 2005, www.brehmcenter.com/mediafiles/Buturain_paper.pdf, June 24, 2008.

21. Springer and Deutsch, *Left Brain, Right Brain,* 1–17, 272.

22. F. Holmes Atwater, "The Hemi-Sync Process," The Monroe Institute Research Division (June 1999).

23. Raymond Moody, *Life After Life* (Harrisburg, Penn.: Stackpole Books, 1976), 29–49; and Gabbard and Twemlow, *Eyes of the Mind,* 136–38.

24. The Nobel Foundation website, www.nobelprize.org, June 20, 2008; and "An Atmosphere of Change," *Breakthrough: The Changing Face of Science in America,* Boston PBS Video: Blackside, Inc., 1996.

25. Eagle Feather, *Toltec Dreaming,* 76–77; and Marcus Chown, *The Universe Next Door: The Making of Tomorrow's Science* (Oxford: Oxford University Press, 2002), 25–26.

26. Paul J. Nahin, *Time Travel* (Cincinnati, Ohio: Writer's Digest Books, 1997), 167–168.

27. Michio Kaku, *Hyperspace: A Scientific Odyssey through Parallel Universes, Time Warps, and the 10th Dimension* (New York: Anchor Books, 1994),

15–16; and James Trefil, ed., *Encyclopedia of Science and Technology* (New York: Routledge, 2001), 463–64.

28. Kaku, *Hyperspace,* 49–51.

CHAPTER 6. STOCKROOM OF A THOUSAND MIRRORS

1. Arthur S. Reber and Emily Reber, eds., *The Penguin Dictionary of Psychology,* 3rd ed. (London: Penguin Books, 1995), 570.
2. Tart, *States of Consciousness,* 264; and Martin Heidegger, trans., John Macquarrie and Edward Robinson, *Being and Time* (San Francisco: HarperSanFrancisco, 1962), 371, 414.
3. Arthur J. Deikman, "Deautomatization and the Mystic Experience," Tart, ed., *Altered States,* 34–57.
4. Tart, *States of Consciousness,* 117; and Castaneda, *The Fire from Within,* 154.
5. Shunryu Suzuki, *Zen Mind, Beginner's Mind* (New York: Weatherhill, 1973), 116–17.
6. Hunt, *Infinite Mind,* 104–11.
7. Castaneda, *The Fire from Within,* 118.
8. Austin, *Zen and the Brain,* 227.
9. Eagle Feather, *Toltec Path,* 109–13.
10. Castaneda, *The Teachings of Don Juan,* 82–87.
11. Castaneda, *The Fire from Within,* 108.
12. Castaneda, *The Teachings of Don Juan,* 82–87.
13. De Laslo, *Basic Writings,* 147–48.
14. More explanation is provided throughout Carlos Castaneda's *The Fire from Within* and in Ken Eagle Feather's *Toltec Dreaming.*
15. Castaneda, *The Teachings of Don Juan,* 87.

CHAPTER 7. CLOSING IN ON FUNDAMENTALISM

1. Barnett and Chambers, *Reiki Energy,* 2.
2. Reber, *Dictionary of Psychology,* 125.
3. Elliot Dacher, *Integral Health: The Path to Human Flourishing* (Laguna Beach, Calif.: Basic Health Publications, Inc., 2006), 139–46.
4. Maslow, *Psychology of Being,* 39–41.
5. Patrick Bernhagen, "Power: Making Sense of an Elusive Concept," *Journal of Postgraduate Research* 2 (2003): 62–82.
6. Gerald M. Edelman, *Second Nature: Brain Science and Human Knowledge* (New Haven, Conn.: Yale University Press, 2006), 95.
7. Maslow, *Toward a Psychology of Being,* 20.
8. Castaneda, *The Art of Dreaming,* 238–39; and Eagle Feather, *Toltec Path,* 110.

9. John Horgan, *Rational Mysticism: Dispatches from the Border between Science and Spirituality* (New York: Houghton Mifflin Company, 2003), 118–19; and Paul E. Johnson, *Psychology of Religion, Revised* (Nashville, Tenn.: Abingdon Press, 1959), 223–26.

10. De Laslo, *Basic Writings,* 54–55; and Maslow, *Psychology of Being,* 166–73.

11. Johnson, *Psychology of Religion,* 104, 220.

12. Castaneda, *The Fire from Within,* 74–75.

13. Castaneda, *The Active Side of Infinity,* 224.

14. Castaneda, *The Fire from Within,* 176.

15. Castaneda, *The Art of Dreaming,* 104; and Arthur Deikman, *The Wrong Way Home: Uncovering the Patterns of Cult Behavior in America* (Boston: Beacon Press, 1990), 96.

16. Deikman, *Wrong Way Home,* 101, 105.

17. John Van Auken, "Guides, Angels, and the Holy One," *Venture Inward* 10, no. 6 (July/August 1994).

CHAPTER 8. BUILDING A CREATIVE LIFE

1. Steven Strogatz, *Sync: The Emerging Science of Spontaneous Order* (New York: Hyperian, 2003), 103–4.

2. Howard Gardner, *Frames of Mind: The Theory of Multiple Intelligences* (New York: HarperCollins, 1983), xii, xviii.

3. J. P. Chaplin, *Dictionary of Psychology* (New York: Dell Publishing, 1975), 263; and Gardner, *Frames of Mind,* 60, 68.

4. Thomas Donaldson and Patricia H. Werhane, eds., *Ethical Issues in Business: A Philosophical Approach,* 5th ed. (Upper Saddle River, N.J.: Prentice Hall, 1996), 3–11.

5. *American Heritage Dictionary,* 284; and Castaneda, *A Separate Reality,* 20–23.

6. Castaneda, *The Active Side,* 179; Castaneda, *The Fire from Within,* xii; and Tart, *Open Mind,* 227.

7. Johann Christoph Arnold, *Why Forgive?* (Farmington, Penn.: Plough Publishing House, 2000).

8. Martin Doblmeir, *The Power of Forgiveness* (Alexandria, Va.: Journey Films, 2007).

9. Castaneda, *The Art of Dreaming,* 73.

10. Castaneda, *The Power of Silence,* 82; and Castaneda, *Tales of Power,* 58.

11. Castaneda, *The Teachings of Don Juan,* 87.

12. Spencer, *Mysticism in World Religion,* 47–66; and Castaneda, *Tales of Power,* 294.

13. Castaneda, *The Fire from Within,* 159–60.

14. His Holiness the Dalai Lama, *Ethics for the New Millennium* (New York: Riverhead, 1999), 161–71.

15. Charles Q. Choi, "Quantum Afterlife," *Scientific American* (February 2009), 24–25.

16. Richard Sennett, *The Corrosion of Character: The Personal Consequences of Work in the New Capitalism* (New York: W. W. Norton & Company, 1998), 10–11, 28–29, 104.

17. Castaneda, *Journey to Ixtlan,* 43.

18. Castaneda, *Tales of Power,* 287.

19. J. C. Cooper, *Taoism: The Way of the Mystic* (York Beach, Maine: Samuel Weiser, Inc., 1972), 20; and Maslow, *Maslow on Management,* 205.

20. De Laslo, *Basic Writings,* 299–304.

21. Castaneda, *The Fire from Within,* 138.

22. Ibid., 14, 80.

23. Ibid., 110, 119; and *The Art of Dreaming,* 33.

24. Colman, *Dictionary of Psychology,* 58.

25. Castaneda, *The Fire from Within,* 14.

26. Cooper, *Taoism,* 13, 85–86.

27. Milo Wolff, "Einstein's Last Question," *Temple University Frontier Perspectives* (Spring 2005); and J. Adriaan Bouwknecht, Francesca Spiga, Daniel R. Staub, Matthew W. Hale, Anantha Shekhar, and Christopher A. Lowry, "Differential effects of exposure to low-light or high-light open-field on anxiety-related behaviors: Relationship to c-Fos expression in serotonergic and non-serotonergic neurons in the dorsal raphe nucleus," *Brain Research Bulletin* 72, no. 1, (April 2, 2007): 32–43.

28. Lipton, *Biology of Belief,* 15–27, 49–73.

29. Donaldson and Werhane, *Ethical Issues,* 424–58; and Michael Lerner, *Spirit Matters* (Charlottesville, Va.: Hampton Roads Publishing, 2000), 138–64.

30. Maslow, *Psychology of Being,* 39–41, 175–76, 197–205.

31. Lipton, *Biology of Belief,* 26–27; and Lionel R. Milgrom, "Entanglement, Knowledge, and Their Possible Effects on the Outcomes of Blinded Trials of Homeopathic Provings," *The Journal of Alternative and Complementary Medicine* 12, no. 3 (2006): 271–79.

32. Oschman, *Energy Medicine,* 175–86, 201–3.

33. David W. Sollars, *The Complete Idiot's Guide to Acupuncture & Acupressure* (New York: Alpha Books, 2000), 25; Hahnemann, *Organon,* 224; and Hunt, *Infinite Mind,* 9–36.

34. Castaneda, *The Fire from Within,* 49, 57.

35. Castaneda, *The Art of Dreaming,* 45; and *The Fire from Within,* 109.

36. David Darling, *Teleportation: The Impossible Leap* (Hoboken, N.J.: John Wiley & Sons, 2005), 168–88.

37. Neil A. Stillings, Steven E. Weisler, Christopher H. Chase, Mark H. Feinstein, Jay L. Garfield, and Edwina L. Rissland, *Cognitive Science,* 2nd ed. (Cambridge, Mass.: MIT Press, 1995), 55–63.

38. Castaneda, *Power of Silence,* 29–32.

39. Dalai Lama, *Ethics,* 219–21; and Johnson, *Psychology of Religion,* 102.

40. Leon R. Kass, *Life, Liberty and the Defense of Dignity: The Challenge of Bioethics* (San Francisco: Encounter Books, 2002), 8–12, 29–49.

41. James F. Drane, *More Humane Medicine: A Liberal Catholic Bioethic* (Edinboro, Penn.: Edinboro University Press, 2003), 1–6.

42. Mastery Learning references: Thomas H. Allen, Humboldt State University, www.humboldt.edu/~that1/mastery.html; www.funderstanding.com/mastery_learning.cfm, May 30, 2007; and http://en.wikipedia.org, December 6, 2007.

43. Kornfield, *Path with Heart.*

44. Castaneda, *Ixtlan,* 26–35.

45. Eagle Feather, *Toltec Path,* 170–72.

46. Stephen Levine, *A Year to Live: How to Live This Year As If It Were Your Last* (New York: Bell Tower, 1997), 39–40, 52.

47. Pearsall, *Beethoven Factor,* 7–19, 31.

CHAPTER 9. LIVING THE UNFOLDING MOMENT

1. Heidegger, *Being and Time,* 22–23.

2. Ibid., 78, 415–18.

3. Maslow, *Psychology of Being,* 85–94.

4. Ibid., 130–37; and Colman, *Dictionary of Psychology,* 443–44.

5. Maslow, *Psychology of Being,* 169.

6. Ibid., 170, 222.

7. Castaneda, *The Fire from Within,* 4–5, 147–48.

8. Castaneda, *Tales of Power,* 97–98.

9. Jones, *Physics,* 212–16.

10. Mihaly Csikszentmihalyi, *Flow: The Psychology of Optimal Experience* (New York: HarperPerennial, 1990), xi; and Goleman, *Emotional Intelligence,* 90.

11. Michael Murphy and Rhea A. White, *In the Zone: the Transcendent Experience in Sports* (New York: Penguin Books, 1995), 149–50.

12. Heidegger, *Being and Time,* 411–15.

13. Castaneda, *The Fire from Within,* 23.

14. Ibid., 170–71.

15. Ibid., 171.

16. Csikszentmihalyi, *Flow,* 26.

17. Ibid., 27.

18. Castaneda, *A Separate Reality,* 84.

19. Goleman, *Emotional Intelligence,* 62, 21.

20. Ibid., 293.

21. Colman, *Dictionary of Psychology,* 369, 379.

22. Malcolm Gladwell, *Blink: The Power of Thinking without Thinking* (New York: Bay Back Books, 2005), 107; and Tart, *Open Mind,* 167; and Rupert Sheldrake, *A New Science of Life: The Hypothesis of Morphic Resonance* (Rochester, Vt.: Park Street Press, 1995), 170–81.

23. Castaneda, *The Fire from Within,* 168–69.

24. Eric R. Kandel, James R. Schwartz, and Thomas M. Jessell, eds., *Principles of Neural Science,* 4th ed. (New York: McGraw-Hill, 2000), 388–92.

25. Russell Targ and Jane Katra, *Miracles of Mind: Exploring Nonlocal Consciousness and Spiritual Healing* (Novato, Calif.: New World Library, 1998), 251; Albert Einstein, *Ideas and Opinions* (New York: Three Rivers Press, 1982), 226; Castaneda, *The Power of Silence,* 14; and David G. Myers, "The Powers and Perils of Intuition: Understanding the Nature of Our Gut Instincts," *Scientific American Mind* (June/July 2007): 24–29.

26. Jerome Groopman, *How Doctors Think* (Boston: Houghton Mifflin, 2007), 44; and Suzuki, *Zen Mind,* 21.

27. Julian Jaynes, *The Origins of Consciousness in the Breakdown of the Bicameral Mind* (Boston: Houghton Mifflin, 1990), 236–46.

28. Eagle Feather, *Toltec Dreaming,* 139–42.

29. Tart, *Open Mind,* 182–83.

30. Sharon Begley, "How the Brain Rewires Itself," *Time* (January 29, 2007): 79; and Targ and Katra, *Miracles,* 257.

31. Castaneda, *A Separate Reality,* 153.

32. Sandra Blakeslee and Matthew Blakeslee, *The Body Has a Mind of Its Own: How Body Maps in Your Brain Help You Do (Almost) Everything Better* (New York: Random House, 2007), 181–89.

33. Castaneda, *The Fire from Within,* 176.

CHAPTER 10. ENERGY MANAGEMENT SKILLS

1. Castaneda, *Ixtlan,* 181–99.

2. Tart, *States of Consciousness,* 117.

3. Castaneda, *The Fire from Within,* 148, 154.

4. Castaneda, *A Separate Reality,* 91.

5. Castaneda, *Ixtlan,* 18–19; and Eagle Feather, *Toltec Dreaming,* 175–76.

6. Castaneda, *Power of Silence,* xii–xiii.

7. Castaneda, *Ixtlan,* 59–70, 88–104.

8. Ibid., 70; and Goleman, *Emotional Intelligence,* 65.

9. Tart, *Open Mind,* 225.

10. Oschman, *Energy Medicine,* 111–15; and Barnett and Chambers, *Reiki,* 43.

11. Taisha Abelar, *The Sorcerer's Crossing: A Woman's Journey* (New York: Penguin Arkana, 1992), 42–65; Castaneda, *Eagle's Gift,* 285–89; Eagle Feather, *Toltec Dreaming,* 185–88; and Victor Sanchez, *The Toltec Path of Recapitulation: Healing Your Past to Free Your Soul* (Rochester, Vt.: Bear & Company, 2001).

12. Suzuki, *Zen Mind,* 29–31; and personal discussions with Tantra teacher Roberta Williams, March 2009.

13. Tart, *Open Mind,* 187–88.

14. Herbert Benson with Miriam Z. Klipper, *The Relaxation Response* (New York: Harper, 2000), xvi; and Rollin McCraty, "From Depletion to Renewal: Positive Emotions and Heart Rhythm Coherence Feedback," *Biofeedback* 36, no. 1 (2008): 30–34; and Antonio Damasio, *Looking for Spinoza: Joy, Sorrow, and the Feeling Brain* (Orlando: Harcourt, 2003), 130–33.

15. Tart, *Open Mind,* 39, 247–50; and Tart, *States of Consciousness,* 25.

16. Gallo, *Energy Psychology,* 4.

17. Castaneda, *The Power of Silence,* 220; and Castaneda, *The Teachings of Don Juan,* 106–7.

18. Suzuki, *Zen Mind,* 119–21.

19. Tart, *States of Consciousness,* 280–81.

20. Castaneda, *A Separate Reality,* 151.

21. Donald B. Calne, *Within Reason: Rationality and Human Behavior* (New York: Pantheon Books, 1999), 243.

22. Ouspensky, *Fourth Way,* 159, 258, 310.

23. Tart, *States of Consciousness,* 156–62, 278.

24. B. Alan Wallace, *The Taboo of Subjectivity: Toward a New Science of Consciousness* (Oxford: Oxford University Press, 2000), 166.

25. Robert Heinlein, *Stranger in a Strange Land* (New York: Ace/Penguin, 2003), references to "Fair Witness" are found throughout the book.

26. Clifford A. Pickover, *Time: A Traveler's Guide* (Oxford, England: Oxford University Press, 1998), 57.

CHAPTER 11. THE HEARTBEAT OF LEARNING

1. Daniel J. Siegel, *The Developing Mind: Toward a Neurobiology of Interpersonal Experience* (New York: The Guildford Press, 1999), 23–24; and Castaneda, *Tales of Power,* 47–48.

2. Siegel, *The Developing Mind,* 24, 60–63; Norman Doige, *The Brain That*

Changes Itself (New York: Viking, 2007), 219–20; and Eric R. Kandel, *In Search of Memory: The Emergence of a New Science of Mind* (New York: W. W. Norton & Co., 2006), 212–18.

3. Doige, *The Brain That Changes Itself,* 117, 203, 224.

4. Pert, *Molecules of Emotion,* 144–45.

5. E-mail correspondence with James Oschman during December 2008 and January 2009. He will examine the role of the extracellular matrix and memory in the second edition of his book, *Energy Medicine: The Scientific Basis.*

6. Kandel, *In Search of Memory,* 116–34; Austin, *Zen and the Brain,* 187–89; Blakeslee, *The Body Has a Mind of Its Own,* 29–32; and Lipton, *Biology of Belief,* 38–39.

7. Tart, *States of Consciousness,* 105–9.

8. Castaneda, *The Power of Silence,* 124–25, 84–86.

9. Castaneda, *The Fire from Within,* 113.

10. Frank T. Vertosick Jr., *The Genius Within: Discovering the Intelligence of Every Living Thing* (New York: Harcourt, Inc., 2002), 5.

11. Steven Pinker, *How the Mind Works* (New York: Scientific American/ W. W. Norton & Co., 1997), 62.

12. Vertosick, *The Genius Within,* 53–55.

13. Doige, *The Brain That Changes Itself,* 250–52.

14. Tart, *Open Mind,* 283; and Copi, *Introduction to Logic,* 444–48.

15. Nancy Andreasen, *The Creating Brain: The Neuroscience of Genius* (New York: Dana Press, 2005), 33–35.

16. "Hollow earth," http://en.wikipedia.org, June 16, 2008.

17. William Byers, *How Mathematicians Think: Using Ambiguity, Contradiction, and Paradox to Create Mathematics* (Princeton, N.J.: Princeton University Press, 2007), 23–24, 59; and Reber, *Dictionary of Psychology,* 774.

18. Wallace, *Taboo of Subjectivity,* 12, 22.

19. Goleman, *Emotional Intelligence,* 145–47, 266.

20. *American Heritage Dictionary,* 791.

21. Castaneda, *The Power of Silence,* ix–xiii.

22. Ibid., 147, 47–48.

23. Castaneda, *The Art of Dreaming,* 75.

24. Schopenhauer, *World as Will,* vol. 2, 72.

25. Castaneda, *The Power of Silence,* xiv; and Castaneda, *The Eagle's Gift,* 54.

26. Norbert Classen, *Das Wissen der Tolteken* (Freiburg, Germany: Hans-Nietsch-Verlag, 2002); and e-mail correspondence, June 15–16, 2008.

Bibliography

Abelar, Taisha. *The Sorcerer's Crossing: A Woman's Journey.* New York: Penguin Arkana, 1992.

Almond, Philip C. *Mystical Experience and Religious Doctrine: An Investigation of the Study of Mysticism in World Religions.* Berlin: Mouton Publishers, 1982.

American Heritage College Dictionary, 3rd ed. Boston: Houghton Mifflin Company, 2000.

Andreasen, Nancy C. *The Creating Brain: The Neuroscience of Genius.* New York: Dana Press, 2005.

Arnold, Johann Christoph. *Why Forgive?* Farmington, Penn.: Plough Publishing House, 2000.

Austin, James. *Zen and the Brain: Toward an Understanding of Meditation and Consciousness.* Cambridge, Mass.: MIT Press, 1999.

Barnett, Libby, Maggie Chambers, with Susan Davidson. *Reiki Energy Medicine.* Rochester, Vt.: Healing Arts Press, 1996.

Becker, Robert O., and Gary Selden. *The Body Electric: Electromagnetism and the Foundation of Life.* New York: William Morrow, 1985.

Ben-Ari, Moti. *Just a Theory: Exploring the Nature of Science.* Amherst, N.Y.: Prometheus Books, 2005.

Benson, Herbert, with Miriam Z. Klipper. *The Relaxation Response.* New York: Harper, 2000.

Berne, Robert M., Matthew N. Levy, Bruce M. Koeppen, and Bruce A. Stanton, eds. *Physiology,* 4th ed. St. Louis: Mosby, 1998.

Blackmore, Susan. *Consciousness: An Introduction.* Oxford: Oxford University Press, 2004.

Blakeslee, Sandra, and Matthew Blakeslee. *The Body Has a Mind of Its Own: How Body Maps in Your Brain Help You Do (Almost) Everything Better.* New York: Random House, 2007.

Brennan, Barbara Ann. *Hands of Light: A Guide to Healing Through the Human Energy Field*. New York: Bantam, 1987.

Byers, William. *How Mathematicians Think: Using Ambiguity, Contradiction, and Paradox to Create Mathematics*. Princeton, N.J.: Princeton University Press, 2007.

Calne, Donald B. *Within Reason: Rationality and Human Behavior*. New York: Pantheon Books, 1999.

Capra, Fritjof. *The Tao of Physics: An Exploration of the Parallels between Modern Physics and Eastern Mysticism*. Boston: Shambhala, 2000.

Castaneda, Carlos. *The Active Side of Infinity*. New York: HarperCollins, 1998.

———. *The Art of Dreaming*. New York: HarperCollins, 1993.

———. *The Eagle's Gift*. New York: Washington Square Press, 1981.

———. *The Fire from Within*. New York: Washington Square Press, 1984.

———. *Journey to Ixtlan: The Lessons of Don Juan*. New York: Washington Square Press, 1972.

———. *The Power of Silence: Further Lessons of Don Juan*. New York: Washington Square Press, 1987.

———. *A Separate Reality: Further Conversations with Don Juan*. New York: Washington Square Press, 1971.

———. *The Second Ring of Power*. New York: Washington Square Press, 1977.

———. *Tales of Power*. New York: Washington Square Press, 1974.

———. *The Teachings of Don Juan: A Yaqui Way of Knowledge*. New York: Washington Square Press, 1968.

Chaplin, J. P. *Dictionary of Psychology*. New York: Dell Publishing, 1975.

Chown, Marcus. *The Universe Next Door: The Making of Tomorrow's Science*. Oxford: Oxford University Press, 2002.

Classen, Norbert. *Das Wissen der Tolteken*. Freiburg, Germany: Hans-Nietsch-Verlag, 2002.

Colman, Andrew M. *A Dictionary of Psychology*. Oxford: Oxford University Press, 2001.

Cooper, J. C. *Taoism: The Way of the Mystic*. York Beach, Maine: Samuel Weiser, Inc., 1972.

Copi, Irving M. *Introduction to Logic,* 6th ed. New York: Macmillan, 1982.

Csikszentmihalyi, Mihaly. *Flow: The Psychology of Optimal Experience*. New York: HarperPerennial, 1990.

Dacher, Elliot. *Integral Health: The Path to Human Flourishing.* Laguna Beach, Calif.: Basic Health Publications, Inc., 2006.

Dalai Lama, His Holiness the. *Ethics for the New Millennium.* New York: Riverhead, 1999.

———. *The Universe in a Single Atom: The Convergence of Science and Spirituality.* New York: Morgan Road Books, 2005.

Damasio, Antonio. *The Feeling of What Happens: Body and Emotion in the Making of Consciousness.* New York: Harcourt Brace and Company, 1999.

———. *Looking for Spinoza: Joy, Sorrow, and the Feeling Brain.* Orlando: Harcourt, 2003.

Darling, David. *Teleportation: The Impossible Leap.* Hoboken, N.J.: John Wiley & Sons, 2005.

Davies, Paul, ed. *The New Physics.* Cambridge: Cambridge University Press, 1989.

De Laslo, Violet S. ed., R. F. C. Hull, trans., *The Basic Writings of C. G. Jung.* Princeton, N.J.: Princeton University Press, 1990.

Deikman, Arthur. *The Wrong Way Home: Uncovering the Patterns of Cult Behavior in America.* Boston: Beacon Press, 1990.

Doidge, Norman. *The Brain That Changes Itself.* New York: Viking, 2007.

Donaldson, Thomas, and Patricia H. Werhane, eds. *Ethical Issues in Business: A Philosophical Approach,* 5th ed. Upper Saddle River, N.J.: Prentice Hall, 1996.

Dossey, Larry. *Reinventing Medicine: Beyond Mind-Body to a New Era of Healing.* New York: HarperCollins, 1999.

Drane, James F. *More Humane Medicine: A Liberal Catholic Bioethic.* Edinboro, Penn.: Edinboro University Press, 2003.

Edelman, Gerald M. *Second Nature: Brain Science and Human Knowledge.* New Haven, Conn.: Yale University Press, 2006.

Einstein, Albert. *Ideas and Opinions.* New York: Three Rivers Press, 1982.

Feather, Ken Eagle. *The Dream of Vixen Tor.* Charlottesville, Va.: Tracker One Studios, 2001.

———. *On the Toltec Path: A User's Guide to the Teachings of Don Juan Matus, Carlos Castaneda and Other Toltec Seers.* Rochester, Vt.: Inner Traditions/Bear & Co., 2006.

———. *Toltec Dreaming: Don Juan's Teachings on the Energy Body.* Rochester, Vt.: Inner Traditions/Bear & Co., 2007.

———. *Tracking Freedom: A Guide for Personal Evolution.* Charlottesville, Va.: Hampton Roads Publishing Co., 1998.

————. *Traveling with Power: The Exploration and Development of Perception.* Charlottesville, Va.: Hampton Roads Publishing Co., 1992.

Gabbard, Glen O., and Stuart Twemlow. *With the Eyes of the Mind: An Empirical Analysis of Out-of-Body States.* New York: Praeger, 1984.

Gallo, Fred P. *Energy Psychology: Explorations at the Interface of Energy, Cognition, Behavior, and Health.* Boca Raton, Fla.: CRC Press, 1999.

Gardner, Howard. *Frames of Mind: The Theory of Multiple Intelligences.* New York: HarperCollins, 1983.

Gerber, Richard. *Vibrational Medicine,* 3rd ed. Rochester, Vt.: Bear & Co., 2001.

Gladwell, Malcolm. *Blink: The Power of Thinking without Thinking.* New York: Bay Back Books, 2005.

Goleman, Daniel. *Emotional Intelligence.* New York: Bantam Books, 1995.

Greene, Brian. *The Fabric of the Cosmos: Space, Time, and the Texture of Reality.* New York: Alfred A. Knopf, 2005.

Groopman, Jerome. *How Doctors Think.* Boston: Houghton Mifflin, 2007.

Hahnemann, Samuel, and Wenda Brewster O'Reilly, ed. *Organon of the Medical Art.* Palo Alto, Calif.: Birdcage Books, 1996.

Hameroff, Stuart R., Alfred W. Kaszniak, and Alwyn C. Scott, eds. *Toward a Science of Consciousness: The Tucson Discussions and Debates.* Cambridge, Mass.: The MIT Press, 1996, 1998, 1999.

Heidegger, Martin. *Being and Time.* Translated by John Macquarrie and Edward Robinson. San Francisco: HarperSanFrancisco, 1962.

Heinlein, Robert. *Stranger in a Strange Land.* New York: Ace/Penguin, 2003.

Horgan, John. *Rational Mysticism: Dispatches from the Border Between Science and Spirituality.* New York: Houghton Mifflin Company, 2003.

Hunt, Valerie V. *Infinite Mind: Science of the Human Vibrations of Consciousness.* Malibu, Calif.: Malibu Publishing, 1996.

James, William. *The Varieties of Religious Experience.* New York: New American Library, 1958.

Jaynes, Julian. *The Origins of Consciousness in the Breakdown of the Bicameral Mind.* Boston: Houghton Mifflin, 1990.

Johnson, Paul E. *Psychology of Religion, Revised.* Nashville, Tenn.: Abingdon Press, 1959.

Kaku, Michio. *Hyperspace: A Scientific Odyssey through Parallel Universes, Time Warps, and the 10th Dimension.* New York: Anchor Books, 1994.

Kandel, Eric R. *In Search of Memory: The Emergence of a New Science of Mind.* New York: W. W. Norton & Co., 2006.

Kandel, Eric R., James H. Schwartz, and Thomas M. Jessell, eds. *Principles of Neural Science,* 4th ed. New York: McGraw-Hill, 2000.

Kaptchuk, Ted J. *The Web That Has No Weaver: Understanding Chinese Medicine.* Chicago: Contemporary Books, 2000.

Kass, Leon R. *Life, Liberty and the Defense of Dignity: The Challenge of Bioethics.* San Francisco: Encounter Books, 2002.

Kornfield, Jack. *A Path with Heart: A Guide through the Perils and Promises of Spiritual Life.* New York: Bantam Books, 1993.

Kuhn, Thomas S. *The Structure of Scientific Revolutions,* 3rd ed. Chicago: University of Chicago Press, 1996.

Lacey, A. R. *A Dictionary of Philosophy.* New York: Barnes & Noble Books, 1996.

Lerner, Michael. *Spirit Matters.* Charlottesville, Va.: Hampton Roads Publishing, 2000.

Levine, Stephen. *A Year to Live: How to Live This Year As If It Were Your Last.* New York: Bell Tower, 1997.

Lipton, Bruce. *The Biology of Belief: Unleashing the Power of Consciousness, Matter, and Miracles.* Santa Rosa, Calif.: Elite Books, 2005.

Lowen, Alexander, *Bioenergetics.* New York: Penguin Arkana, 1994.

Manning, Clark A., and Louis J. Vanrenen. *Bioenergetic Medicines East and West: Acupuncture and Homeopathy.* Berkeley, Calif.: North Atlantic Books, 1988.

Maslow, Abraham H. *Maslow on Management.* New York: John Wiley & Sons, 1998.

———. *Toward a Psychology of Being,* 3rd ed. New York: John Wiley & Sons, 1999.

Mauskopf, Seymour H., and Michael R. McVaugh. *The Elusive Science: Origins of Experimental Psychical Research.* Baltimore, Md.: The Johns Hopkins University Press, 1980.

McCraty, Rollin. *The Energetic Heart: Bioelectromagnetic Interactions Within and Between People.* Boulder Creek, Calif.: Institute of Heartmath, 2003.

McMoneagle, Joseph. *Memoirs of a Psychic Spy: The Remarkable Life of U.S. Government Remote Viewer 001.* Charlottesville, Va.: Hampton Roads Publishing Co., 2006.

———. *Mind Trek: Exploring Consciousness, Time, and Space Through Remote Viewing.* Charlottesville, Va.: Hampton Roads Publishing Co., 1997.

Mindell, Arnold. *Dreaming While Awake: Techniques for 24-Hour Lucid Dreaming.* Charlottesville, Va.: Hampton Roads Publishing Co., 2000.

Monroe, Robert. *Journeys Out of the Body.* New York: Doubleday, 1971.

Moody, Raymond. *Life After Life.* Harrisburg, Penn.: Stackpole Books, 1976.

Murphy, Michael, and Rhea A. White. *In the Zone: the Transcendent Experience in Sports.* New York: Penguin Books, 1995.

Myss, Caroline. *Anatomy of the Spirit: The Seven Stages of Power and Healing.* New York: Harmony Books, 1996.

Nahin, Paul J. *Time Travel.* Cincinnati, Ohio: Writer's Digest Books, 1997.

Oschman, James L. *Energy Medicine: The Scientific Basis.* Edinburgh, Scotland: Churchill Livingston, 2000.

Ouspensky, P. D. *The Fourth Way.* New York: Vintage Books, 1971.

Pearsall, Paul. *The Beethoven Factor: The New Positive Psychology of Hardiness, Happiness, Healing, and Hope.* Charlottesville, Va.: Hampton Roads Publishing Co., 2003.

Pert, Candace. *Molecules of Emotion.* New York: Scribner, 1997.

Petroski, Henry. *Design Paradigms: Case Histories of Error and Judgment in Engineering.* Cambridge, UK: Cambridge University Press, 1994.

Pickover, Clifford A. *Time: A Traveler's Guide.* Oxford, England: Oxford University Press, 1998.

Piel, Gerald. *The Age of Science: What Scientists Learned in the Twentieth Century.* New York: Basic Books, 2001.

Pinker, Steven. *How the Mind Works.* New York: Scientific American/W. W. Norton & Co., 1997.

Reber, Arthur S., and Emily Reber, eds. *The Penguin Dictionary of Psychology,* 3rd ed. London: Penguin Books, 1995.

Restak, Richard M. *The Brain: The Last Frontier.* New York: Warner Books, 1979.

Runes, Dagobert. *Dictionary of Philosophy.* Totowa, N.J.: Littlefield, Adams, and Co., 1980.

Sanchez, Victor. *The Toltec Path of Recapitulation: Healing Your Past to Free Your Soul.* Rochester, Vt.: Bear & Company, 2001.

Schopenhauer, Arthur, and E. F. J. Payne, ed., *The World as Will and Representation,* vols. 1, 2. New York: Dover Publications, 1969.

Sennett, Richard. *The Corrosion of Character: The Personal Consequences of Work in the New Capitalism.* New York: W. W. Norton & Company, 1998.

Sheldrake, Rupert. *A New Science of Life: The Hypothesis of Morphic Resonance.* Rochester, Vt.: Park Street Press, 1995.

Siegel, Daniel J. *The Developing Mind: Toward a Neurobiology of Interpersonal Experience.* New York: The Guildford Press, 1999.

Smith, Houston. *The World's Religions.* New York: Harper Collins, 1991.

Sollars, David W. *The Complete Idiot's Guide to Acupuncture & Acupressure.* New York: Alpha Books, 2000.

Spencer, Sidney. *Mysticism in World Religion.* Gloucester, Mass.: Peter Smith, 1971.

Springer, Sally P., and Georg Deutsch. *Left Brain, Right Brain,* 4th ed. New York: W. H. Freeman and Co., 1993.

Stillings, Neil A., Steven E. Weisler, Christopher H. Chase, Mark H. Feinstein, Jay L. Garfield, and Edwina L. Rissland. *Cognitive Science,* 2nd ed. Cambridge, Mass.: MIT Press, 1995.

Strogatz, Steven. *Sync: The Emerging Science of Spontaneous Order.* New York: Hyperion, 2003.

Suzuki, Shunryu. *Zen Mind, Beginner's Mind.* New York: Weatherhill, 1973.

Targ, Russell, and Jane Katra. *Miracles of Mind: Exploring Nonlocal Consciousness and Spiritual Healing.* Novato, Calif.: New World Library, 1998.

Tart, Charles T., ed. *Altered States of Consciousness.* New York: HarperCollins, 1990.

———. *Open Mind, Discriminating Mind: Reflections on Human Possibilities.* Lincoln, Neb.: iUniverse.com, Inc., 2000.

———. *States of Consciousness.* Lincoln, Neb.: www.iUniverse.com, Inc., 2000.

Tedlock, Dennis, and Barbara Tedlock, eds., *Teachings from the American Earth: Indian Religion and Philosophy.* New York: Liveright, 1975.

Trefil, James, ed., *Encyclopedia of Science and Technology.* New York: Routledge, 2001.

Vertosick, Jr., Frank T. *The Genius Within: Discovering the Intelligence of Every Living Thing.* New York: Harcourt, Inc., 2002.

Wallace, B. Alan. *The Taboo of Subjectivity: Toward a New Science of Consciousness.* Oxford: Oxford University Press, 2000.

Whale, Jon. *The Catalyst of Power: The Assemblage Point of Man.* Findhorn, Scotland: Findhorn Press, 2001.

Zelazo, Philip David, Morris Moscovitch, Evan Thompson, eds. *The Cambridge Handbook of Consciousness.* New York: Cambridge University Press, 2007.

Index

Page numbers in *italics* refer to illustrations.

About the Author

Kenneth Smith, writing under the name Ken Eagle Feather, has published several books on Toltec philosophy, including *On the Toltec Path* and *Toltec Dreaming*. After his apprenticeship to Toltec seer Juan Matus, he served on the staff of the Association for Research and Enlightenment, part of the Edgar Cayce legacy, and the staff of The Monroe Institute, founded by sound and consciousness researcher Robert Monroe. Leaving a career in the book industry as the vice president of sales and marketing of a publishing company in order to study scientific perspectives and technologies of healing, Smith serves as the communications director of Beech Tree Labs, Inc., a discovery and early-stage development biopharmaceutical company, and as the executive director of Beech Tree's sister company, The Institute for Therapeutic Discovery, a nonprofit organization focused on bridging biochemistry and biophysics. He lives in Richmond, Virginia.